EXPANDING

THE AMERICAN MIND

D0062752

EXPANDING
THE AMERICAN MIND

Books and the
Popularization of Knowledge

BETH LUEY

University of Massachusetts Press
AMHERST AND BOSTON

LC 2010003404
ISBN 978-1-55849-817-4 (paper), 816-7 (cloth)

Designed by Sally Nichols
Set in Monotype Bell
Printed and bound by Thomson-Shore, Inc.

Library of Congress Cataloging-in-Publication Data

Luey, Beth.
Expanding the American mind : books and the popularization of knowledge /
Beth Luey.
    p. cm.
Includes bibliographical references and index.
ISBN 978-1-55849-816-7 (library cloth : alk. paper) — ISBN 978-1-55849-817-4
(pbk. : alk. paper)
1. Books and reading—United States—History. 2. Communication in learning
and scholarship—United States—History. 3. Authors and readers—United States—
History. 4. Publishers and publishing—United States—History. I. Title.
Z1003.2.L84 2010
028´.90973—dc22
                                                                    2010003404

British Library Cataloguing in Publication data are available.

For my mother and the memory of my father

Some books are to be tasted, others to be swallowed, and some few to be chewed and digested.

FRANCIS BACON

CONTENTS

ACKNOWLEDGMENTS

Like any historian, I owe a great deal to librarians, especially those at Arizona State University, the Columbia Rare Books and Manuscripts Library, the Harry Ransom Humanities Research Library, and the Library of Congress. I am also grateful to supportive colleagues at Arizona State University and to my students, especially my research assistant, Paul Tsimahides. Most of all, I wish to thank my friends and colleagues in the Society for the History of Authorship, Reading and Publishing, whose creative work and varying approaches to the history of the book have informed and inspired my own thinking.

EXPANDING
THE AMERICAN MIND

INTRODUCTION

Francis Bacon knew his books, but he got one thing wrong: knowledge is not power. The *control of knowledge* is power. In any university office one is surrounded by people whose brains are bursting with knowledge yet who have no meaningful power. But people in a position to withhold knowledge are powerful. The intelligence analyst who withholds information from a policymaker, the doctor who fails to explain a diagnosis to a patient, a president who distorts events in speeches to Congress or the nation, the corporate executive who misrepresents accounting methods to Wall Street analysts—all of these people are enhancing their power by preventing others from acquiring the knowledge they themselves have acquired.

The most basic tool to acquire knowledge is literacy, and in the Western world the powerful long acknowledged its importance by denying it to others. The first line of defense is to prevent people from becoming literate. As late as the nineteenth century, in parts of the American South it was illegal to teach a slave to read. But people do learn to read despite enormous barriers. Once that happens, the best method of control is to limit the material available to readers through language, price, or censorship.

Most people learn first to read the language they speak, but early European books were in the dead languages of learned discourse: Latin, Greek, and Hebrew. Christian churches used language to limit access to knowledge of God. In the Western world, the way to know God was to read the Bible, and until the Renaissance and Reformation only those who could read ancient languages could acquire that knowledge independently. Laypeople depended entirely on the clergy. Translating the Bible into vernacular languages was often contentious. In England, when John Wycliffe translated the Bible into English, his works were banned. In 1428, more than forty

1

years after Wycliffe had died, the pope ordered his bones exhumed and burned. William Tyndale's English translation formed the basis of the King James Bible, but by then he was dead, executed for his work in 1536. In nineteenth-century Russia the clergy used a Bible in Old Church Slavonic, a language that few Russians continued to speak. When a translation into modern Russian was begun, the clergy resisted, and a modern version became available only toward the end of that century. The printing press and vernacular literature, both sacred and secular, advanced together, and by the sixteenth century a well-read person had no practical need to know an ancient language, though such knowledge continued to carry considerable social cachet.

Being able to read gives immediate access to free information, but little information (let alone knowledge) is free. Official information—government decrees, news of royal deaths and successions, of wars and conscription—was freely distributed not only to those who could read but, through public oral reading, to those who could not. (Understanding of the meaning of those decrees and events, much less the opportunity to influence them, was limited to those who were well enough educated to read critically and discuss events with others.) Once literacy was fairly widespread, information was made available in newspapers, periodicals, and other printed matter. Print expanded access, but not as much as you might think. Printed material of all kinds was expensive, not only because the technology was new and the materials costly but because governments frequently taxed those materials and the finished products heavily, further raising the price. Even after printing became more economical and taxes were lowered or eliminated, books especially were far too expensive for working people. Only in the nineteenth century, when printing technology advanced and a used book market and free or inexpensive lending libraries were established, were books readily available to large numbers of people. Even then, there was much discussion among the elites about what sort of books should be made available in cheap editions or placed on library shelves. Reading suitable for the ruling classes might not be suitable for their servants. (Class distinctions about suitable reading died hard: when paperback books flourished after World War II, "objectionable" language and passages deemed acceptable in the cloth editions might be expunged from the paperbacks, with or without the authors' knowledge.)

Once vernacular publishing took hold, churches and governments sought to restrict access to knowledge by controlling the press. In England, the Stationers' Company until 1710 licensed printers and decided what they could publish, combining the modern functions of a copyright office, a trade union, and—in conjunction with a government officer—an official censor. Governments' right to control their citizens' reading was generally assumed until the Enlightenment, when freedom of the press began to be recognized as a civil right. Despite this recognition, freedom to read was accepted only gradually and far from universally. Governments at both ends of the political spectrum have always exercised censorship, as have theocracies.

In democratic nations, with literacy nearly universal and the right to read an established principle of human rights, control of knowledge becomes much more difficult. The control of politically sensitive information remains a government concern, and the definition of "politically sensitive" may include morally controversial topics as well as material that threatens national security or the incumbent's security in office. But the control of knowledge more often is a cultural issue: Whose version of history will be told? Who will decide what is worth reading? What will schoolchildren be taught about evolution? Under these circumstances, control is impossible. Cultural arbiters, whether official or self-appointed, turn instead to *direction* and *guidance*.

In Great Britain and the United States, a mass audience developed in the middle of the nineteenth century. At that point, nearly everyone could read and gain access to books through libraries or booksellers. Intellectual, political, and religious leaders became concerned about *what* this audience would read. "The masses" were not identical in the two nations: in England and Scotland the native working classes were the source of concern, while the United States had also to consider the waves of immigrants who needed to be educated in the ways of American citizenship. In both countries, cultural authorities sought to provide material that was politically and morally uplifting, and to avoid having readers come into contact with reading matter that might create or improperly channel political discontent or radical ideas. One positive way to do this was to make "good reading" available in inexpensive editions and to stock libraries with it. Working-class readers did not always cooperate. They resisted bland pablum and sought out the very same books that their "betters" chose for themselves.

As citizens' level of education rose, another approach to directing the reading of both the working classes and the expanding middle class arose:

the recommended reading list or prefabricated library. In England, several publishers issued reasonably priced editions of classic literature. In the United States, university professors and presidents took on the role of general guides to self-education. Charles W. Eliot, after leaving the presidency of Harvard, lent the institution's name to a five-foot shelf of books that, if read carefully and studiously, would provide a sound education to those who were not fortunate enough to attend his alma mater. Robert M. Hutchins, president of the University of Chicago, started the Great Books Program, which is still functioning. His colleague Mortimer Adler wrote books to tell people not only what to read but how to read it. Even such purely commercial ventures as the Modern Library performed an advisory function as readers planned reading programs to include these "modern classics."

It is possible, of course, to see these efforts as well meant, and to some extent they were. But, as we will see, their rhetoric and the way they were received by intellectual elites reveal a good deal of condescension and disdain for the audience. This was the era when brows were divided among low, middle, and high—a division that ends, I would argue, only at the turn of the twenty-first century. Snobbery is the last gasp of social control over reading: everyone is literate, everyone has access to the same books, and the only way to distinguish yourself from the mass audience is to show that your reading (either the books or your manner of reading them) is superior.

The academy, which exists to extend and disseminate knowledge, is in some ways the last bastion of knowledge control. What scholars collectively know about the world—as scientists, social scientists, and humanists—has expanded greatly, but what each knows individually has narrowed. Much of academic life outside the classroom is spent communicating exclusively with one's peers in language that is too specialized (and sometimes deliberately too obscure) to be understood by laypeople. This kind of specialized communication, although vital to research and the extension of knowledge, makes it difficult to communicate with policymakers and other nonspecialists. Specialized communication can be privileged over general communication to the point where it is legitimate to talk about controlling, or even hoarding, understanding.

The desire to restrict access to knowledge has always puzzled me. As a citizen and teacher, I believe that the more people know, the better. I am offended by the notion that there are things that "they" cannot understand, and even more so by the idea that helping ordinary people understand complex ideas is a laughable or unworthy use of one's time. The economic principle of scarcity probably explains this tendency best. Knowledge grants power only if not everyone has it. Investment is a good example. If you know that the CEO of a major corporation is about to step down, and you know enough about the company to predict that this will cause the value of its shares to plummet, you are in a position to profit from that knowledge. Once everyone knows, it's too late. But the principle works outside finance as well. Knowing the latest gossip before one's colleagues or neighbors has social value. (Really good gossip may have economic value as well, at least to the extent of a few free drinks.) At an intellectual level, being able to understand things that other people don't supplies cachet and a sense of importance. Once everyone understands the latest literary, economic, or political theory, it's time for a new one. Of course, the popularizer who interprets these theories to those outside the inner circle is going to come in for some criticism from intellectual peers. To me, though, the popularizers are the heroes who, having acquired esoteric knowledge, are eager to share it with others rather than to hoard it. They view knowledge as a commodity whose value is enhanced rather than diminished by accessibility.

By *popularization* I mean writing that makes new or complex research and ideas accessible to nonspecialists. Researchers may write two versions of their work: one for peers and one for general readers, as Stephen Jay Gould and Deborah Tannen have done. Other scholars may write about their research in ways that simultaneously satisfy both peers and general readers, as Laurel Thatcher Ulrich and Annette Gordon-Reed have chosen to do. Science writers like John McPhee and Jonathan Weiner describe research done by others so that nonspecialists can understand it.

I have studied popularization as a way to understand the dissemination of knowledge. Too often, dissemination is considered to be accomplished with publication in a peer-reviewed journal or a specialized monograph. For a great deal of research, at least in its early stages, these media are adequate. But when specialized research is brought together into a unifying theory; when its results affect society, culture, or polity; when it changes the way we should think about the planet and our lives—then this knowledge must escape the walls of the academy. That liberation is the mission of the popularizer.

In the pages that follow, I examine how nonfiction differs from fiction, and how popularization differs from other forms of nonfiction (chapter 1). I then look at the history of popularization to better understand the preconditions for its existence and the conditions in which it flourishes (chapter 2). Next, I describe how these conditions—an educated public, a research-oriented professoriate, and a publishing industry oriented toward a mass readership—were met in the United States after World War II (chapters 3–5). Chapter 6 explores the ways popularizers practice their craft, and chapter 7 explains how publishers develop, design, and market their books. In chapter 8, I discuss motivations for reading, based on psychological studies, publishing history, and my own survey of nonfiction readers. I have ended the book with thoughts about how electronic media are continuing the process of disseminating knowledge to a broad audience. Although this book is based on archival research, surveys, and reading in peer-reviewed journals and specialized monographs, I have tried to follow the example of the authors I studied by making what I have learned accessible to all interested readers.

1

NON: THE PREFIX THAT CHANGES
WHAT—AND HOW—WE READ

When you walk into most public libraries, you come to the Great Divide: fiction is on one side of the building, nonfiction on the other. We all know what fiction is—novels, short stories, works of the imagination. But nonfiction is harder to define because it is everything else, encompassing many different subjects, purposes, and even genres. How can you define a category that includes the *Encyclopedia Britannica, The Papers of George Washington,* the complete works of Sigmund Freud and Martha Stewart, *Java for Dummies,* and *The Wicca Cookbook?*

This book is about popularization, a subset of the nonfiction genre: the books that explain complicated subjects and ideas to nonexpert readers. I have not included self-help books, celebrity biographies, cookbooks, diet books, or sensationalized accounts of real-life events. It's not that I don't read such books, or that I discount their value (in fact, I've written books that could be called self-help). But the kinds of books I am writing about are very different from these: they are written by a different sort of author using different narrative techniques, they present different challenges to publishers, and they are read for different reasons.

Popularization in its present form is also different from other varieties because it is relatively new. Charles Darwin and some of his contemporaries wrote successfully for general readers, who could understand their writing without a background in arcane theories, complex methodologies, or esoteric vocabulary. Darwin wrote before the scholarly specialization and professionalization of the twentieth century created a gap between researchers and readers that for a time seemed unbridgeable. Since World War II, researchers—as well as professional science writers, nonacademic historians, and others—have developed ways to bridge that gap, and it is their work that this book examines. We cannot understand how the gap arose, or how it was bridged, without looking at changes in higher education—in the number of Americans attending college, in the kinds of intellectual experiences they have had, and in the goals and ambitions of faculty members and administrators. I will look at changes in education, but before I do, I want to return to the library to examine the two sides of the building and what is on the shelves.

Fighting Fiction

Today's American public libraries are usually organized according to the Dewey Decimal System, which many of us learned in elementary school. Its creator, Melvil Dewey, proposed the system in the 1870s, when he was a student at Amherst College. (Dewey was christened "Melville," but simplified spelling was another of his causes.) Books at that time were shelved alphabetically by author, and Dewey suggested a decimal system of subject categories that gets more specific as you move to the right of the decimal point. Libraries quickly adopted his system.[1] As a library patron, you know that Dewey's system is generally used only for nonfiction. Like most librarians of his time, Dewey disdained fiction and did not really care how it was cataloged. His goal was to make it easier for librarians to catalog, and readers to locate, the more ennobling variety of literature, nonfiction. Fiction continued to be shelved alphabetically by author, untouched by the new system.

The American clergy, community leaders, and educators who promoted nonfiction in the eighteenth and nineteenth centuries almost universally opposed the reading of novels. (Their British and Canadian counterparts were no more favorably disposed.) In the words of Carl Van Doren, "The dullest critics contended that novels were lies; the pious, that they served no virtuous purpose; the strenuous, that they softened sturdy minds; the utilitarian, that they crowded out more useful books; the realistic, that they painted adventure too romantic and love too vehement; the patriotic, that, dealing with European manners, they tended to confuse and dissatisfy republican youth."[2] The first fiction works published in America were sentimental novels, typified by Samuel Richardson's *Pamela* and *Clarissa* or Susanna Rowson's *Charlotte Temple.* So strong was the opposition to such fiction that novelists sometimes presented their work as truth—as edited diaries or collections of letters—and themselves as editors or translators, rather than authors. This ruse was adopted by Daniel Defoe, Eliza Haywood, Horace Walpole, and Samuel Richardson. Readers frequently believed them. Another trick, employed by Richardson and Tobias Smollett, was to confuse the matter by interpolating nonfiction excerpts into novels.[3]

Despite strong opposition, the genre thrived. By the 1820s fiction dominated book sales, and by the early twentieth century almost everyone who read books read novels. Whether as leatherbound volumes, dime pamphlets, or newspaper serials, fiction ruled. And because novels were available in cheap formats and through lending libraries, working people joined the middle and upper classes in reading them. The cheaper the format, the louder the objections of the anti-novel factions. Perhaps the upper classes (or at least the male half of them) could read fiction without endangering their immortal souls, but their servants (and their wives and daughters) remained at risk. As a contributor to the *Church of England Quarterly Review* fretted, "The great bulk of novel readers are females; and to them such impressions (as are conveyed through fiction) are peculiarly mischievous; for, first, they are naturally more sensitive, more impressable, than the other sex; and secondly, their engagements are of a less engrossing character—they have more time as well as more inclination to indulge in reveries of fiction."[4]

Benjamin Franklin brought out the first American edition of Richardson's *Pamela* in 1744. It was an enormous success and encouraged American printers to import more British novels for reprinting. It also inspired American writers to write in the new genre. American authors were also encouraged by passage of a federal copyright law in 1790. Although it did not protect American work abroad (that event awaited the copyright law of 1891), it did provide domestic protection and bargaining power to authors. As a result of market demand, legal protection, technological advances (steam-powered printing presses and stereotyping), and improved distribution (railroads and favorable postal rates), the number of American novels increased, bringing new prosperity to domestic publishing. In the 1820s, only one hundred novels by American authors were published; in the 1840s, a thousand were published. The most successful of those hundred novels in the 1820s sold five or six thousand copies; their counterparts in the 1850s sold sixty to a hundred thousand copies. And the book publishing industry, which had revenues of $2.5 million in the 1820s, had increased its revenues to $12.5 million in the 1850s.[5]

As public libraries expanded throughout the nineteenth century to serve the growing reading public, librarians joined the struggle against fiction in some imaginative, forceful, but ultimately ineffective ways. "Through the late 1880s many public libraries regularly published and analyzed the figures for the percentage of fiction in the total yearly circulation. An increase in the percentage brought dark self-questioning. A decrease of one-tenth of a point was cause for joy." The public's hunger for novels was a serious concern. Charles A. Cutter, an eminent librarian of the late nineteenth century, in 1883 described the hoped-for library of a hundred years thence in which fiction circulation would have fallen from 75 percent to only 40 percent. Libraries limited their acquisition of fiction, but that did not seriously affect circulation. In 1895, for example, three California libraries whose collections were less than 15 percent fiction had fiction circulations of 53 to 79 percent.[6]

One ploy used in the 1890s was the "two-book system." Patrons were normally allowed to borrow only one book at a time, but if they took out a book that was *not* a novel, they could borrow a second book. In 1912 the New York Public Library's quota for borrowers was four books, but only one could be fiction. Some readers continue to equate nonfiction with spinach and novels with dessert. Novelist and philosopher Rebecca Goldstein, writing in 2002, recalled: "Soon after I learned to read, I was given a library card, and I made a strict rule for myself. On each trip to the library I would take out two books: one would be a 'good for me book,' meaning science or history or at the very least biography; and the other would be a 'fun book,' which meant a storybook, pure make-believe. . . . I did not altogether approve of make-believe or of myself for loving it so much." As one library historian points out, however, librarians' efforts were hampered by ambivalence: despite their fears for the tastes and morals of their patrons (especially the working-class ones), they realized that novels brought readers into the library, and they stocked their shelves accordingly.[7]

The opponents of the novel did not give up, but by the middle of the nineteenth century the battle was lost. "Sensational" novels were joined by moral, domestic novels that supposedly used the wiles of fiction for higher purposes. Thus, next to *Pamela* and *Tristram Shandy* on the bestseller lists were the works of Mrs. E. D. E. N. Southworth, T. S. Arthur's *Ten Nights in a Bar-Room,* Horatio Alger's uplifting tales, and Martha Finley's saccharine Elsie Dinsmore books. Of varying quality and longevity, these books offered overt moral messages that made them acceptable to many critics.[8] Also available were adventure novels whose promoters could claim social value as well as readability: the works of James Fenimore Cooper, for example, were not only good stories, but they were distinctly *American*—an important quality in a young nation. As Euro-Americans moved west, novels of the frontier grew more numerous and popular.

American publishers continued to import British novels that today are considered of higher quality than the sentimental and sensational novels, such as those of Charles Dickens and William Makepeace Thackeray. Translations of French novels were also imported. Americans wrote novels of high quality, too, but their works were not so commercially successful as the sentimental bestsellers: Nathaniel Hawthorne and Herman Melville relied on government posts to support themselves. On the whole, though, fiction writers and publishers prospered. Gothic novels, romantic novels, realistic novels, mystery novels, historical novels, and fantasy were gradually added to the shelves of bookstores and libraries. Opposition eased, although it is hard to sort out the reasons. As fiction grew more varied in both genre and quality, it became difficult to condemn it wholesale. Its popularity led librarians to see it as a necessary evil—a way to attract patrons who at some point might be converted to higher things. And, of course, American society became less religious and moralistic—not, I suspect, solely because of novel reading.

Nevertheless, the novel has never been properly tamed, and claims for the superiority of nonfiction are still made. Nonfiction, it is argued, may not always serve a "virtuous purpose," but it does not lie; it strengthens minds rather than weakening them; it is useful; it does not deliberately exaggerate emotions; and it clarifies the mind instead of confusing it. Unfortunately, early nonfiction did not always rise to the standards of truth that its critics claimed. Mason Weems, in his biography of George Washington, stretched the truth in the service of nation building. Indian captivity narratives, though presented as diaries or in other nonfiction forms, are more statements of faith and dramatizations than accurate renderings of the encounters between Native Americans and white settlers. Early biographies and memoirs were entertaining, but often not truthful. (This tradition lives on: at the turn of the twenty-first century, memoirs by James Frey, Margaret Seltzer, Benjamin Wilkomirski, and Misha Difonseca were exposed as exaggerations or complete hoaxes.)[9] When early nonfiction *was* truthful, it was often didactic and boring. Only at its best—generally in the short journalistic writings of fiction writers such as Mark Twain or Stephen Crane—could nineteenth-century nonfiction compete with fiction.

The Varieties of Nonfiction

Since colonial times nonfiction has been a staple of reading in this country: books of psalms, religious tracts, and practical manuals of advice and instruction were the first books printed here and were the most popular imports. Even as novels rose in popularity, the traditional nonfiction genres prospered and evolved.[10]

Religious books remain among the bestselling works in the United States. The Bible is the nation's all-time bestseller, and although collections of sermons are no longer popular, other religious titles thrive. At the millennium, a series of apocalyptic novels about the "end times" of Revelation topped bestseller lists.[11] Secular inspirational titles appeared as well, serving many of the same purposes: they provide comfort, reassurance, strength in times of trial, and occasionally some moral backbone. Because newspaper and magazine bestseller lists historically were compiled from sales reports by secular booksellers, religious titles rarely appeared on them, but retrospectively compiled lists and sales figures gathered in other ways are more informative.

Frank Luther Mott's classic discussion of bestselling books, *Golden Multitudes*, lists eight titles whose total sales were equal to 1 percent of the population of the American colonies in the seventeenth century. Six of these were religious titles: Michael Wigglesworth's *Day of Doom*, Richard Baxter's *Call to the Unconverted*, Lewis Bayly's *Practice of Piety*, Samuel Hardy's *Guide to Heaven*, John Bunyan's *Pilgrim's Progress*, and Jonathan Dickinson's *God's Protecting Providence*. In the eighteenth century, although tastes broadened and the reading public grew, a few religious titles, such as John Fox's *Book of Martyrs*, sold at bestseller levels. In the nineteenth and twentieth centuries such books nearly disappeared from the lists, although religious novels such as *Ben Hur*, *The Robe*, and *Quo Vadis* sold very well.[12]

A variant originating in the twentieth-century is the book that combines a religious message with some other genre. A 1920s bestseller was *The Man Nobody Knows*, by Bruce Barton, which described Jesus as a successful business executive. Norman Vincent Peale's *Power of Positive Thinking* and Harold Kushner's *When Bad Things Happen to Good People* are religious titles that also belong to the self-help tradition. Marabel Morgan's *Total Woman*, a religiously oriented book of marital advice, and Charles Colson's *Born Again*, an unlikely combination of inspiration and political memoir, also crossed genres.

By the middle of the twentieth century, religious titles were generally published by specialized houses and sold in specialized bookstores, but they continued to sell in large numbers. In the 1980's New Age books, generally classified as inspirational if not actually religious, experienced enormous sales growth. In the 1990s Stephen Carter's *The Culture of Disbelief: How American Law and Politics Trivialize Religious Devotion*, which argued for the reinclusion of religion in American life, appeared on the *New York Times* bestseller list. In the first decade of the twenty-first century, Americans made bestsellers of such inspirational titles as Rick Warren's *The Purpose-Driven Life* and its many spinoffs, Don Piper's *90 Minutes in Heaven*, and Eckhart Tolle's *The Power of Now* and *A New Earth* (an Oprah's Book Club selection). Mitch Albom's *Tuesdays with Morrie, The Five People You Meet in Heaven*, and *For One More Day* dominated the secular inspirational genre. Religious books, whether narrowly or broadly defined, continue to be an important part of American readers' lives.

Practical manuals, a genre dating back to the dawn of print, also remain popular. Early manuals taught basic skills—farming, surveying, husbandry, navigation, spelling, bookkeeping, and so forth—as well as household skills such as sewing and cooking. Today these ends are served by textbooks—one of the most profitable products of the publishing industry—and by how-to books, also perennial profit makers. Today's how-to books continue to teach basic skills, such as do-it-yourself plumbing and carpentry, but they also teach more frivolous subjects, such as setting beautiful holiday tables or arranging silk flowers. The "how-to" genre experiences some competition from DVDs, but it still flourishes. In the person of Martha Stewart, it has become an industry that exploits several media. And anyone who has been in a bookstore since about 1980 knows that when consumers have problems with the preeminent technology of our time, the computer, they turn to books. In the long run, electronic media may replace many kinds of printed materials. In the short run, however, they have been a boon to the publishing industry.

Books also teach less concrete skills. Readers have sought the secrets of success in financial affairs since colonial times, when Benjamin Franklin's *Poor Richard* provided advice to ten thousand readers a year for many years.[13] The dominance of business in the late nineteenth century gave a boost to this literature, with such titles as Orison Swett Marden's *Pushing to the Front* (1894) and Russell Conwell's *Acres of Diamonds*, first published in 1888 and still in print. The tradition has continued. One long-lived bestseller is Dale Carnegie's *How to Win Friends and Influence People*, first published in 1936 and continuously popular since. In the 1990s it experienced great success among would-be entrepreneurs in former Communist countries.[14]

Books on etiquette, improving one's speech, what to read, and how to behave in social situations increased in number and popularity as American society matured. More than a hundred etiquette manuals were published before the Civil War.[15] In the nineteenth and early twentieth centuries, such books were usually written by ministers and schoolteachers, but by the middle of the twentieth century the ministers were joined by psychologists, psychiatrists, and other doctors. Readers continue to seek advice on etiquette (though many questions now answered went unasked a century ago), wardrobe, and other aspects of public behavior. Emily Post's *Etiquette*, first published in 1923, and Amy Vanderbilt's *Complete Book of Etiquette* (1952) have been through numerous editions and were joined in the 1970s by the advice of "Miss Manners," Judith Martin.

Readers also now seek help on more private matters, such as sex. The first bestsellers about sex were not written as self-help books, but they were marketed to general readers, who used them for guidance, or at least reassurance. The two "Kinsey Reports"—*Sexual Behavior in the Human Male* (1948) and *Sexual Behavior in the Human Female* (1953)—were written as reports of scientific research and initially issued by a medical publisher, but Simon Michael Bessie, an editor at Harper & Row, later convinced Alfred Kinsey that they should be published as books for general readers.[16] The Kinsey Reports' successors were the equally scientific, and equally popular, works by William H. Masters and Virginia E. Johnson, *Human Sexual Response* (1966) and *Human Sexual Inadequacy* (1970).

There is a good reason for the success of advice books: they serve genuine social needs. Benjamin Spock's *Baby and Child Care* has been continuously in print since 1946 and is the second best-selling title in the United States (after the Bible). The success of his book, as well as the controversy it occasionally provokes, has inspired a host of competitors. Spock's book appeared at the end of World War II, when Americans became more mobile and new parents found themselves living far from their own parents and other family members who might have offered advice on the same matters that Dr. Spock covered. Suburban homes equipped with modern appliances offered middle-class mothers time to spend with their children, leisure to contemplate how best to raise them, but no servants to turn them over to. When child-rearing advice began to be included in domestic manuals in the 1830s, the reasons were similar. As Richard Brodhead explains, "Books like [Lydia H.] Sigourney's *Letters to Mothers,* or Catherine Sedgwick's *Home* (1835), or Lydia Maria Child's *The Mother's Book* (1831), quite overtly posit as their audience a family closed off from extended relations; a family prosperous, but not luxuriously wealthy; a family whose home life is relieved from the heavy labor of primary economic production; a family in which the mother, now the chief presence in the home, is able to devote her whole attention to raising her children. They address, in short, exactly the family formation that historians have shown to be emerging as a new middle-class paradigm in the decades around 1830."[17]

Self-help books are most likely to succeed in an egalitarian society. As Cathy Davidson notes, writing about the 1820s, the "proliferation of these self-improvement books attests to an emerging, broadly based interest in education that encompassed men and women, city and country citizens, and specifically addressed unprivileged readers. The manuals encouraged self-reliance, free thinking, inductive reasoning, and a questioning of principles and authority."[18] More than many European countries, the United States remains a place where improving one's social status is both possible and approved. Some stigma still attaches to being "self-taught" and, in the upper classes, to "social climbing," but in our better moments Americans admire and encourage upward educational, social, and economic mobility. Many popular nonfiction books have been designed to assist people in such aspirations, and their continuing presence in the market suggests that they have succeeded.

Another perennial nonfiction genre is the reference book. Over the years, Americans consulting the *Farmer's Almanac,* the *World Book Encyclopedia,* or the various world almanacs have found facts in abundance. Books of lists, bibliographies, dictionaries, encyclopedias, and compound interest tables have long been available and valued. The nature of the information sought has changed, and—as in the case of how-to- books—electronic media now offer competition, but reference books still represent an important source of publishing revenue.

Until World War II, then, nonfiction books were mostly utilitarian. They offered spiritual guidance, taught people how to do things, or offered lists of facts or other information. There were exceptions, of course. In the early years of the republic, readers of general nonfiction favored history (usually ancient or English), law, natural history, philosophy (especially the writings of the Deists), and politics (very popular during the Revolutionary era). The Civil War gave an immediate boost to history books, and that war remains the most popular subject for history readers. (World War II may be catching up.) Biographies and histories could be interesting to read, as well as encouraging spirituality or patriotism. Books of essays could be enjoyed as works of literature as well as sources of moral guidance.

Shortly after World War II, nonfiction began to change. No longer primarily utilitarian, it became an entertainment medium, what one might call "luxury nonfiction." One kind of luxury nonfiction is what critics label "literary nonfiction" or "literary journalism." It can be regarded as a continuation of the tradition of essay writing or quality journalism, with American roots as varied as the writings of Ralph Waldo Emerson and those of Mark Twain. Critics debate the reasons for its flourishing in the middle of the twentieth century, but clearly many people who earn their living as writers began to find the essay, the magazine article, and longer forms of reportage more congenial than fiction forms. The works of writers such as Annie Dillard, Tracy Kidder, and John McPhee exemplify this genre. Their books are widely read and critically applauded.[19]

Another kind of luxury nonfiction is written by academic authors for general readers. These books are different from those written by professional writers mainly because the authors are writing about their own research and that of professional colleagues rather than reporting solely on the work of others. The authors are scientists such as Carl Sagan, Stephen Hawking, Stephen Jay Gould, and Edward O. Wilson; social and behavioral scientists such as John Kenneth Galbraith, Robert Coles, Lester Thurow, and Robert Bellah; and humanities scholars such as Daniel Boorstin, Elaine Pagels, Henry Louis Gates, and Richard Rorty. These authors have opened the American mind to current research and thinking directly, without intermediaries and without condescension. To use a distinction proposed by Roland Barthes, I would call them "writers" (*écrivants*) rather than "authors" (*écrivains*) because their writing has an end or purpose beyond the act of writing itself, whether it be reporting, explaining, or teaching. But as

Barthes himself pointed out, the distinction has become blurred, and many of the scholars and literary journalists are in fact writer/authors.[20]

Are popularizations written by literary journalists truly different from those written by research scholars? Scholars believe they are. A professor of anthropology wrote to an editor at Knopf in 1955 to complain about an advertising brochure that promoted books in his field by both journalists and academics: "They are amateurs writing about high points in investigation. . . . Coon's book is the synthesis of a very brilliant professional. Carl is on the inside looking out. They are on the outside looking in."[21] More recent literary journalists, however, make a point of going inside and staying inside. McPhee, Jonathan Weiner, and others immerse themselves not only in the literature of the fields they investigate but in the lives and work of the researchers doing the work. They are not true insiders, but they are much closer to the work they describe than their predecessors.

In *Wonderful Life*, Stephen Jay Gould insisted on the distinction, but for different reasons:

> I am caught between the two poles of conventional composition. I am not a reporter or "science writer" interviewing people from another domain under the conceit of passive impartiality. I am a professional paleontologist, a close colleague and personal friend of all the major actors in this drama. But I did not perform any of the primary research myself—nor could I, for I do not have the special kind of spatial genius that this work requires. Still, the world of Whittington, Briggs, and Conway Morris is my world. I know its hopes and foibles, its jargon and techniques, but I also live with its illusions. If this book works, then I have combined a professional's feeling and knowledge with the distance necessary for judgment, and my dream of writing an "insider's McPhee" within geology may have succeeded. If it does not work, then I am simply the latest of so many victims—and all the clichés about fish and fowl, rocks and hard places, apply.[22]

Gould's distinction is not based on the ability of an "outsider" to understand the science but on the writer's ability to understand the scientists, their culture, and their mindset.

From the point of view of authorship, I think Gould is right: there is a difference between inside and outside that grows out of being part of a culture for the whole span of one's professional life, of depending on one's subject for a living, for a way of life, and for a meaning to life. The professional writer derives professional meaning from the act of writing; for the academic author, the writing is secondary.

The two kinds of author pose different challenges for the publisher. The literary journalist can write well and usually needs little editorial guidance (though publishers do sometimes suggest subjects and commission books), but the publisher must be assured of the reliability of the information and must in turn assure readers of the writer's authority. The academic author presents fewer concerns about reliability but often needs a great deal of help with writing. Readers may also want some assurance that Professor X has written something they can understand without returning to graduate school, and advertising copy for the work of academics tends to emphasize readability.

For the reader, the distinction is less important. As the Knopf editor replied to the complaining anthropologist, "From the point of view of the public, all three books help the general reader to see more deeply into the dim dawn of human history."[23] Readers are looking for well-written, authoritative books, and these can come from the computers of journalists or those of academics. When writing for general readers, both kinds of writers use similar language and similar rhetorical devices. In most cases, readers know which kind of writer they are dealing with only because of introductory material and authorial comments scattered throughout the book. The narratives and explanatory sections of the two kinds of books are indistinguishable.

Academics began writing for general readers after World War II because of changes in the American system of higher education and in the nature of knowledge. First, the number of college-educated Americans increased dramatically, and the nature of the education that colleges offered changed. Concurrently, large numbers of faculty members became not only teachers but researchers, charged with creating new knowledge as well as disseminating it. And as they met that challenge, knowledge grew more rapidly and became more specialized. In other words, at the middle of the twentieth century, the United States created a new generation of readers and a new generation of authors, both of whose needs could be met best by a new kind of writing.

Fiction and Nonfiction

Melvil Dewey and his colleagues may have been too dismissive of fiction, but they were right in drawing a distinction between the two sides of the library. Fiction and nonfiction are very different. In fact, one of the differences is reflected very clearly in the dual cataloging system itself.

As a reader of fiction you can find all novels by a given author—say, Jane Austen—in one place. But once you have read all of Austen's novels, you have no further resources within most cataloging systems for finding a similar novel—one by a woman, one written in the eighteenth century, a comedy of manners, or any other way you wish to categorize her novels. As you stand at the shelf, there is no reason to think that the books to the left of *Emma* or to the right of *Sense and Sensibility* will be to your taste. But if you go back to the shelf where you found a book about evolution, or Mars, or fractals, you can find every book the library holds on the subject.

This shelf pattern reflects the way fiction and nonfiction are usually selected. Readers choose novels according to who wrote them and nonfiction books according to what they are about. (An exception might be a writer like John McPhee, whose readers are generally willing to tackle any subject he writes about.) But there are also differences between the importance of the author of a novel and the author of a nonfiction book in the composition of the book. Fiction almost always begins in the imagination of the author, where it takes shape and becomes a book. Sometimes an agent or editor has a part in this process; usually this role is minor. For nonfiction, a publisher rather than the author may have initiated the project, determined its scope and content, set all relevant guidelines for the author to follow, selected the author, dictated extensive revisions, and copyedited heavily. Contracts for nonfiction may be offered on the basis of what novelist Gail Godwin called "a scant proposal and tentative outline," whereas all but the most established novelists must offer a detailed plot synopsis and some sample chapters. The nonfiction author is certainly not incidental, for had a different author been chosen the book would have turned out differently. And some nonfiction authors do achieve the kind of name recognition usually reserved for fiction writers. But in most cases the author of a nonfiction book is far less important than the novelist in determining the content of the book and the style and form in which that content is delivered to the reader. Friends and colleagues sense this difference, too. As Godwin noted, when she was working on a novel, people "respectfully hung back from suggesting content." When she talked about her nonfiction project, however, "people feel entitled, perhaps duty bound, to supply material."[24] That is why, in writing this book, I have used the correspondence, editorial evaluations, and marketing memos to be found in publishers' archives. The author's intention is not the only intention that must be considered, and it may not even be the most important. If composition is ever to be viewed as a social or communal process, nonfiction is the place.

The books on either side of the library also differ in the stability of their text. Once a novel is published, the author rarely alters it. The book may be reprinted in cloth and then again in paperback, and minor errors may be corrected, but rarely are significant changes introduced. There are exceptions, like John Updike's *Rabbit, Run,* in which Updike restored cuts made in the first edition.[25] But sometimes even an author who is given the opportunity to restore deleted material to a new edition declines to do so. Perhaps this is because he or she decides the editor was right, or perhaps it is because of a desire to preserve the text as it has been read by the first generation of readers. Nonfiction, though, it if is reprinted, is frequently revised, updated, and corrected. These changes are most commonly initiated by the author or the publisher because what is known about the subject changes. In the sciences especially, knowledge advances rapidly, and books must be revised to reflect new information, theories, and understanding.

But often, too, changes are suggested by readers. It is hard to imagine a reader suggesting that a novelist rewrite a book. Readers and critics may disagree with a novelist's choices, of course. When *Sophie's Choice* was published, some readers criticized William Styron for making Sophie Catholic rather than Jewish. But neither critics nor readers thought for a moment that Styron might wake up one morning and say, "You know, you're right. I'll rewrite the book." Perhaps because it is seen as so thoroughly the work of a single imagination, fiction is granted a formal immutability that nonfiction lacks.

Publishers' archives reveal that readers of nonfiction send in corrections and updates at an alarming pace. After checking with the author, the publisher may revise subsequent printings and editions to reflect that correspondence. The most extreme example that I have found is Carl Sagan's *Cosmos,* which was widely read, in part because it accompanied a television series. Sagan had checked and rechecked the manuscript very carefully, as had the publisher's editors, and they had hired a Columbia graduate student to check the math. Nevertheless, letters poured in from readers with new data, different interpretations, newer citations, and other suggestions. The publisher checked all of these with other sources and with Sagan. The first edition was reprinted thirteen times, and each printing had several substantive changes, many initiated by readers.[26]

Another important difference between fiction and nonfiction has to do with readers' motivations and their ways of selecting books. For fiction and poetry, readers' motivations are complex and sometimes ineffable. Readers of novels rely on word of mouth, reliable recommendations, and their previous reading. For nonfiction, motivations are sometimes complex but more often straightforward: to get information, learn a new subject, or update knowledge. If fiction is read for pleasure, if it is what psychologist Victor Nell refers to as "ludic reading," nonfiction might be called "telic reading," reading with a purpose or end in mind.[27] For the researcher, this simplifies considerably the task of understanding, via questionnaire, survey, or interview, readers' motivations for reading nonfiction and ways of selecting what to read.

There are differences, too, in actual reading practices. Unless a novel severely disappoints or repels us early on, we generally finish it. We care about the characters, we want to know how it turns out, and so forth. In writing about Italo Calvino's *If on a Winter's Night a Traveler,* a novel in which every other chapter is the first chapter of a novel that does not continue, one of my students described the experience of reading without conclusion as a sort of literary coitus interruptus: frustrating and unproductive.

When reading nonfiction, though, readers are more likely to put a book aside once they have learned what they want to know, accomplished what they set out to do, reached a point where they can no longer follow or understand the text, or simply prefer to move on. A good example is the bestselling *Brief History of Time,* by Stephen Hawking, often cited as a prime candidate for the least-read bestseller. Informal surveys reveal that, while almost no one finishes the book, most people do read part of it. (Most people quit at chapter 4, where Hawking moves into the fourth dimension.)

I suspect, though, that the reason that nonfiction readers are more likely not to finish books is that nonfiction (with the exception of biography and narrative history) generally lacks a strong narrative line. You can read the first part, or just the middle, or just the chapters that you are interested in. There's rarely any question of whodunit, who gets the girl, who gets the horse, who destroys the alien, or who wins the race. To prevent reader drop-out, the best nonfiction writers structure their books like old-fashioned novels, with strong narrative lines and characters the reader will care about.

Another area in which the two genres differ is critical evaluation. In fiction, critics commonly make distinctions between highbrow and lowbrow, high culture and mass culture, literature and trash, literary novels and genre fiction. These are often, though not always, spurious and shifting distinctions. Sometimes the argument is circular: Mass fiction is by definition lowbrow. Therefore if a book sells well it can't be any good. What, then, do we say about books that achieve critical acclaim as high culture and then—because they win a Pulitzer or are selected by Oprah—become bestsellers? Do they cease to be good books? Do they fall from high to mass, literature to trash? Jonathan Franzen clearly lost some sleep over this when Oprah selected his novel *The Corrections* for her book club, demoting it in his eyes from the category of high art.

In nonfiction, we use a much more straightforward (though not necessarily more valid) criterion: practical and useful versus abstract and of purely intellectual value, how-to and self-help versus books of no immediate use. As an example, take *The Beak of the Finch*, by Jonathan Weiner. This is a superb book that explains and illustrates evolution by describing ongoing studies of Galapagos finches. Reading this book will not influence anyone's choice of mate, and evolution will continue whether we read the book or not. Scientists whose work might be influenced by the studies described would have learned about them earlier, from articles in peer-reviewed journals. The book's value has nothing to do with its practical application. A diet book, though, is good only if it helps people lose weight. And even if it does, it will not get the same kind of critical attention or be assigned the same kind of cultural value that the Weiner book has. As a litmus test, you might see the Weiner book on a friend's coffee table, but you are unlikely to find the diet book there.

Also, since the advent of modernism, critics have tended to equate good fiction with difficult fiction. Innovation, experimentation, and varying degrees of obscurity have been valued over straightforward narrative and clear description. In nonfiction, though, the level of difficulty either is irrelevant or is valued in the opposite way. That is, a good nonfiction book may be easy or hard to read. What is important is the *source* of the difficulty. If the subject matter causes the difficulty, readers and critics tolerate or even welcome it. If poor writing causes the difficulty, they do not. Most valued, perhaps, is the book on a difficult subject written with great clarity and an engaging style. This would account, in large measure, for the popularity of *A Brief History of Time.* Even if you can't understand all of it, Hawking's book is challenging and fun to read. Because we use different standards in evaluating nonfiction than the ones we apply to fiction, reading reviews is a useful way of understanding what nonprofessional readers value in nonfiction. Reviews of fiction are rarely useful in this way.

The final distinction between fiction and nonfiction is lifespan. We speak of fiction reaching classic status by "surviving the test of time." We still read the works of Shakespeare, Trollope, Austen, Dickens, and other playwrights and novelists with pleasure hundreds of years after they were written. How much of the nonfiction written by their contemporaries survives? In fact, the number of nonfiction books that last more than a generation is very small. As George Sarton, a historian of science, explained, "The classics of science are essentially different from the literary classics in that the latter are eternal, while the former are ephemeral."[28] If you eliminate the personal essays and memoirs and the books that survive only as curiosities or for their literary value (rather than, say, their historical or scientific value), it is even smaller.

Information and interpretations presented in nonfiction books are superseded. If most readers of nonfiction are trying to learn something that is currently thought to be true, they do not seek out a book that is a hundred, or fifty, or even five years old. "It is all right to study English in Shakespeare; it is all wrong to study astronomy in Newton."[29] Readers look for the latest thing (and in some fields, given the time it takes to publish a book, even the latest thing may already be out of date). To that extent, it is simply the nature of the beast to have a short life.

For some books, the relevant intellectual issues are resolved, or just die out, and researchers move on to new questions. Many nonfiction books become popular because they are controversial. Some are controversial enough that they inspire other researchers to write books disputing the original, and these in turn inspire responses. The sociobiology debate is a good example of this phenomenon in the natural sciences; the nature-versus-nurture debate can serve for the behavioral sciences; and the no-longer-new "new Western history" might do for the humanities. Once the controversy is resolved or dies down, most of these books cease to be interesting and end up on remainder tables or at recycling plants.

And few nonfiction books are well enough written that, once the information becomes outdated, or the issues are resolved, there is any reason to read them. To the extent that these books serve only to inform, they do not survive. They do not entertain, engage, or charm their readers sufficiently to ensure longevity. In order to survive, nonfiction must be stylish (in the literary rather than the fashion sense), personal, and original. That is, lasting nonfiction books must be more *authorial* than most. That is one reason we still read Darwin. There are briefer, more efficient, and more up-to-date books on evolution than *The Voyage of the Beagle* or *The Origin of Species.* Yet these books remain in print and continue to be read simply because, in addition to their historical value as the work of one of the founders of the field, they are fun to read. The nonfiction books that last more than a season are those with a strong narrative line, a narrator or characters whom readers can care about, and engaging language. Readers can sense the author's presence and share the author's developing ideas and convictions.

Authorial style is also important because it strongly influences the impact the book and the ideas it expresses have on the reader. Most nonfiction subjects are open to interpretation. The more important the subject, the more books are likely to be written about it. Yet few readers have time to read every book written about evolution, the cosmos, or the economy. The reader unsatisfied and unconvinced by a poorly written book may seek further information from another source. A well-written book that gains the reader's confidence and conviction will probably determine that reader's views on the issues it discusses. Clifford Geertz justifies the study of his fellow anthropologists' writing styles for this reason: "The ability of anthropologists to get us to take what they say seriously has less to do with either a factual look or an air of conceptual elegance than it has with their capacity to convince us that what they say is a result of their having actually penetrated (or if you prefer, been penetrated by) another form of life, of having, one way or another, truly 'been there.' And that, persuading us that this offstage miracle has occurred, is where the writing comes in."[30] For nonfiction, the author's ability to speak with authority is crucial, and authority derives not only from knowledge and status, but also from the ability to write persuasively.

Melvil Dewey was right, even if it was for the wrong reasons. It is time to look seriously at the library books with all of those decimal points on their spines.

2

A BRIEF HISTORY OF POPULARIZATION

Serious nonfiction is commonly called popularization, popular science, popular history, and the like. These words, although useful until recently, are now imprecise because, beginning in the middle of the twentieth century, the borders between the popular and the scholarly shifted. The word *popularization* is also somewhat loaded with negative connotations. (It could be worse, though: the French call it *vulgarisation*.) The beginnings of popularization are difficult to date, and the vagaries of its status are hard to fathom.

It is important, first, to distinguish between *popular* and *popularized*. Popular history and popular literature have been around as long as people have used language, and written popular literature has existed since language was first recorded. There has always been popular "science," although what we now call science is a modern, post-Enlightenment phenomenon. *Popularization*, though, is more recent. In its relevant definition, "the presentation of a technical or specialized subject in a generally intelligible or appealing form," the *Oxford English Dictionary* dates its first appearance to the 1830s, with *popularizer* first used in 1831. This places it just ahead of the Victorian age, when mass production of inexpensive books, as well as efforts to educate a larger portion of the population, became common in the English-speaking world.

Another reason that this timing makes sense is that during the middle and late nineteenth century the sciences and the secular humanities first established themselves firmly among academic professions. In order to popularize, one must have something that is *not* popular to work from. The starting point might be called elite science, academic history, or highbrow literature; what is important is that it be distinguishable from its popular version. The distinction might be its author: a scientist in a research establishment versus a science journalist, a history professor versus a bestselling writer of presidential biographies. It might be its audience: other research scientists versus interested general readers, history professors versus history buffs. It might also be the medium: a peer-reviewed chemistry journal versus *Scientific American*, a university press monograph versus a paperback from a New York trade house. What is popular is often defined largely in terms of what is not.

Today, the popularizer may teach or do research at a university. At least in the English-speaking world, though, that was unlikely before the twentieth century. Scientists did not hold university posts until the late nineteenth century. Before then, universities in the British Isles remained bastions of theology, classics, and mathematics. In England, most scientists were amateurs. Some were gentlemen, or at least men with enough leisure and independent income to pursue science on their own. Others were working people, often living in rural areas, who devoted their scarce time outside work to collecting natural history specimens or observing natural phenomena. Nor were humanities scholars or social scientists to be found in academe. The great universities granted posts to a few academic historians in a few areas of the discipline, but not nearly so many as there are today; the amateur tradition was strong. Literary criticism, anthropology, sociology, economics, and politics were not recognized as legitimate fields of study. In the United States and the colonies that formed the nation, colleges trained clergymen and, they hoped, pious laymen. The modern research university, with its scientists, social scientists, historians, and literary scholars, was a late-nineteenth-century phenomenon in the English-speaking world.

Popularization also requires a sizable audience. Academic authors may settle for a few hundred readers (indeed, in some fields, they are grateful for that many). Popularizers, though, are looking for thousands or tens of thousands of readers. Popular nonfiction cannot be said to exist until there are enough people with the ability, interest, leisure, and money to read and buy books. Although statistics about literacy are notoriously unreliable, only in the mid-nineteenth century can we say with confidence that a large majority of the population in the United States and Great Britain were literate enough to read books frequently and with pleasure.

And, of course, someone must select, edit, design, print, and publicize the books, as well as provide the capital to finance the enterprise. Although popular literature might have been oral or written in manuscripts, popularizations require print—and relatively cheap print at that. The technology of the Nineteenth-century—papermaking, printing, and transportation—made mass production possible for the first time. Only then did publishers acquire the confidence and expertise to gamble on books for a mass market.

Roy Porter describes the prerequisites for medical popularization as "a body of authorized regular medicine; doctors or writers eager to undertake the work of spreading it; a medium of diffusion, be it printed book, flysheet, handbill, pamphlet, or newspaper column; and, finally, a literate audience keen, prepared, or possibly compelled to imbibe such publications."[1] Much the same can be said of the popularization of other sciences, of history, indeed of any sort of knowledge. Although all of these things fall into place in the middle of the nineteenth century, popular nonfiction did not appear overnight. It has clear antecedents in the Enlightenment. A few scholars have placed it earlier, and their claims are worth examining.

Popularization before Printing

One nineteenth-century scholar claimed to have found scientific popularizations dating back to the Middle Ages. Thomas Wright compiled a collection of three medieval treatises written in or translated into Anglo-Saxon, Anglo-Norman, and English. Because they were in vernacular languages rather than Latin, he argued, they were meant for a popular audience. "We are wrong," he asserts, "in supposing that our forefathers endeavoured to conceal science from the unlearned; at all times they published treatises for the uninitiated." More recent scholarship, particularly in the history of medicine, also argues that the existence of vernacular literature is evidence of a lay audience.[2]

The texts themselves look like they were intended for an audience other than learned clerics and laypeople. Cursive script and the omission of abbreviations familiar only to scholars imply that a work was intended for general readers.[3] While some medieval collections of medical advice "include sophisticated recipes containing Latin terms and exact measurement indications," suggesting an educated audience, "there are also recipe collections that belonged to household literature. Some treatises originating in learned contexts . . . show efforts to accommodate a learned treatise to an expanded audience literate in Middle English." Indeed, the author of one such treatise explained that he translated it "be-cause whomen of oure tonge cvnne bet-tyre rede & vnderstande thys langage than eny other & every whoman let-tyrde [may] rede hit to other vnlettyrd."[4] As this explanation suggests, those who could read frequently read aloud, in public or at home, to those who could not. Clergy read from the pulpit, and official decrees and announcements were read aloud in town meeting places. Books were also read aloud in loftier venues. "Even as late as the 12th century there is the cautionary example of Count Baldwin II of Guines, who was extremely learned and possessed a splendid library, but who never learned to read: he had his books read to him by his *clerici et magistri*."[5]

If there were books for general readers, the audience for them remained very small. "At no point" between 1000 and 1300 "was a significant percent-age of laymen able to read and write. . . . [T]here was a tiny minority who were truly literate and a much larger majority for whom communication could take place only by word of mouth." Among the "tiny minority" were clerks, scribes, and merchants who could read for practical purposes like keeping records for estates and for commerce but who would have been hard pressed to read a book from cover to cover.[6] M. B. Parkes, in his study of medieval texts and reading, describes three kinds of literacy: "that of the professional reader, which is the literacy of the scholar or the professional man of letters; that of the cultivated reader, which is the literacy of recre-ation; and that of the pragmatic reader, which is the literacy of one who has to read or write in the course of transacting any kind of business."[7] At this time, most of the literate few were professional readers. The few literate lay-people were pragmatic readers. Cultivated readers were virtually unknown.

The variety of literature available and the number of people who could read it began to expand in the twelfth and thirteenth centuries with an increase of works in the vernacular. Noble men and women—cultivated readers—read poetry and didactic treatises along with religious works. In this period, those who could afford books bought them and shared them with others, nobles commissioned books about their families, and literacy began to extend beyond the clergy and nobility. A middle class grew in numbers and literacy, so that by the end of the fourteenth century it was possible to speak of a genuine, if small, commercial book market.[8]

If, on the eve of the appearance of the printing press, both literacy and book production were increasing, is it yet legitimate to talk of populariza-tion? Is the mere fact of translation into English (from Latin or French), or the creation of new vernacular texts, evidence of a popular audience? In the late fourteenth and the fifteenth century, English replaced Latin in the courts, schools, and guilds, giving access to those who did not know Latin. In science, too, texts in English gave a larger audience access to knowledge. Medicine was the first of the sciences to be presented in the vernacular. Scholars of medieval medicine divide the literature into treatises for academics, texts for practitioners, and remedy books for nonexperts, and they argue that books in the last class were widely read. "As matters of health are of universal interest, the potential audience for vernacular medical texts includes all those who could read—a heterogeneous group in terms of social status, education, and profession."[9] Given the actual numbers of "those who could read," however, the extent to which that potential was realized remains in doubt.

In the mid-fifteenth century, then, we can find a distant ancestor of modern popularization. Some writers were trying to make specialized knowledge available to larger numbers of people, and their audience was growing. But the distance is as important as the ancestry: literacy rates remained low, books were a luxury, they were not mass produced, and they were by and large meant for practical use—to help readers in their everyday work, to improve their spiritual standing, or to save them from the plague and other ailments. Except for the Bible, books were consulted rather than read.

Popularization and Print

Printing eased the spread of literacy because printed letter forms were fairly standard, as opposed to the great variety of scripts that had been in use. As more titles were printed, the availability of varied reading material made the ability to read a more useful and attractive skill. By the end of the sixteenth century, editions of histories and romances were being published with modernized spelling and glosses—evidence that the authors and printers had a nonscholarly audience in mind.[10]

Despite these advances, the market for books remained small. Owen Gingerich estimates that the first and second editions of Copernicus' *De Revolutionibus*, published in 1543 and 1566, each had a print run of perhaps five hundred copies, achieving what was for the time "relatively wide distribution."[11] Those thousand copies were sold worldwide, over the course of more than two decades, to scholars who could read Latin. Historians of literacy agree that even in the seventeenth century "England was massively illiterate."[12] Estimates of literacy in England around 1650 are roughly 20 percent, while in New England they were double that. But being literate— then as now—did not necessarily imply that one would buy and read books. "Those who could read and write," even in the seventeenth century, "often used their skills in a strictly limited context, to read a letter or make out a bill. They did not necessarily become habitual book-readers."[13] Books were expensive, not only because of the costs of materials and production but because English law limited the size of printings, forcing printers to issue small editions at high prices.[14]

Literacy increased rapidly during the eighteenth century, and the number of readers able to read and buy books grew large enough to support publishers in their efforts to disseminate and create popular literature. Acceptance of Enlightenment doctrines throughout Europe and North America meant more than valuing reason over faith and intellectual freedom over the imposition of dogma. These philosophical beliefs found practical application in movements for reforms that, it was thought, would advance the general progress of humanity. Among these reforms was a commitment to extend education and literacy—enlightenment with a small *e*—to all members of society. By mid-century, perhaps 70 percent of English men and 32 percent of English women could read. In New England, male literacy reached more than 80 percent, and more than half of women could read.[15] Wealthy residents of the American colonies emulated the gentry of England in establishing private libraries. William Byrd II, who lived in Virginia, had a "library of 3500 volumes that he painstakingly imported from England." The collection was "a balanced assortment of titles including the most highly regarded scholarship and literature of Byrd's era [and] reflected his desire to remain in the same intellectual milieu he had known in England," including both classic works and "modern English and European works on philosophy, history and travel, natural sciences and technology, religion, law, and literature."[16]

One result of increased literacy was the emergence of the professional author. Professional writers—those who earn their living at least in part by their pens—did not appear until print was well established. Until the seventeenth century, poets and other writers were supported by patrons, and this practice continued through the eighteenth century, although it declined as an audience large enough to support both author and publisher developed. Even then, professional authors in the eighteenth century earned most of their authorial income not from books but by writing articles for encyclopedias and for periodicals like the *Tatler, Spectator,* and *Guardian.* Sometimes writers of fiction supported themselves through church or government posts, often a disguised form of patronage. Jonathan Swift spent thirty-two years as dean of St. Patrick's in Dublin. Henry Fielding wrote his novels while in the post of London's first stipendiary magistrate, in which capacity he organized the precursor of Scotland Yard.[17] Only later, as the market for books expanded, could authors support themselves solely with payments from readers, via publishers.

Authors of popular nonfiction books were rarely academics. Until the nineteenth century, few university posts went to scholars outside theology, classics, mathematics, and ancient history. The people who held those posts were not subject to today's law of publish or perish. They lived in a closed circle, and their work was circulated among themselves and was often written in Latin. This meant that scholars in other countries could read it, but few laypeople in their own country could do so. In the eighteenth and nineteenth centuries, when publishers sought out authors to fill volumes of history, science, and philosophy for general readers, they looked first to journalists, doctors, amateur scientists, and scientists in government posts. The subjects of most interest to their readers—especially the sciences—were rarely taught in universities. Even in the nineteenth century, the situation at England's leading universities could hardly be said to promote creative thinking in the sciences: "Science teaching at Cambridge and Oxford was not intended to institute a modern, professional education, but rather to educate Christian gentlemen. Half of the students became clergymen, and most of the college fellows were in holy orders. Geology, chemistry, and botany were taught as optional lectures, not examinable until after mid-[nineteenth] century. . . . By the mid-1840s advocates of scientific education despaired of Oxford, where studies were devoted almost entirely to classics and theology." At Cambridge, "instead of being taught geology, many now prepared for examinations in scriptural chronology, where they were expected to affirm the reality of the Flood, and the Creation of the world in 4004 B. C.."[18]

Writing about the controversial subjects of most interest to general audiences, such as the origins of the universe and of humankind, was risky business for academics. The universities remained largely in the control of churchmen, so a certain orthodoxy of opinion was required of the faculty. David Hume, for example, despite excellent family connections and well-regarded scholarship, was denied a post at the University of Edinburgh because of his religious views. He supported himself as the Keeper of the Advocates' Library in Edinburgh and briefly as an undersecretary of state in the Home Office.

The eighteenth century did boast some successful academic authors. Sir William Blackstone, a legal scholar, based his widely read *Commentaries on the Laws of England* on lectures he delivered at Oxford. Adam Smith, who held the chair of moral philosophy at the University of Glasgow, published his *Theory of Moral Sentiments* in 1759 and *The Wealth of Nations* in 1776. Most of his colleagues in political economy, however, were not academics. Jeremy Bentham, trained as a lawyer, was independently wealthy; John Stuart Mill worked for the East India Company; David Ricardo was a securities dealer.

Eighteenth-century publishers and authors developed new media to reach their expanding audience. Periodicals flourished in the eighteenth century, and they sought "a readership beyond scholars . . . the educated, but not just the learned."[19] The *Spectator* and *Tatler* reached a large middle-class audience, many of whom had not been habitual readers. Each issue of the *Spectator* sold three to four thousand copies, and because these were read in coffeehouses and other gathering places, the readership was much larger than the sales.[20]

The eighteenth century was the age of the encyclopedia—not just the *Encyclopédie* of Diderot, but of a whole range of books that attempted to digest and organize knowledge. "Deriving from an ancient classical heritage, the encyclopedia is also closely linked with the emergence of modernity, with assumptions about the public character of information and the desirability of free intellectual and political exchange that became distinctive features of the European Enlightenment." As Richard Yeo, a historian of science, explains, encyclopedias came into being when it became clearly impossible for any one person to assimilate all the knowledge possessed by mankind. Reflecting this development, encyclopedias ceased to be written by single authors but were compiled by editors who commissioned articles from a variety of experts.[21]

The creators of encyclopedias at first tried to organize them as maps of knowledge, emphasizing the relationships among subjects in a systematic way. Always an intellectual challenge, such systematization became increasingly difficult as the range of subjects to be covered expanded. Enlightenment encyclopedias, no longer limited to history and biography, attempted to include the sciences and the practical arts. The sheer volume of information, along with the desire to serve a broader audience, led to the adoption of the system earlier introduced in dictionaries: alphabetical arrangement. Yeo writes that "the notion that alphabetical order offered the practical advantage of accessibility to a wider group of readers—by avoiding issues of classification or theory—is largely an eighteenth-century one." In an attempt to retain the advantages of systematic organization, the encyclopedists "included diagrams showing how various subjects . . . were in fact related to each other in logical, conceptual or historical ways."[22] The encyclopedias of the eighteenth century were not "mere popularizations"; that is, they did not offer merely simplified versions of more complex knowledge. They were useful to specialists who needed to find information quickly, as well as to those wishing to learn something in areas about which they had no knowledge. Some of the encyclopedias first published in the eighteenth century—*Chambers* and the *Britannica*—survived in some form into the twenty-first century. And, interestingly, a late-twentieth-century edition of the *Britannica* reverted to a modified version of the "knowledge map," to extremely mixed reviews.[23]

The encyclopedias succeeded not only because of their content and arrangement but because of the business practices of their publishers. The books were sold serially and by subscription, making them far less expensive than multivolume sets sold as a whole. The encyclopedia developed most fully in the nineteenth century, when technology made cheaper production possible, enlarging the market. And it was in the nineteenth century that the difficulty of creating a single encyclopedia for all readers became clear.

Although the encyclopedia is the most noticeable development in eighteenth-century popularization, books by single authors extending knowledge to laypeople were published successfully as well. Works of philosophy and political economy by Hume, Ricardo, Smith, Mill, and Bentham reached a popular audience in the English-speaking world and were translated into French, German, and other European languages. Smith's *Wealth of Nations* became a canonical text in France during the revolution, when it was "marketed as a work that citizens were duty-bound to read," with editions aimed in design and price at a wide range of audiences.[24]

Sir William Blackstone published his *Commentaries on the Laws of England* between 1765 and 1769. The *Commentaries* explained the English legal system clearly and elegantly to educated laypeople. Blackstone explained his motivation: "a competent knowledge of the laws of that society in which we live, is the proper accomplishment of every gentleman and scholar," not just lawyers. "He was read by the intellectuals. . . . He was studied by the nobility and the squirearchy. A generation or two later, knowledge of the *Commentaries* was so widespread that *Punch* could satirize it."[25] Blackstone's work traveled to the United States, where it influenced lawmaking in the new republic.

Other disciplines—or at least some members of them—were eager to make themselves understood to the expanding literate public. Prominent among these was medicine, which may have been the first profession to "establish clearer boundaries between itself and non-professionals," in part to grant medical practitioners higher status. By 1800, although physicians no longer used only Latin in their writing, vernacular languages gave them specialized vocabularies that effectively shut out lay readers. Medical popularization, then as now, was in part a reaction against professional elitism.[26] Medical advice for laypeople became a staple of English and American publishing. Works published in the United States between the 1790s and 1830s included *The Family Advisor, The American Domestic Medicine, The American Medical Guide*, and *Domestic Medicine*. These books differed in tone from their British equivalents. "Early American writers of domestic medical guides wrote as if their readers were their potential equals or lay colleagues." Although they imitated British models in format and content, they used descriptive names rather than technical ones for diseases, recommended native botanical remedies, and offered optimistic anecdotes. "In an American domestic medical guide no one ever dies of a curable disease brought to the physician writer in time."[27]

Historical writing, too, was transformed "from the minor pastime of a small number of monastic chroniclers and civic officials into a major area of study and leisurely pursuit of university students, lawyers, aspiring courtiers, and ordinary readers, and thence into a much more broadly appealing genre that straddled the worlds of scholarship and literary culture." By the eighteenth century, histories were competing successfully with novels for readers' attention. Historians such as David Hume and Edward Gibbon learned from fiction writers the importance of a well-structured narrative and emotive language, and history had the advantage of being more respectable than fiction.[28] "It was possible to take up with a clear conscience any book, however fantastic, that had the word 'history' displayed on its title page."[29] Like encyclopedias, historical works were often published by subscription. Abridgments and serials of historical works were issued for the larger audience of those who could not afford the time, effort, or money required to read the full-length books, and cheaper pirated editions offered another alternative.[30]

The eighteenth century, then, witnessed a dramatic increase in the accessibility of knowledge. People who were educated but were not scholars could read about practical developments as well as more esoteric knowledge in periodicals, encyclopedias, and books, all written in the vernacular and all accessible to the educated. Those with the ability and the leisure to read books were not yet numerous enough to support a robust publishing industry (the usual first printing for nonfiction was five hundred to two thousand copies),[31] and that industry did not have the technology to produce books at prices that could expand the market beyond the educated, prosperous upper middle class. Yet innovations in business practices were beginning to open the doors to new readers, as were institutions such as commercial and public lending libraries. Within a few decades, publishers would have access to steam-powered presses, machine-made paper, and railroads that could transport their products throughout their countries. The opening of new markets, both geographical and social, made possible the true beginnings of popularization as a genre and as an occupation for writers.

The Nineteenth Century

If popularization requires both academic and professional authors, writing different kinds of books for different kinds of audiences, we can safely say that it appears in the middle of the nineteenth century. What we also see, though, is that the subjects that received popular treatment were not yet so technical or specialized that they needed "translation" for the educated general reader. Darwin's books are accessible to anyone with a college education, for example, not only to other scientists. Yet they could not be said to have reached a mass audience. The number of "educated general readers" remained too small to support such a claim. A mass audience could be reached only by simplification, excerpting, and other popularizing measures, and such writing was generally undertaken by someone other than the original creator, discoverer, or theorist.

Literacy expanded rapidly during the nineteenth century. By the 1880s, nearly 90 percent of English men and women could read, and by the end of the century illiteracy was rare.[32] In the United States, the same numbers held for native-born whites. A somewhat lower percentage of immigrants could read, and the literacy rates of black Americans lagged significantly behind as a lingering result of slavery and laws against teaching slaves to read. These gaps closed during the early twentieth century.[33] Although levels of reading proficiency undoubtedly varied, the important question became not whether people could read but whether they had access to books and a desire to read them.

As long as books remained expensive, access required free or inexpensive libraries and alternative publication forms or retail outlets. Commercial lending libraries had been founded throughout England during the late eighteenth century. Members could pay an annual fee or rent books by the day, and by the mid-nineteenth century their members included working-class people as well as the middle class. Beginning in the 1820s mechanics' institutes joined the mix. These institutes were specifically designed to educate workers through lectures, newspaper reading rooms, and libraries. They made a measurable impact on working-class reading. By 1850, 610 institutes owned about seventy thousand volumes and were circulating nearly two million books a year. The institutes remained active into the 1890s.[34]

Commercial libraries and mechanics' institutes did not serve rural areas very well, and church groups tried to fill the vacuum. But the village libraries they opened generally stocked only tracts and other books that passed the relevant theological tests. As Richard Altick notes, groups that encouraged reading for solely utilitarian purposes lacked "any sense of the intellectual and spiritual enrichment—or the simple relaxation—that an individual man or woman, boy or girl, may derive from reading."[35] The absence of fiction, science, and controversial literature encouraged people to form book clubs whose members pooled their funds to buy books. It was the readers themselves, of whatever social class, who created the market for novels and for entertaining, thought-provoking nonfiction.

In the United States, by the time of the Civil War large personal libraries could be found in wealthy homes in cities and in the country. More important, "public and quasi-public libraries of various types, almost unknown in the colonial era, were now commonplace through much of the North, and apprentices, artisans, and clerks, as well as mill girls and domestic servants, were afforded the opportunity to read extensively."[36] Free public libraries became widespread in Great Britain and the United States when Andrew Carnegie contributed funds for the purpose beginning in the 1890s.

American women in both cities and rural communities formed literary societies that not only promoted reading but provided forums in which women could develop civic skills such as speaking in public, conducting meetings, and presenting reports. African Americans also used literary societies for these purposes and—like the women—to demonstrate their capacity for full citizenship. The creation of library collections was not a major purpose of such groups, but they did promote reading and the appreciation of books.[37]

Cheaper formats enabled both libraries and individuals to increase their book purchases. Publishers in Great Britain and the United States had experimented successfully with serialization in the eighteenth century, and they continued this approach in the nineteenth. Nonprofit organizations joined church groups in producing tracts—pamphlets sold at low prices or given away—to promote the right sort of reading among the working classes. Opinion was divided, of course, over what exactly the right sort of reading might be, although there was general agreement that it should not be fiction. Beginning in the 1820s, evangelical Christian groups worried about the availability of modern scientific works in cheap formats. "Readers who did not have intellectual safeguards might be seduced . . . into believing that new scientific discoveries could be interpreted only in an anti-religious manner, and they might end up as unbelievers." The solution to this problem was to create a new genre: Christian popular science. The Religious Tract Society rose to the challenge in 1845 with a monthly series of inexpensive popular science books and, a few years later, the weekly *Leisure Hour*. Unlike religious tracts, which were given away, these publications were sold at a modest price and were so popular that their sales completely covered the Society's costs.[38]

Commercial publishers and groups such as the Society for the Diffusion of Useful Knowledge took note of the Tract Society's success. Although a number of cheap book series had failed in the 1820s, technological advances (and perhaps a leap of secular faith) made several houses risk them again in the 1840s. Steam-powered printing presses, machine-made paper, and stereotyping (printing from reusable plates rather than standing type) made cheap production possible, but it took a large market to make it profitable. Because so many of the costs of book publication occur before the books actually go to press, the size of the print run has a great impact on the price at which the book must be sold. The publisher's overhead, editing and design, and typesetting costs remain the same whether the publisher is issuing a hundred copies or ten thousand. The costs of paper, printing, and binding vary with the size of the print run, of course, but even there economies of scale come into play. Publishers in England had long adhered to a model of small editions sold at a high price per copy. They were slow to shift to a model of large editions sold at lower prices. Yet, in the middle of the nineteenth century, this shift did take place. In 1811, only 20 percent of the books published in England sold for 3s 6d or less; by 1855, nearly half of all books were in this cheapest category, and in 1865 the figure rose to more than 60 percent.[39] Altick suggests that this conversion took place after publishers witnessed the financial success of five- or six-shilling reprints of three-decker novels that had earlier sold for 31s 6d: "Between 1827 and 1832, therefore, London and Edinburgh publishers behaved as if they stood on a peak in Darien, beholding for the first time a vast sea of common readers." By the end of the century, expensive first editions were a rarity. Instead of trying to sell fewer than a thousand copies at high prices, publishers were printing tens of thousands at six shillings.[40]

But this new publishing model, and these new numbers, applied mainly to fiction. Many more people wanted to buy a Dickens novel—whether serialized or bound—than wanted to read history or science. To appeal to the vast sea, publishers of nonfiction had to do more than make books cheap: they had to make them intellectually accessible and entertaining for a literate but not highly educated mass audience. Publishers and authors in England recognized the need for a new style of writing, but until mid-century they had failed to understand what Altick called "the art of popularization."[41] In the end, secular publishers encouraged authors to adapt the narrative techniques of novelists to their task, and evangelical publishers followed suit, seeking "a balance between the requirement for Christian content and the equally strong need to avoid scaring off potential readers."[42]

American publishers saw their market expand even more dramatically than their British colleagues. In part this was a function of population growth: at the turn of the nineteenth century, there were around 4 million Americans, but by the beginning of the Civil War there were more than 32 million.[43] Almost all of them, both men and women, could read. Public schooling was readily available, at least through the elementary grades, and schoolbooks were needed. Libraries, too, flourished. As long as there was no copyright agreement between the United States and England, American publishers could issue current English works without paying royalties. (Although English publishers could have reciprocated, they found little American literature worth pirating.) But American publishers also published American works, many of which were nonfiction. Establishing a national identity required history books, biographies, natural histories, and eventually fiction reflecting national issues and culture. History and biography became major American cultural enterprises. By the 1830s, Jared Sparks "was making a small industry out of the lives and letters of Washington and Franklin, and his *Library of American Biography*"; and George Bancroft, W. H. Prescott, and Washington Irving all wrote histories that sold extremely well. James Fenimore Cooper's historical novels were far more successful than his other fiction. Of these writers, only Sparks held an academic post.[44] "In the 1840s and 1850s, dozens of histories intended for the masses exploded into the market. The rise of 'popular history' as an independent genre" started with the publication of inexpensive comprehensive histories that often sold as well as fiction.[45] At least one American biographer, James Parton, wrote successfully for both elite literary audiences and the masses. Parton wrote for "the broad, literate middle class, whose tastes lay somewhere above dime novels and somewhere beneath fancy European literatures and esoteric science and philosophy." Writers of less talent, "hack biographers [who] allegedly degraded the genre by pandering to masses of readers," also experienced financial success.[46]

Publishers in the United States were quick to adopt new technologies, marketing techniques, and business methods. After all, most were starting from scratch and had no attachment to previous ways of doing business. Printers like the Harper brothers quickly became publishers, underwriting and organizing the whole process of manufacturing and marketing books. The number of publishing enterprises grew rapidly. Boston, for example, had roughly a hundred editorial offices during the 1820s but nearly seven hundred a mere twenty years later. In addition to publishing inexpensive books and extremely inexpensive chapbooks, American houses sold books by subscription, employing sales representatives to recruit buyers before publication. A large subscription meant a large guaranteed sale.[47]

By the middle of the nineteenth century, writing for a mass audience became appealing to authors on both sides of the Atlantic as a way to generate support for the fields and ideas that interested them, but also as a way to earn money. These writers, for the most part, were not academics. They were journalists, lawyers, doctors, or men of independent means. Publishers turned to them for books about science, history, and travel. When publishers contracted with academic writers, they were generally seeking textbooks or books for "school series." The mid-nineteenth-century lists of the Harper Brothers and Henry Holt, for example, are full of books by academics (both British and American) written for their various school library series.[48]

The vast sea of common readers did not come into being because an educated elite granted them literacy and guided their reading. Indeed, parallel to the reformist desire to educate the masses ran conservative resistance. "Culture was a force for equality and was destructive of ideology, including the ideology supporting the British class structure."[49] Once unleashed, however, literacy proved a powerful force. People of all classes developed a desire to read—in some cases an emotional and intellectual *need* to read—that publishers rushed to satisfy once they recognized that it existed.

Desire is hard to document. It may well be that people in the Middle Ages longed to read as much as their nineteenth-century descendants did. But only when ordinary people became sufficiently literate to keep journals and write letters was this need expressed in a way that is useful to historians. Jonathan Rose, in *The Intellectual Life of the British Working Classes* (2001), used such documents from the late nineteenth and early twentieth centuries to show not only the profound hunger for learning of ordinary people but also the high level of intellectual and political consciousness that ran parallel to it. Although many readers began with simplified works, and some never moved beyond them, others used such works as stepping stones to more serious reading. Despite the predictions and recommendations of university-educated reformers, working-class readers devoured the same books recommended to upper-class readers in universities and salons. They read the ancient and modern classics, Shakespeare, the English poets, and—most relevant here—popular, but unpopularized, nonfiction. T. A.

Jackson, a typesetter and lecturer for the Communist Party of Great Britain who was born in 1879, wrote in his autobiography, "Incongruous though it may seem, it was Macaulay as much as anybody who gave me a push-off on the road from the conventional conception of history as a superficial chronicle-narrative to the wider philosophical conception of history as an all-embracing world-process as understood by Marx." Another Communist, J. T. Murphy, a few years younger than Jackson, found that in reading Macaulay's essay on Milton "it is only necessary to transpose 'bourgeois revolution' to 'proletarian revolution' and you can soon think you are reading an essay by Trotsky, whose style of writing is not unlike Macaulay's, on the Russian Revolution."[50] Working-class readers chose their books with little regard for the recommendations of cultural arbiters, and they interpreted them "against the grain," extracting messages to which upper-class readers might have been blind.

In a study of what was perhaps the first popular science bestseller—Robert Chambers's anonymously issued *Vestiges of the Natural History of Creation*, published in many editions beginning in 1844—James Secord shows not only the wide range of readers the book attracted with variously priced editions, but the wide range of reactions to it. Although religious conservatives opposed the book strongly, and some scientists were critical of its facts and interpretations, most readers were enthusiastic about the knowledge it transmitted and the quality of the writing. Working-class reactions were both enthusiastic and critical: readers did not accept or reject Chambers's conclusions unthinkingly. The responses that readers recorded in their journals and letters show the value placed on the book and the care with which it was read. Eighteen-year-old apprentice surveyor Thomas Archer Hirst read *Vestiges* "with devouring attention more closely in fact than any book up to this point in his life other than the Bible." He read critically, intensely, with an eye to self-improvement. "By the time he checked *Vestiges* out of the library, he had already read Lyell's *Principles of Geology*, Humboldt's *Cosmos*, Mantell's *Wonders of Geology*, . . . Combe's *Constitution of Man*, Jeremiah Joyce's *Natural Philosophy*, Cuvier's *Theory of the Earth*," and many volumes of theology. Hirst compared *Vestiges* with his other reading, creating "a continuous narrative of his own experience." Hirst discussed these books with friends who also, despite leaving school at young ages, continued their education and their self-formation through their reading.[51]

The Twentieth Century

The readers whom Rose and Secord describe were self-educated. Their hunger for knowledge had not been satisfied by the limited educational opportunities available to them, and books filled the gap. The most important development for nonfiction in the twentieth century, in the United States before Great Britain, was the expansion of educational opportunity. High school became available to more and more people. The age at which children could leave school was raised, and states required communities to provide free schools for all. A college education, however, remained beyond the reach of most.

Recognition that many people who were unable to attend college wished to continue their education led to two collaborations between distinguished academics and commercial enterprises: the Harvard Classics and the Great Books. Both projects sought to make the education (or at least the reading) offered at the nation's great universities available to all. The texts, translated into English when necessary, were accompanied by guidance to readers in introductory lectures, notes, and—for the Great Books—the two-volume *Syntopicon*, an elaborate index.

The Harvard Classics were selected by Charles W. Eliot, who had recently retired as president of Harvard, and published by Collier between 1909 and 1914. This "five-foot shelf" of books was offered as "a good substitute for a liberal education in youth to anyone who would read them with devotion, even if he could spare but fifteen minutes a day for reading."[52] Eliot's goal was "to open that collection of literary materials to many ambitious young men and women whose education was cut short by the necessity of contributing in early life to the family earnings, or of supporting themselves."[53]

The Great Books grew out of the ideas of John Erskine, a member of the Columbia faculty; Mortimer Adler, one of his students; and Robert M. Hutchins, the president of the University of Chicago. Unlike the "five-foot shelf," the Great Books were more than a publishing project. They were designed to revolutionize the college curriculum and to provide a focus for adult education through guided discussion groups. They were, however, also a publishing project: in 1952 the Encyclopedia Britannica launched the fifty-four-volume series *Great Books of the Western World*, eventually marketed so aggressively that the Federal Trade Commission was moved to investigate.[54]

Neither of these projects constitutes popularization as I have defined it. The texts—whatever their original purpose and intended audience—are unaltered. The editors were making specialized knowledge accessible to nonspecialists only by providing convenient editions, translating into English, and adding general advice and background. But these projects are part of the history of popularization because of their intention (the commercial aspect aside) to disseminate knowledge to a mass audience and their recognition of a desire for "higher learning" beyond the academy.

Another early twentieth-century precursor of modern popularization was the summary, digest, or outline volume. H. G. Wells's *Outline of History* (1920) and Hendrik Willem Van Loon's *Story of Mankind* (1921) led the way. But the most famous and longest lasting were *The Story of Philosophy*, by Will Durant (1926), and the multivolume *Story of Civilization*, by Durant and his wife, Ariel (1935–75). These books ran counter to the academic trend of specialization: no academic historian or philosopher would attempt to summarize centuries of events or thought unless writing a survey textbook. Will Durant recognized that his projects were both unfashionable and—in the case of *Civilization*—grandiose. But Durant's approach struck a chord: *The Story of Philosophy* was a bestseller and is still in print; *Civilization* was a financial success as well.

Philosophy attracts general readers because it tackles questions of eternal interest, but its difficulty and abstractness are barriers to independent understanding. Durant sought "to humanize knowledge by centering the study of speculative thought around certain dominant personalities"—anticipating an approach to popularization that would flourish in the early post–World War II era.[55] He summarized and simplified their arguments in a lively, direct narrative, and he engaged his readers with rhetorical questions and humor. In *Civilization*, he and his wife wrote the history of the world, including the non-Western world, in sweeping narratives of cultural and social change, moving beyond politics and economics.

The enthusiastic reception of the Durants' work (including a Pulitzer prize and a Presidential Medal of Freedom) was not echoed by professional historians, who were critical of the volumes' accuracy, selection of sources, uncritical acceptance of earlier work, and neglect of recent scholarship. In the history of popularization, the Durants' work is important because it "increased the need for mediation between the academy and the public that had helped to create the 'outline' vogue in the first place."[56]

By the end of World War II, then, the prerequisites of successful popularization were in place. Professional scientists, historians, social scientists, and humanities scholars held academic posts and were creating new knowledge for transmission to a variety of audiences. Publishers had the technology to publish large numbers of books at reasonable prices, and they had developed business methods and a view of the market that made large-scale activity profitable. (Paperbacks had been technologically possible for some time, but a workable distribution system and access to adequate numbers of titles were achieved only in the 1940s.) Readers had the same desire to read that we have seen in their parents and grandparents. What was about to change was their preparation to appreciate and assimilate advanced scholarship, for when World War II ended, the United States expanded educational opportunities in ways that previous generations had only dreamed of.

3

A HIGHLY EDUCATED PUBLIC

Since the settling of the American colonies, Americans have valued literacy and education, at least for some members of society. In colonial times, men were far more likely to be literate than women, and whites were far more likely to be literate than Native Americans (most of whose cultural traditions were oral and who did not have written languages) or African Americans. Slaves were rarely taught to read, and as fear of slave rebellion increased, many southern states made it illegal to teach them. Even though this ban was not entirely effective, it certainly prevented most African Americans in those states from reading. Free blacks had far higher literacy rates. In addition, city dwellers were generally more literate than the rural population, and the affluent were taught better and longer than the poor.[1]

As the nation developed, the differences between opportunities offered to urban white males and those available to citizens of color, immigrants, women, and the poor gradually diminished, and the number of Americans receiving primary and, later, high school education increased. By the 1920s, almost every American attended elementary school, educators were promoting universal public secondary education as a reasonable goal, and most communities provided free public high schools. As George S. Counts wrote in a 1922 report, "The conception of secondary education as education for the selected few, whether by birth or by talent, appears to be giving ground before the assaults of political democracy and the demands of a society of increasing complexity and wealth." As in the nineteenth century, children of uneducated parents, African Americans, and rural young people were the least likely to find high school accessible; girls, however, were *more* likely to attend high school than boys. Compulsory high school for all children through age sixteen was not accomplished nationwide until 1960. Equal quality of public education remains elusive, but by the 1970s court cases had begun to change school funding formulas, and equity is at least on the national agenda.[2]

After World War II, the American vision of educational opportunity expanded to include the availability of a college education. Increased college attendance was expected to provide a better-educated electorate, to improve the American economy by raising the quality of the workforce, and to heighten America's chances to compete technologically against the Soviets during the Cold War and economically against the Germans and Japanese later in the century. Equality of opportunity for women and minority students also became a social goal. Whatever the motivations, this broadened educational policy was effective. Beginning in the late 1940s, more Americans were attending college than even the most optimistic educators had predicted in 1945. While in college, and after leaving, those Americans supported an expansion of book publishing that was also unprecedented.

Education and Reading

Studies of literacy and reading all show that the more education people receive, the more likely they are to read. Those who have completed high school read more than those who have not, and those who have attended college read more than those whose education stopped at high school.[3] The possible reasons for this relationship are many, and though none of them has been adequately tested, they are probably all correct, at least for some people at some times.

One possibility is that people are better educated because they are readers, rather than vice versa. That is, children who develop the habit of reading—because their parents read to them, because a librarian or teacher introduced them to reading, or for some other reason—may be more likely to succeed in school and to continue their education longer. Of course people may develop the habit of reading later in life. We know from the memoirs of writers and other educated readers that a love of books can be formed in one's adult years. For example, some people became readers because they were given novels in Armed Services Editions, paperbacks distributed free to service personnel, while in the military during World War II. The poet and novelist James Dickey recalled that he had gone to college to play football. During the war, though, he began to read, and when he returned he transferred to another university and became a serious student of literature. Helen MacInnes, whose work appeared in the Armed Services Editions, received a letter from a veteran who had read her work as an enlisted man. He "said he had read little until [the Armed Services Editions] got him *enjoying* literature. From there he read constantly, and after his service went to college. He ended with a Ph.D. and sent me a copy. It was dedicated to me, the writer of the novel that started his reading."[4] But for many people, childhood reading becomes a lifetime habit that also promotes educational aspirations.

Among children of educated upper- or middle-class parents, reading generally begins at home. In her memoir, *One Writer's Beginnings*, Eudora Welty wrote, "I learned from the age of two or three that every room in our house, at any time of day, was there to read in, or to be read to. . . . I live in gratitude to my parents for initiating me—and as early as I begged for it, without keeping me waiting—into knowledge of the word, into reading and spelling, by way of the alphabet. They taught it to me at home in time for me to begin to read before starting to school." Jorge Luis Borges recalled, "I was lucky to have been educated not only in schools—that was second-ary—but in my father's library. . . . When I remember my childhood, I think less of the neighbourhood than of my father's library, and I think of those books that revealed the world to me." For Richard Rodriguez, the son of Mexican immigrants, books and reading did not become important until school began, but reading and educational success were, if anything, more closely linked: "In fourth grade I embarked upon a grandiose reading pro-gram. . . . Each time I finished a book, I reported the achievement to a teacher and basked in the praise my effort earned. . . . Librarians who ini-tially frowned when I checked out the maximum ten books at a time started saving books they thought I might like. Teachers would say to the rest of the class, 'I only wish the rest of you took reading as seriously as Richard obviously does.'"[5]

It is also possible that a single set of characteristics underlies success in both reading and education. Such characteristics might include innate intelli-gence, parental guidance, ambition, the ability to sit still and concentrate, or simply a lack of distractions (such as television) in childhood. In other words, reading may not cause educational success and educational success may not cause a love of reading: they may both be effects of the same causes.

The most straightforward explanation of the relationship is that more education provides people with better reading abilities, so that reading becomes easier and more pleasurable. This argument is especially compelling when we look at the differences between young readers and nonreaders. If a limited vocabulary or poor grasp of grammar makes reading a chore, then other forms of entertainment become far more attractive. Yet this is true even at higher levels of education: one or two college courses in literature enable students to read novels, plays, and poetry with a clearer awareness of what they are reading and why it is written as it is than they would have if they had never been exposed to the subject. Reading is not necessarily "easier," but it is more rewarding.

One reason for reading nonfiction is to find information or explanations. It seems likely that education increases curiosity, or at least broadens the range of subjects about which one might be curious. One study has shown that the more education people receive, the more likely they are to follow election campaigns, keep up with public affairs, and seek information about health matters. Even more likely, education trains us to use books, rather than other media, to satisfy our need for facts or knowledge.[6] When trying to understand an event in some distant part of the world, a less educated person might call a radio talk show, while a more educated person would head for the library. One person might be satisfied with a summary account on the nightly news, while the other might want the kind of background analysis available only in print. A study in the 1960s showed that college graduates read more than other adults and watched less television.[7] The World Wide Web has not replaced books: people often search the Web for quick answers (it may be replacing reference books), but for extended accounts and explanations, they seek out books (often bought via the Web).

A survey by the Gallup Organization showed that college-educated people, especially in middle age, prefer nonfiction to fiction. In my own survey, a fifty-year-old reader explained: "The older I become the less patience I have with modern fiction. Perhaps I figure I'm running out of time to spend on that which pays no other dividend than escape."[8] The elderly man in the comic strip *Pickles* offered another explanation: "At my age, I only read stuff that will make me look good if I die in the middle of it." Other theories about education and reading support the *Pickles* character, reminding us that people may read, and select what to read, for reasons that have little to do with the books themselves. People may read the books most talked about in their own social circles simply to keep in step with everyone else. That is one reason why a book's selection by a book club, or its appearance on a bestseller list, leads more people to read it: if it's so popular, it must be good, and even if it isn't good, everyone is talking about it, and no one likes to be left out. Nor is this merely a "lowbrow" or "middlebrow" phenomenon. The "highbrow" reader simply relies on different authorities: the *New York Review of Books*, for example, or the *Times Literary Supplement*, instead of the Literary Guild or Oprah's Book Club. As Pierre Bourdieu pointed out, the decision to read at all, or to read more elite literature, may result not from what one learned in college but simply from the fact that one attended. It is a matter of living up to expectations, whether they are society's or one's own. One reader noted that there are some books we read out of a sense of duty shaped in our late adolescent years—"all that foundational reading you forgot to do in college because you were too stoned."[9]

A related reason for reading at all—or for reading "good" books—is guilt. People who have benefited from a college education may feel that their usual occupations do not fully exercise their intellectual capacities, and that by watching television or reading "junk" they are somehow behaving badly. This theory may sound farfetched until one thinks about selecting books to take on vacation. Into the box with the paperbacks recently picked up for that purpose go the "difficult" novel bought with good intentions back in February and the new book on quantum mechanics that is supposed to be more comprehensible than the last one, still on the bedside table unfinished. Harry Scherman, the founder of the Book-of-the-Month Club, subscribed to this theory and claimed that the club's advertising campaigns appealing to guilt were uniformly successful.[10]

A variant on the guilt theory is that of competitive reading. In a 1989 article in the *New Republic*, Lawrence Lipking described competitive reading as the scramble to find new meaning in texts. Within the academy the competition is between selections of books (my reading list is better than yours) and "rival interpretations . . . my reading can beat your reading." This kind of competition grows heated in classrooms (especially graduate seminars) and in book discussion groups. But another form of competitive reading takes place between individuals. In explaining why she ruined a Maine vacation by reading Steven Pinker's *How the Mind Works* instead of something lighter, writer Jennifer Moses confessed: "My husband had loved *How the Mind Works*, and as he and I are competitive readers, I knew that if

I gave up on it, I would lose the advantage I'd held over him ever since I'd finished reading Thomas Mann's *Magic Mountain.*" And readers also compete with themselves: Am I a good enough person to set aside that trashy thriller in favor of a classic novel or new elucidation of the space/time continuum? (And where did I learn that the thriller was trashy?)[11]

Each of us is motivated to read by a combination of curiosity, habit, a desire to impress others, an intellectual need to understand the changing world, and a search for enjoyable ways to use our time. And each of us reads different sorts of books in response to these different motivations. We may read mysteries to entertain ourselves, self-help books to figure out how to talk to our teenaged children, "quality" fiction to impress in conversation at parties, computer books to save us from technological disaster, and nonfiction to understand what is happening in Africa or what we should think about genetic engineering. Education affects all these choices, even if we do not understand exactly how. We may choose to read a book because we have seen favorable reviews (and our choice of which review media to read is affected by how well educated we are), because friends or colleagues have recommended it (our friends and colleagues are, in all likelihood, similarly educated), because the book appeals to us aesthetically (our tastes in design are influenced by our education), or because the subject concerns us (the level and nature of our education influence the breadth of our curiosity and concerns).

It is probably impossible to formulate with any precision the exact nature of the relationship between reading and education. In fact, accepting the simple fact of the relationship, as well as the extreme complexity of its workings, may be the best way to approach the subject. Certainly the dramatic improvement in the educational attainments of the American people in the second half of the twentieth century increased the number of potential book readers and altered their reading tastes.

Going to College

In 1945 a group of book publishers and manufacturers commissioned a study of American reading and book-buying habits. Publishers had prospered during the war (despite paper rationing and other exigencies), and they were eager to know whether they were likely to thrive when it was over. Because textbook publishing is an important segment of the industry, a hundred college and university administrators were polled to determine what they saw as the future of higher education. Of those hundred, twenty-five expected no increase in enrollment. Some had no opinion, but the sixty-eight who anticipated growth expected it to be in the range of 40 percent over the next decade.[12] They could hardly have been more mistaken.

In fact, between 1940 and 1950 (and presumably mostly between 1945 and 1950), college enrollment in the United States increased by 78 percent. Much of this increase can be explained by a single event: on June 22, 1944, the Congress had passed the G.I. Bill of Rights, which provided economic support for veterans who wished to continue their education. College administrators were not alone in underestimating the impact of this legislation. The political economist Peter Drucker wrote: "It was seen by practically everybody as pure public relations. President Truman regretted all his life that his father's bankruptcy prevented him from going to college before World War I. But even he would not have signed the GI Bill of Rights had he not been assured by all his advisers (foremost among them the then president of Harvard) that practically no one among the veterans would avail themselves of the bill's educational benefits." By the time the program expired in 1956, 2.8 million veterans had used it to attend college. And the growth continued. When the children of the G.I. Bill generation (and there were a great many of them) grew to college age in the decade between 1960 and 1970, enrollment grew by 140 percent. In 1940, 1.6 million people had been enrolled in college. By 1960, enrollment had risen to 3.7 million; in 1969, to 7.8 million; in 1980 to 12 million, and in 2000, to 15.3 million.[13]

This increase was due to more than population growth. The period after the war was one of prosperity and rising expectations. People who have attended college expect their children to do so as well, so that increased college enrollments for one generation beget increased enrollments for the next—assuming that places and tuition money are available. The federal government supported its citizens in these aspirations. The G.I. Bill was only the beginning of an almost unfathomable expansion of federal aid to higher education. In addition to research funding, discussed in the next chapter, the government introduced new forms of student financial assistance. In 1960, federal student aid amounted to $300 million; by 1980, it was $10 billion (both figures are in 1980 dollars); by 1990 it was nearly $20 billion, and in 2002 it was nearly $38.6 billion.[14]

Another important reason for the expansion of college enrollment was the extension of educational opportunities to new groups of Americans. The G.I. Bill sent African American veterans to college, making educational aspirations achievable for many who had only dreamed of continuing their schooling. The civil rights movement in the 1950s and 1960s both assisted the growth of traditionally black colleges and made it possible for African Americans to attend previously segregated institutions. As a result of these advances and of activism by other minority groups, minority enrollment in colleges and universities increased from 10 percent in 1968 to 17 percent in 1980. The students who enrolled under the G.I. Bill changed faculty attitudes as well, engendering "an appreciation among academics of admission policies based on merit rather than family history," which also facilitated the admission of other previously excluded groups.[15]

Women's expectations also changed. The 1950s may have been the decade of suburbs, domesticity, and large families, but in 1960, 37 percent of the students enrolled in colleges and universities were women. As the women's movement gained strength in the following decades, college enrollment grew more balanced, so that by 1980, 51 percent of all college students were women.[16]

The enlargement and diversification of the student body had profound effects on both the publishing industry and the college curriculum. More students needed more books, and new kinds of students demanded new courses—which required more books. The expansion of the publishing industry began in the textbook companies.

A Growth Industry

In 1959, *Fortune* reported that textbook publishing was "the fastest-growing, most remunerative and most freely competitive branch of book publishing."[17] Many publishing companies that had neglected textbooks in favor of their trade branches began investing in them, expanding their educational divisions, acquiring smaller textbook companies, or merging with companies whose textbook lists complemented their own. Harper's, a leader in textbook publishing in the nineteenth and early twentieth centuries, had actually stopped publishing schoolbooks in 1951. To correct their mistake they merged with Row, Peterson in 1962, becoming the firm long known as Harper & Row, with a strong textbook list. Holt, Rinehart & Winston, another leading textbook firm, was created when Henry Holt (with a strong high school list) bought Rinehart (with a large college list) and John C. Winston (a publisher of elementary texts). The new firm provided schoolbooks for students from kindergarten through college. Simon & Schuster, which had begun as a publisher of crossword puzzle books, became the country's largest publishing house by expanding into more general trade books and by acquiring large numbers of trade and textbook companies.[18]

The fastest growth in textbook sales between 1940 and 1970 occurred in college-level publishing. Some of the companies that published elementary and high school texts also published college textbooks, but others published only for higher education. John Wiley & Sons had published scientific and technical books along with college textbooks before World War II. With the end of the war and the dramatic increase in college enrollments, the company expanded from 99 employees in 1945 to 229 in 1948. W. W. Norton had started a college division in 1930 to increase the sales of its trade books by getting them into classrooms and gradually began publishing books exclusively for classroom use. Throughout the 1970s and 1980s, textbooks were the primary source of Norton's growth. As the publisher of the *Norton Anthology of English Literature*, the company has helped to define the literary canon.[19]

The growth of textbook publishing was both dramatic and predictable, given the nation's demographics, but sales of books for general readers also skyrocketed, due in large part to the growth of the paperback industry. Paperbound books had been sold in a variety of forms since the nineteenth century, but modern paperbacks made their appearance in the United States just before World War II, when Pocket Books and Penguin Books entered the business. Their growth was slowed by wartime paper shortages, but as soon as the war ended, they rapidly increased the number of titles they published and the number of copies of each that they printed.

Paperbacks succeeded so quickly because they were inexpensive (then, as now, mass-market paperbacks cost about one-fifth as much as hardback books) and because they were sold at many outlets other than bookstores—newsstands, drugstores, railroad stations, and airports. Early paperbacks were mostly reprints of classics and new issues of genre fiction—mysteries, adventure stories, and science fiction. But their profitability enabled the paperback houses to form alliances with hardback publishers and to acquire paperback rights to current titles. By 1959, despite their far lower prices, paperbacks were responsible for more sales dollars than hardbacks. Paperback sales rose from roughly $14 million in 1947 to $67 million in 1959.[20]

In the early years, fiction dominated paperback lists, but a rapid shift took place in the early 1960s. In 1959, slightly fewer than 2,000 paperback fiction titles were published, compared to 1,200 nonfiction titles. Three years later, fiction titles rose to about 2,800 while nonfiction rose to 6,115. Industry analysts attributed much of the growth to the use of paperbacks in schools and colleges.[21] Most of the paperbacks used in classrooms were "trade" paperbacks: larger format books with higher-quality paper and higher prices than the mass-market paperbacks found on drugstore racks. These more respectable-looking volumes were also more appealing to booksellers, who had generally refused to stock cheap paperbacks but found room on their shelves for the trade paperbacks.

Respectability is important in the sale of nonfiction. The reader looking for a good novel is willing to buy a cheap paperback because the author's name or the title is a known quantity. But the reader seeking authoritative information about the economy or the human genome, or a better under-standing of Islam, probably will not recognize an author's name. The trade format, in addition to looking more reliable, generally provides more infor-mation about the author and, if the book appeared first in hardback, offers excerpts from reviews of the original edition. Trade paperbacks are also more durable and therefore more appealing to people who value and keep their books.

The publishers of quality nonfiction benefited not only from the increased number of college graduates and the appearance of an appropriate medium. Reform and diversification of the curriculum led to a demand for more titles, not only for use in the classroom but also for general readers. It also led to some fairly acrimonious debates, which publishers managed to turn into bestsellers.

Curriculum Development and Debates

In 1960, half of U.S. college students were enrolled in private, generally liberal arts, colleges. By 1980, 80 percent of the enrollment was in public institutions not committed exclusively to the liberal arts. In 1960, the cur-riculum was dominated by departments of sciences and letters. By 1980, the curriculum was dominated by professional subjects such as those taught in business or engineering schools. Between 1969 and 1976—a mere seven years—undergraduate enrollments in professional curricula rose from 38 to 58 percent.[22]

This transformation reflected a dramatic change in students' goals. As Christopher Jencks and David Riesman wrote in a 1968 study: "Until World War II many if not most undergraduates came to the old special-interest colleges in order to kill time, get away from home, make new friends, enjoy themselves, acquire salable skills, and so forth. . . . Today a substantial fraction of the undergraduate population wants not only a degree but an undergraduate transcript sufficiently distinguished to ensure entry into a competitive professional school of some sort."[23] The changes in women's goals were even more dramatic: the importance of college in seeking a husband lessened, and women began to earn not only B.A.'s and B.S.'s but Ph.D.'s, M.B.A.'s, M.D.'s, and J.D.'s in numbers that by the 1990s often equaled the numbers of degrees awarded to men.

After World War II, then, the United States had more college students, who were more serious about their studies, more career-oriented, and more narrowly educated than the prewar student population. The narrowness of their education began with the shift to professional curricula. According to one writer, "the recipients of [professional] degrees have usually taken as few courses as possible outside of their major and, within the professional specialization, have given little or no attention to, say, the philosophy and ethics of law, the social psychology of medicine, the aesthetics of engineering, the ideological basis for business."[24] Also, if a professional student *did* take a course in philosophy, it would in all likelihood be the philosophy *of* engineering, law, or medicine rather than a more general course. But professionalism was not the only source of narrowness.

Since the late nineteenth century, college administrators and faculty, as well as the interested public, have been arguing over what students should learn. At first the question was what, beyond the classics, is important? Should modern languages (as opposed to Greek and Latin) be taught? How much time should be allotted to the sciences? Is American (as opposed to English) literature worthy of study? Gradually other questions were raised, focusing in part on how to accomplish curricular reform, and the presidents of Harvard, Columbia, and Chicago took competing stands that were debated and copied throughout the nation.

As the discussion was phrased in the post–World War II era, the arguments were at first simply over questions of breadth versus specialization. To what extent should students be required to take courses outside their major fields? Should this breadth be achieved through a "core curriculum," "general education" courses, distribution requirements, or some other set of regulations? A core curriculum requires all students—regardless of their fields—to enroll in a common set of courses in the humanities, social sciences, and hard sciences. "General education" may require students to choose from broader offerings of specially designed interdisciplinary courses in these three areas of knowledge. "Distribution requirements" solve the problem by requiring that students take a certain number of courses from each of these areas.

The question of breadth grew complicated as specific goals, some more controversial than others, were added to the debate. Many faculty members argued for including required courses in response to technological change—courses imparting "numeracy" and "computer literacy," for example. Although such requirements seemed reasonable to most faculty members, they were sometimes offered as substitutes for courses in foreign languages or other traditional requirements. Aside from the merits of the case, this would mean a shift in enrollments—and money and faculty positions—from foreign languages to mathematics and computer science. Curriculum debates became turf battles, as they frequently do.

The more hotly debated issues revolved around what the core should contain. Should all students be exposed not only to disciplinary breadth but also to cultural breadth: to women's studies, Asian philosophy, African American history, Hispanic literature, and American Indian religion, for example? More narrowly, on what texts should general education or core courses be based—what is "the canon"? What should "every educated American" have read? This argument was carried on beyond the campuses in bestselling books (E. D. Hirsch's *Cultural Literacy* and Allan Bloom's *The Closing of the American Mind*), in newspaper columns, and in political speeches. It was too often characterized in either/or terms: should students read Plato or Angelou? Thomas Wolfe, Virginia Woolf, or Tom Wolfe? Men or women? Europeans or Latin Americans? As the rhetoric cooled, it became clear that the notion of a fixed canon, hallowed by tradition, has always been an illusion. It has also become clear that students can read more broadly than the traditional, classically based surveys allowed and gain a better understanding of the roots of American culture—which have become far more varied than the turn-of-the-century educators who introduced general education could have known or predicted.[25]

The merits of the arguments over general education and the canon are less important than their effects. Somehow, general education has failed to educate students more broadly, though not for want of trying. As one historian of education notes, the main effect of the general education movement was, perversely, "early disciplinary or professional specialization."[26] Critics on the right complain that students can graduate from college without courses in American history and literature; critics on the left complain that they can graduate without having studied anyone but dead white European males. Students simply complain that there isn't enough time to learn everything they want to know.

For college students, the goal of becoming a generally educated person conflicts with the goal of acquiring professional credentials. Students have only a limited amount of time to spend in college, and the requirements for professional training have expanded. For the student whose main educational goal is to become a certified public accountant, courses not directly applicable to accounting become obstacles rather than opportunities, mandated rather than desired.

The requirements of cultural diversity, coupled with the specialization of faculty, have had similar effects. At a minimum, the visibility and volume of the debate force students and graduates to face the fact that, no matter how the arguments were resolved on their own campuses, they have missed a lot. Where the "conservatives" won, students are taught the classics, but not contemporary and non-European works. Where the "liberals" won, the opposite is true. Even where both sides agreed on a reasonable compromise, students understand that the canon is not a fixed entity, and that there are plenty of important books to be read that didn't make it onto any syllabus.

The use of distribution requirements rather than a core curriculum may also contribute to narrowness. Students in a traditional core curriculum take a survey course exposing them to the works of what at least one faculty agreed were the standards of Western or world culture. But with distribution requirements a student who must meet a humanities requirement and a requirement for, say, non-Western civilization might pass up the survey in favor of a course in premodern Asian philosophy. A U.S. history requirement and a requirement for gender studies might be met by completing a course on African American women's history. Courses on Asian philosophy and African American women are important, but they are unquestionably narrower than a survey course in philosophy or American history.

If learning ended with college graduation (or with a graduate degree, which is even narrower), professional overspecialization and smatterings of narrow bits of other disciplines could hardly create well-educated citizens. Education does not end at graduation, however, and it cannot be described merely by the content of courses. College education includes habits of mind, the generation of curiosity, a need to know. These habits can be cultivated not only by what is taught but by how it is taught and—oddly enough—by what is not taught.

Students all have expectations of what college will do for them, and those expectations usually extend beyond achieving economic security. Sometimes those expectations are submerged during college only to reappear five or ten years later. The economics graduate with a dream job in an investment bank takes a customer to the theater and experiences a sudden urge to read Shakespeare, Shaw, Ibsen, or Pinter. The internist with an established practice remembers the course on Russian novelists that conflicted with biochemistry lab and heads for the bookstore to stock up on Tolstoy. The lawyer who took Asian philosophy wonders what Europeans were thinking. All of these people may have been just as curious in college, but there wasn't room in the schedule for everything. Professionalization and specialization, whatever their impact on students while in college, have a very clear impact on alumni: they recognize large areas of knowledge of which they are ignorant. In fact, that realization was probably implanted before they arrived at college, when they received the university catalog in the mail. The dazzling variety of courses, the breadth of knowledge, the enticing titles—there was never any possibility of learning it all!

The rapid pace at which knowledge has been increasing enhances graduates' unfortunately accurate recognition of their limitations. Imagine a member of the class of 1965, who completed a relatively balanced undergraduate curriculum, suddenly facing the world of today. Among the things that the curriculum could not have included (because they were undiscovered, unrecognized, or unpublished) were computer technology, the structure and mechanisms of DNA, ecology, social history, women's literature—a host of topics that fill the pages of the daily newspaper and with which our hypothetical graduate's children are quite comfortable. Even if graduates recall almost no content from their college courses after twenty or thirty years, they are likely to recognize what they do not know and to want to fill in the gaps.

And filling in the gaps usually means reading. The vastly increased number of people graduating from college in the last half of the twentieth century not only have a propensity to read but a recognition that they *need* to read in order to keep up with their professional fields, learn what they missed in college, and master emerging knowledge. As Clark Kerr noted, writing in support of liberal education, "A person lives a life as well as earns a living, and . . . a life involves citizenship duties and the effective use of leisure as well as work. And I note that alumni particularly wish they had spent more time on liberal education." Another student of education remarked, "Education ought to contribute to one's capacity to earn a living. At the same time, the earning of one's living does not necessarily explain why it is worth earning—why it is worth staying alive."[27] Books meet both the practical needs to keep up with the times, or to understand events and natural phenomena, and intellectual or spiritual needs to understand life and to use time in a meaningful way. And good books meet these needs whether the motivation is to find information, satisfy curiosity, assuage guilt, meet others' expectations, or satisfy the standards we set for ourselves.

The broad expansion of literacy in England in the eighteenth century created a similar demand—"a veritable hunger"—for books that made new discoveries in natural philosophy accessible to the reading public. Early in that century, readers wanted short, simple books, but "these books grew lengthier as the century wore on and as their authors assumed a readership far more adept in natural science than earlier readers had been." "By 1760 or 1770 the public was caught, the time was ready for bestsellers among a readership thirsting for them . . . the trend was toward reasonably priced books written in a language and style the educated layman could understand. . . . Booksellers recruited well-known authors to write books about natural history and paid them far more than they paid for novels."[28]

Today's audience for quality nonfiction had a similar genesis. American society now includes record numbers of college graduates with unmet needs for information, knowledge, and understanding. They are used to meeting these needs through reading, as well as through other media. Their standards for what they read are high: they want reliable information and explanations from recognized authorities. But these readers make other demands as well. Their time is valuable, and books must compete with television and film for their attention. They seek books that are well written, concise, and entertaining.

The ability and willingness of academic authors to meet these needs was influenced by changes in universities that went far beyond increased enrollment. In the second half of the twentieth century, academic work became more specialized, arcane, and competitive. Scholars found the syntheses of Wells and the Durants inadequate, but the demands of academe pushed them toward writing for one another, rather than for general readers. Popularization and its readers were in danger of being abandoned in the widening gap between the ivory tower and the marketplace.

4

FROM SNOW TO SOKAL

A major battle in the culture wars of postwar academe began when C. P. Snow, a scientist and novelist, delivered the Rede Lecture at Cambridge University in 1959. More than fifty years later the title of its first part, "The Two Cultures," remains part of the vocabulary of every educated person. The differences between the sciences and the humanities continue to be debated: Is one branch of learning more "objective" than the other? Does either lead to truth, or Truth? Is the benchmark of difficulty rocket science or *Ulysses*? Snow was not the first to raise the question of the relative value of science and literature—the matter had been debated in American universities from the mid-nineteenth century—and he did so with a heavy hand. Yet the lecture, which was published in the same year in both England and the United States, created a firestorm of responses on both sides of the Atlantic. In Great Britain, academics were outraged. There was "no name to equal Snow's as a signal, at a university party, for every guest to get out his malice and all together start enjoying themselves."[1] In the United States, the responses were less personal and hostile, but concern was intense: essays were written, conferences were held, courses were launched. Indeed, the "two cultures" debate now encompasses an enormous literature that is still discussed and taught. In March 2009, a *New York Times Book Review* essay urged readers to "spend less time merely citing 'The Two Cultures,' and more time genuinely reconsidering it," and a Web search for "Two Cultures" discloses the remarkable extent of continuing interest, yielding more than two million results.[2]

What Snow Actually Said

Snow argued that scientists and "literary figures" (among whom he included in the course of his essay novelists, literary critics, and scholars in other humanities fields) were unable to communicate with each other, even though they were "comparable in intelligence, identical in race, not grossly different in social origin, earning about the same incomes." The two groups, he concluded, had virtually nothing in common in "intellectual, moral, and psychological climate." Their images of each other were "distorted," with humanists seeing scientists as "shallowly optimistic, unaware of man's condition," while scientists saw humanists as "totally lacking in foresight, peculiarly unconcerned with their brother men, in a deep sense anti-intellectual." Snow described a seemingly unbridgeable communications gap. Humanists did *not* understand science and were bound to the cultures of the past. Scientists did *not* read literature and did not see its relevance; they cared little for the past but were bound to the future. According to Snow, both sides were ignorant and overspecialized. Moreover, they were not even civil: "Thirty years ago the cultures had long ceased to speak to each other: but at least they managed a frozen smile across the gulf. Now the politeness has gone, and they just make faces." Snow's solution—long-term and partial at best—was a rethinking of British education to make it less elite and less specialized. Students in the arts and humanities needed to learn about science. He had less to say about scientists being educated in the humanities. The future, Snow implied, belongs to the scientists. Everyone else had better get in line.[3]

Snow's proposed solution is probably what fueled the lively conversation at British university parties. Not only did Snow criticize British education, but he compared it unfavorably with what went on in American, Russian, and Scandinavian schools. In his second edition of the lecture, written in 1963, Snow made this inferiority explicit, claiming that the gap between the cultures was less severe in the United States because of the multidisciplinary requirements of liberal arts education and the development of social sciences, which represented "something like a third culture" that was in touch with the other two (69–70). British intellectuals disagreed with much of what Snow said, and they did not like being compared unfavorably to their American colleagues.

Responses

The most virulent attack on Snow was delivered by F. R. Leavis in the 1962 Richmond Lecture, also at Cambridge. Leavis conceded that Snow *might* know something about science but insisted that in matters of literature he "exposes complacently a complete ignorance." He went on to disparage Snow's novels, his rhetorical powers ("Snow's argument proceeds with so extreme a *naïveté* of unconsciousness and irresponsibility that to call it a movement of thought is to flatter it"), his grasp of history, and his understanding of literature ("he doesn't know what literature is"). Leavis's least personalized criticism was that Snow's recommendations for educational reform were inadequate. Fifty years later, Leavis's own vision does seem more prescient: "The advance of science and technology means a human future of change so rapid and of such kinds, of tests and challenges so unprecedented, of decisions and possible non-decisions so momentous and insidious in their consequences, that mankind—this is surely clear—will need to be in full intelligent possession of its full humanity. . . . What we need, and shall continue to need not less, is something with the livingness of the deepest vital instinct; such as intelligence, a power—rooted, strong in experience, and supremely human—of creative response to the new challenges of time." For Leavis, Snow's solution would fall far short of this goal.[4]

In the United States, Lionel Trilling took on Snow with a more substantive argument than Leavis had offered. He found Snow's thesis both obvious ("perhaps nothing in our culture is so characteristic as the separateness of the various artistic and intellectual professions") and inadequate, because it failed to bring politics into the equation. Trilling tried to make sense of Snow's argument by extrapolating from Snow's concern with world peace and his conviction that scientists all understand one another intuitively. "The position of *The Two Cultures* is to be explained by Sir Charles's preoccupation . . . with the assuring of peace. . . . An understanding between the West and the Soviet Union could be achieved by the culture of scientists, which reaches over factitious national and ideological differences." But despite his generosity, Trilling could not endorse this naïve view: "We can be perfectly certain that the world will not be saved by denying the actualities of the world. Among these actualities politics is one." For Trilling, both science and literature were necessary for the survival of the world and humanity.[5]

Snow's lecture could easily have been dismissed: both Leavis and Trilling were right in criticizing its obviousness and naïveté. Yet it touched a nerve and has remained extraordinarily influential. When Snow published his lecture—whether or not the gulf in values and understanding was real—many measurable gaps in resources and status were developing between the sciences and the humanities. Communicating with each other was a peripheral issue for many academics. What they could see and feel was the increasing influence, status, and funding of the sciences, often at the expense of the humanities. If academic scientists and humanists were now making faces at each other, it was not because they could not communicate but because they no longer saw themselves engaged in a common effort—education—but rather in a struggle for attention and money. Competition and rivalry were beginning to displace collegiality.

The Cold War in the University

In describing what he would like the university to be, Leavis made very clear what higher education in the 1960s was not: "something (that is) more than a collocation of specialist departments." He hoped it would become "a centre of human consciousness: perception, knowledge, judgment and responsibility."[6] The expansion of higher education, and the infusion of funds that made it possible, had altered not only the student body but the composition, motivation, disciplines, and rewards of the faculty.

During the Great Depression and World War II, scholars became involved in national affairs to a far greater extent than they had earlier been. Franklin Roosevelt recruited academics into New Deal programs to solve the nation's economic and social problems, making their work visible to the public. Most influential was the Manhattan Project to build the atomic bomb, which demonstrated the possibility of massive, government-funded scientific research directed toward a specific objective. It became the model for such diverse endeavors as the space program, the war on poverty, and the Reagan-era defense initiative known as "Star Wars." The Cold War added urgency and competitiveness as motivations for government promotion of scientific research. The Soviet Union's launching of the first of the Sputnik satellites in 1957 was the sharpest reminder of competition, because the USSR won that particular race.[7]

The end of World War II and the beginning of the Cold War started the

United States on a program of massive federal involvement in research and education, especially in the sciences. "The period from 1939 to 1945 was the beginning of a deeply sustained surge of national appreciation of the importance of possessing a broad base of science. Postwar confidence in the likely *uses* of science was justified first and in large part on the ground that new weapons might be needed for national security. Yet the national goals for a federal policy about science, originating during the late 1940s, went well beyond the compelling argument of defense."[8] In 1941 the National Defense Research Committee became the Office for Scientific Research and Development; beginning in 1942, National Laboratories were founded at Brookhaven, Los Alamos, and Oak Ridge; in 1950 the National Science Foundation was created; in 1957 the Council for Science and Education was established and the post of Special Assistant to the President for Science and Technology was created; and in 1958 the National Defense Education Act was passed and the National Aeronautics and Space Administration was established.[9] Funding for the humanities and arts lagged behind, in terms of both time and money, but in the 1960s the National Endowments for the Humanities and the Arts were established, in part to promote research.

Scientific research became a national priority, and acquiring government research funds became an institutional priority at many universities. In Massachusetts, for example, "the federal government created new funding programs to support scholarly research and promote graduate education, and the region's universities obediently adopted the new priorities. As the aims of federal programs evolved in the postwar years, the concerns of scholars shifted with them."[10] Government grants changed the nature of academic life for those in fields where funding was abundant. "For the first time in Western history, professors and scholars were thrust into the unwonted position of entrepreneurs in incessant search for new sources of capital, of new revenue, and, taking the word in its larger sense, of profits."[11]

Vast amounts of federal funding became available for university research. Total research and development funds provided by the federal government to universities and colleges grew from $169 million in 1955 to $405 million in 1960; by 1970 they had risen to $1.6 billion and, by 1980, to $4.1 billion (the last two figures are both in 1987 dollars). Some fields benefited more than others. Public expenditures for medical research increased from $1.7

billion in 1970 to $11 billion in 1990, while the National Endowment for the Humanities granted $10.5 million in 1970 and $141 million in 1990. But no matter what the field, and even allowing for inflation, the federal government's investment in university-based research rose rapidly.[12]

The professoriate grew in response to increased enrollments and the availability of research funding as well as the introduction of new academic fields and specialization within existing fields. According to the historian Walter Metzger: "Almost 80 percent of all academics in 1980 occupied positions that did not exist thirty years before. The 1940 census put the number of academics at 190,000. By 1960 the number had grown to 281,000; by 1970 to a whopping 532,000. . . . The overall academic rate of growth between 1880 and 1960 doubled every fifteen years." The social origins of the faculty changed as well. Metzger writes: "Prior to World War I, the academic profession took its membership from a relatively narrow band of society. A study of a thousand scientists in 1906 and 1910 revealed that they came mostly from Protestant professional merchant families and were overwhelmingly white and male. . . . Not until the 1940s would the Columbia English Department appoint a professor of Jewish origin, a 'cultural alien' by the name of Lionel Trilling. True, Jews had been appointed to the Columbia University Department of Economics. This *was* a career open to talents—provided the talents conformed to ancient stereotypes."[13] After World War II, the influx of refugee scholars ended the homogeneity and insularity of faculties, leading to the rise of meritocracy over social snobbery. Not until the 1970s, however, were women and people of color hired in significant numbers.

The research of this enlarged faculty is difficult to measure. In the sciences, we might count the number of vaccines, surgical techniques, newly discovered stars, useful plastics, and the like that have been discovered or developed in university laboratories. It would be hard to aggregate these into a meaningful figure, though, and there is no way of counting new theories or more abstract discoveries. In the social sciences and humanities, the results are even less quantifiable. One approximate measure, however, is the number of scholarly publications. Almost every discovery or theory is documented in a book or journal article, and books at least are not difficult to count.

In the humanities and some social sciences, books are the most common medium for disseminating new discoveries and ideas, and most academic writers publish their books through university presses. If we are willing to accept a rough measure, then, university press book output approximates the amount of new knowledge generated in fields such as history, literature, philosophy, and sociology. In the 1950s, 40 university presses together issued about 750 books each year. Ten years later, 60 university presses were publishing 2,300 books a year. By the mid-1980s, 80 university presses were publishing 5,600 books annually, and in 1990, roughly the same 80 presses published 7,100 books. Scholarly book production in 1990, then, was nearly ten times as great as it had been forty years earlier.[14]

This growth reflects an increase in the total number of college faculty, but also an increase in the research orientation and productivity of that faculty. "In 1955, the presses published one new title for every 266 of the 250,000 faculty members, while their 1965 rate was one title for every 181 of the 370,000."[15] By 1980, that calculation yields one title for every 122 faculty members. In fact, those figures probably understate productivity, because the greatest increase in university faculties has been in fields—such as business and the sciences—in which researchers tend to publish journal articles rather than books. The total number of books is understated as well, because some faculty members, especially in the sciences, publish with for-profit scholarly publishers or trade houses. A study conducted by the U.S. Department of Education estimated that in 1986 and 1987, full-time faculty members published an average of 0.6 books and 2.0 journal articles each.[16]

Journals and journal articles are harder to count. Most estimates set the number of scholarly journals at between 100,000 and 180,000. One study, for example, shows growth from 10,000 scholarly serial titles in 1951 to 40,000 in 1970, to 62,000 in 1980, and to 118,500 in 1991. By far the majority of journals published worldwide are in the sciences, and they have the largest circulations. The same study shows the number of biomedical journals rising from 3,937 in 1949 to 7,888 in 1959, to 14,338 in 1969, and to 19,316 in 1977.[17]

The predominance of the sciences notwithstanding, the number of journals in the humanities and social sciences is large and continues to grow. The Modern Language Association estimated that about 3,200 journals were published worldwide in literature, linguistics, language, and folklore in 1990. A different national study in 1979 reported growth in humanities journals published in the United States (in classics, English and American literature, history, and philosophy) from 148 in 1960 to 317 in 1975. (The figures in other studies suggest that these numbers are probably low, or were based on a very restrictive definition of a scholarly journal.) In sociology, one study showed a trebling of the social scientific literature between 1969 and 1977, with 254 new social science periodicals starting up in 1975 and 334 starting in 1976. Nor do the numbers of periodicals, as large as they are, reflect the full amount of growth, because many journals, especially in the sciences, increased their frequency of publication or the number of pages in each issue.[18]

Historians of science and science policy frequently cite an estimate by Derek J. De Solla Price that scientific knowledge doubles every ten to fifteen years. Price based this estimate on a variety of statistics, including the number of doctorates granted in the sciences, the number of scientists listed in various biographical directories, and the numbers of journals and journal articles. This doubling is usually cited to support the idea that knowledge has "exploded" in the mid-twentieth century. But Price himself was very careful to note that the rate of doubling has been roughly constant since the eighteenth century, and that scientific knowledge is increasing so dramatically simply because the numbers that are being doubled have gotten so large—on the same principle as compound interest. Price was also careful to note that such increases cannot continue indefinitely; if they did, we would confront ridiculous—indeed, impossible—predictions. As one impossible example, he pointed out that if government spending on research continued to increase at 1970s rates, by early in the twenty-first century the United States would be spending twice its gross national product on such research.[19] In other words, the kinds of growth and productivity in research that universities have experienced since World War II cannot continue much longer. Indeed, some reduction in that pace is already visible, and we may even see actual shrinkage within a decade or two.

It would be inspiring, but unfortunately naïve, to think that the vast increase in publication that has occurred over the past fifty years represents an equivalent increase in what we know about important things. A good portion does represent expansion of useful knowledge. But two other forces complicate the picture. The first is the rise of specialization (in research as in teaching), and the second is the increased emphasis on research in the evaluation of college and university faculty.

The tree of knowledge is a familiar image and a useful metaphor. It has a sturdy trunk (what every American should know?) and substantial branches—the humanities, the arts, the social sciences, the natural sciences. Nowadays, however, the tree of knowledge is looking very bushy. It burgeons with twigs: the large branch of history, for example, has smaller branches broken down chronologically, geographically, methodologically, and in some cases ideologically. These in turn have even smaller twigs, so that a historian may specialize in eighteenth-century German social history, or in the economic history of Hispanics in the American Southwest in the early twentieth century. A university that fifty years ago simply had a department of biology may how have departments of botany, zoology, and microbiology. These offer courses in subfields that include lichenology, plant ecology, mycology, palynology, phycology, paleobotany, physiology, genetics, biogenetics, anatomy, entomology, sociobiology, neurophysiology, ornithology, mammalogy, ichthyology, herpetology, bacteriology, immunology, virology, and neuroimmunology. And both historians and biologists have links to other disciplines, which generate interdisciplinary fields.

Each of these disciplinary twigs and interdisciplinary grafts has at least one journal, and each of the sturdier branches has many. Fifty years ago, a handful of journals in a field such as history could serve the profession adequately, but as readers' interests have narrowed, they have come to want journals in which they can quickly learn what colleagues in their specialties and subspecialties are doing without having to plow through material in dozens of other subspecialties that are of little interest. The work in these specialized journals may be of very high quality, but it is of interest to very few people. Most subdisciplinary journals in the humanities have fewer than a thousand subscribers, including libraries. Some have only two or three hundred.

The more general journals survive because they are the official organs of the major professional societies, because having work published in them is considered prestigious, and (in fields like history) because they publish reviews of all new books in the general field. These journals have large numbers of subscribers (the top three in history each have between 15,000 and 20,000), in part because a subscription is an automatic benefit of membership in the professional society and membership is akin to holding a union card. But it is unlikely that every subscriber reads every article; in fact, some editors claim informally that readership surveys show that many subscribers read only the book reviews.

Some articles in academic journals may not be read by anyone at all. A 1990 analysis of citations of articles in science journals concluded that more than half of the articles were never cited in the five years following publication, which suggests either that the articles were not read or that they were read but found useless.[20] There is no reason to think that a similar study of the literature in other fields would have different results.

Clearly, much scholarly journal publishing is not driven by readers' demands. Rather, it responds to the demands of scholars as writers. As research has become a priority of universities, the need has grown for faculty to publish. Research universities appeared in the United States in the late nineteenth century, with Johns Hopkins the first institution to base itself on the German model. Other universities gradually added research to their activities, and by the midwar period most universities included research as part of their mission. (Indeed, universities are distinguished from colleges by their ability to offer graduate degrees, which requires a graduate faculty active in research.) By the end of World War II, academic prestige—both institutional and individual—began to derive almost entirely from research productivity rather than from the quality of teaching. "The graduate school replaced the college as the most important component of many universities, and research productivity became a vital measure of institutional standing. In this context, well-known scholars became increasingly valuable contributors to campus reputations, and judgments about research carried greater weight in decisions on hiring and promotion."[21]

The rise of the research university gave faculty members new goals for their work, but also for their status. Beginning in the late nineteenth century, university teachers sought standing as professionals along with doctors and lawyers. Professionals are distinguished by self-governance, control over entry into the group, and specialized knowledge. Doctors and lawyers, like those holding doctorates in English or classics, acquire their specialized knowledge through university study. But doctors and lawyers are *practicing* professionals, not teaching professionals, and that has set them off from university professors. Teaching, no matter the level, is less respected and less well paid than other professions. In a quest for professional status, academic disciplines tried to distance themselves from teaching. For example, the flagship journal of the Modern Language Association stopped publishing its section on teaching in 1902. The MLA amended its constitution in 1916, changing its main goal from "advancement of the *study* of the Modern Languages and Literatures" to "advancement of *research*." And in 1929, "the president of the association declared with finality that 'henceforth, our domain is research.'"[22]

Since the 1960s, it has been nearly impossible for a faculty member in a research university to gain tenure without at least some publications, and since the 1970s, when the academic job market contracted, that requirement has spread to all universities and to many liberal arts colleges. In a survey undertaken in 1979, "70 percent of the senior scholars responding . . . report they have felt institutional pressures to publish and believe that their positions and prestige are dependent on publishing," and the researchers concluded that "the pressures to publish have increased in the 1970s. . . . They are being felt even at the less prestigious four-year colleges and, not surprisingly, have led to an increase in article writing."[23] At research universities, extensive publication is required for tenure and promotion. Whereas at selective liberal arts colleges, 5 percent of faculty members reported spending over 20 hours per week on research in 1990, at the top-ranking research universities, the figure was 33 percent. At the liberal arts colleges, 17 percent reported spending no time on research, while at the research universities the figure was 7 percent.[24]

The pressure to "publish or perish" has led to some well-publicized scandals in which researchers falsified results or reported experiments that were never performed. It has also added some colorful phrases to the journal editor's vocabulary. Editors in the sciences refer to "salami publishing," in which researchers reduce their work to the thinnest possible slices, thus generating the longest possible list of publications. Another expression is the "LPU," or "least publishable unit"—the smallest amount of information one can derive from research to constitute a publication. If they do nothing else, such practices inflate the numbers of articles and even journals that are needed to meet the authors' (not the readers') needs. This inflation, in turn, makes it difficult for libraries to find the money for all the journals that are being churned out. It also makes it difficult for scholars to read everything in their fields, although most say that if they read the top five or ten journals they don't risk missing much.

Research and publication are encouraged by both sticks and carrots. Faculty members know that if they do not publish they will lose their jobs or fail to be promoted. If they do publish, and especially if their research generates outside funding, they will be rewarded not only with tenure and promotion, but with prestige and the opportunity to reduce their teaching loads in order to do more research. The notion that teaching and research compete for time, rather than complementing each other, is relatively new. Before World War II, the scholar-teacher was the model: faculty members were expected to keep up in their fields, publish occasionally, and teach. But when the scale of research was stepped up so dramatically, some faculty and administrators began to see teaching as an obstacle to research productivity. As Robert Nisbet noted: "Instead of conspicuous consumption as the hallmark of affluence, we may refer to *conspicuous research.* Ordinary research was not enough. It must be made conspicuous not merely through sheer bulk of project, but through one's conspicuous exemption from all ordinary academic activities. One must first be exempted from teaching, or from a significant share of teaching. . . . One must also obtain, if possible, a title— whether Director or Research Professor—that made plain beyond all possible doubt that one's teaching was as minimal as one's research was maximal."[25] Statistics on teaching loads from the late 1980s confirm Nisbet's observations. At the leading research universities, 31 percent of the faculty reported spending no time at all teaching, 35 percent spent only 1 to 4 hours, and 34 percent spent 5 to 15 hours. At the selective liberal arts colleges, which continue to pride themselves on the quality of teaching, only 3 percent of the faculty reported spending no time on teaching, and only 9 percent reported 1 to 4 hours; 84 percent spent 5 to 15 hours per week teaching.[26]

The tendency is clearest at prestigious private universities. At Harvard and MIT, "decisions about hiring and promotion were increasingly dominated by judgments about scholarly work as distinct from teaching effectiveness. Indeed, keeping time-consuming instructional commitments to a minimum was essential in research universities and lower-level instructional work was often delegated to graduate students."[27] Henry Rosovsky, writing as dean of the Faculty of Arts and Sciences at Harvard, put an imaginative spin on this situation for prospective students: "Research is an expression of faith in the possibility of progress. The drive that leads scholars to study a topic has to include the belief that new things can be discovered, that newer can be better, and that greater depth of understanding is achievable. Research, especially academic research, is a form of optimism about the human condition. . . . Persons who have faith in progress and therefore possess an intellectually optimistic disposition . . . are probably more interesting and better professors. They are less likely to present their subjects in excessively cynical or reactionary terms."[28] And Leonard Levy, then dean of the faculty at Brandeis, wrote in 1964 that "teaching and related activities . . . are almost impediments toward advancement in the profession. The road to preferment, position and profit only passes through, and sometimes passes by, the classroom. . . . The scholar who crystallizes DNA or wins a Bancroft prize receives all the publicity, advancement and take-home pay, regardless of how much or how well he teaches."[29]

State institutions sometimes experience pressure in the opposite direction from taxpayers and legislators. Legislators may recognize the economic benefits of university research, especially if it is directed toward local industry. But they also hope to get their money's worth from the faculty by imposing higher teaching loads and deemphasizing research. The latter tendency is aimed especially at the humanities, where research has a cultural rather than an economic impact. The pressure to publish is felt equally in all academic departments, but the resources for research are far from equal. In the academic world, as in the larger world, inequality breeds discontent.

Rivalry and Status

Whether or not the sciences and the humanities constitute two cultures, they certainly constitute two classes within academe. W. H. Auden once wrote that "when I find myself in the company of scientists I feel like a shabby curate who has strayed by mistake into a drawing-room full of dukes."[30] The shabbiness was probably metaphorical, referring to the power and influence of scientists relative to those of poets rather than to their affluence. Nevertheless, the image is telling. Scientists have more grant opportunities, the funding available to them is far greater, their salaries are higher, and they have more graduate assistants and other employees to help with their work. In part, this is due simply to the nature of science. The experimental sciences require large laboratories with expensive equipment. Much of the work in these fields is done by teams of researchers, rather than individuals, and not all of these are teaching faculty. Some scientific work is drudgery that senior scientists happily delegate to postdoctoral fellows and graduate students; the latter are grateful for the employment and the experience. Scholars in the humanities and social sciences are more likely to work alone, and their expenses are generally limited to photocopying and travel to archives or fieldwork sites. Differentials in salary are explained partly by the fact that many scientists could find employment outside the university should they wish to do so. Chemists quite simply are more employable than philosophers. The same reasoning explains the higher salaries of faculty members in business schools and economics departments.

Humanities scholars understand all of this, and most accept the differences. What is galling—what perhaps causes the humanists to make faces at faculty parties—is that the higher salaries and more abundant outside funding are accompanied by higher status within the academy and among the public. University administrators have good practical reasons to smile on the science faculty. The grants they bring in include "indirect costs," sums that in many cases amount to half again as much as the actual costs and go to the university administration. These funds are used to pay the costs of administering the grant and to cover overhead. Each university distributes such income differently; typically some of it goes to the investigator who wrote the proposal, some to the department, some to the college, some to the library, some to support the grants administration office, and some to the central administration for use as it sees fit. Some grants in the humanities provide indirect costs, but the individual fellowships and foundation grants that are most common do not.

It is also easier for university administrators to make the case for supporting the sciences to state legislators and voters, because much scientific research makes a material contribution to the economy and to the welfare of citizens. Humanities research may be equally important and valuable, but its impact is usually less tangible and immediate. Most administrators appreciate the academic importance of the humanities and the value of work in literary criticism, philosophy, languages, and history. They all appreciate the fact that humanities classes attract large numbers of students. But the humanities are not a source of revenue. Humanities scholars know all of this, and they often feel underappreciated.

Their feelings are not assuaged by conversations with their colleagues in the sciences. Scientists are not generally aware that they hold privileges that their colleagues across the quadrangle do not. Scientists' grants fully fund their travel to conferences in more interesting cities and at hotels with more stars than those the humanities faculty attend—with their expenses less likely to be paid. Scientists have all the graduate assistants they need. If they do not wish to teach freshman survey classes, they can usually buy out their time with grant money. Try as they may, humanities scholars have a hard time fighting back the envy.

The public perception of the two cultures adds to the rivalry. In fact, the differences in political and economic support are in large part a reflection of public evaluations of the disciplines. Both scientists and humanities scholars have therefore tried to make a public case for the value of their work, but they have gone about it in very different ways, with very different results.

Making One's Case

Researchers in the humanities have always had relatively easy access to the public. History and biography have long been among the most popular subjects of nonfiction. Readers enjoy the chronological narrative, the insight into the lives of others, and the accounts of events that have shaped the present. Those who are not experts in theology or philosophy nevertheless seek out books about religion and ideas. In the humanities, the distinction between writing for one's peers and writing for the general public is a late twentieth-century phenomenon. Scientists have typically had a more difficult time explaining their work to lay readers. Yet in the period since World War II, it is the scientists who have captured the public's attention, while research and writing in the humanities have become more specialized and less accessible.

Scientists have many reasons to write for nonscientists. The first is the desire, nearly universal among academics regardless of discipline, to have others understand one's work, to appreciate its importance and fascination, and to share one's excitement. This motivation may be regarded as an extension of the desire to teach—only with more status and without having to grade papers. In order to understand the importance of a scientific discovery or innovation, general readers need some background in the field. Scientific authors must help them understand the problem, the principles underlying the work, the reasoning that led to the scientist's hypothesis, the design of the experiments, and the interpretation of the results. Most scientists believe that understanding a specific experiment or discovery is inadequate. Readers must understand the scientific method: the way scientists think and work. "Just the facts, ma'am" doesn't do the job. As a way of teaching, this makes a good deal of sense, because it allows the reader to think the way the researcher does, even if the author must supply a lot of the answers as the questions are raised, rather than having the readers figure them out themselves. Rhetorically, too, it is extremely useful, because it humanizes science. Instead of being a dense mass of experiments, data, and theories, the subject becomes a thought process conducted by human beings. Very often these narratives of discovery include the less intellectual side of the protagonists, portraying their rivalries, failings, and foibles along with their inspiration and intelligence.

Another reason that scientists feel they should make sure the public understands their work is that, since the bombing of Hiroshima, scientists, policymakers, and the public have become more aware that scientific research raises ethical concerns and generates public policy. The bomb was only the beginning. The discovery of the structure and function of DNA led to research in applied genetics that raises possibilities troubling to many people, such as choosing the gender of a child, engineering the appearance or intelligence of children, and creating embryos for medical or pharmaceutical use. These ethical concerns rapidly become legal and legislative concerns: Who is the mother of the baby created from the egg of one woman, in the uterus of another, at the request of a third? Is the baby conceived from the frozen sperm of a dead man that man's heir? We hope that such decisions will be made by legislators and judges with some understanding of the underlying science. Should governments forbid, regulate, or ignore genetic engineering of food? The response depends largely on one's understanding of the processes and the science upon which these processes are based. Cloning, whether of sheep or humans, is not only a scientific challenge but the subject of religious debate and congressional hearings. In such situations, it is only sensible for scientists to make their work comprehensible to laypeople. In fact, if legislators do not understand what scientists do, they are likely to prevent some kinds of work from proceeding.

In communicating with laypeople, scientists must reveal the complexity and frequent ambiguity of scientific evidence. Scientists similarly trained, using similar methods and sharing an identical body of data, may reach very different conclusions. Global warming is perhaps the most obvious example. Policymakers and the public have learned that you cannot ask to what extent human activity influences global warming and get a single answer. In such cases, we may rely on the scientific community for guidance, but not for definitive solutions. For both researchers and the public, this is a strong argument for making science accessible to nonscientists. It is also an opportunity to let people know how scientists think and work, and why they may disagree.

More practically, scientists know that public funding depends on public appreciation and understanding of their work. The American space program benefited enormously from Carl Sagan's television appearances and popularizations of astronomy. The space program has generated few practical discoveries relative to its costs, but it has captured a popular imagination primed by information, enthusiastically imparted, about the sun and other stars, other planets, and the possibility of extraterrestrial life. Had NASA relied on transmitting straightforward technical reports to the Congress, it might have disappeared long ago. But the agency has made a point of publicizing its work in terms that television viewers, schoolchildren, and Congress can understand.

The editors of *Nature*, one of the leading journals in the life sciences, expressed some of these motivations in a 1996 editorial, "In Pursuit of Comprehension":

> To have "intimate relations with the little band . . . of nature's servants in every civilized region of our planet" was one of this publication's expressed intentions at its outset, in November 1869. But intimacy can breed withering exclusiveness, rather than stimulating inclusiveness, if it expresses itself in private language and with hidden rules. Such an approach is at odds with one of *Nature*'s original prime ambitions: "to place before the general public the results of scientific work . . ." and downright harmful to another: "to aid Scientific Men themselves by giving early information of all advances made in any branch of natural knowledge throughout the world and by affording them an opportunity of discussing the various scientific questions which arise from time to time."

The editors then went on to explain to prospective authors how they might write more accessible prose and to warn them that the editors would be more diligent about such matters. Their modest goal was to make at least the introduction of every article comprehensible to all readers.[31]

The work of social and behavioral scientists—sociologists, political scientists, economists, and psychologists—also has policy implications and frequently receives government support. But the social sciences are easily distinguished from the "hard" sciences. Most are not experimental sciences, and those that have human beings as research subjects cannot employ the strict standards of control possible in the hard sciences. With human behavior (whether individual or group) as their subject matter, they are less likely to produce consistent results and conclusions.

One reason the social sciences do not enjoy the public confidence that benefits the natural sciences is that they are more subject to influence by the researcher's political and ideological commitments. A chemist's political affiliation is unlikely to be evident in lectures or journal articles, but most economists and political scientists are easily placed on the political spectrum by anyone who reads their work. The work itself is frequently politicized by others, with policymakers whose programs it supports lauding the results and those who are offended by its implications writing angry letters to book review editors. *The Bell Curve* (1994), in which Richard J. Herrnstein and Charles Murray purported to show differences in intelligence among the races, is an excellent example. The social sciences are quite simply more political and ideological than the natural and physical sciences. It would be strange indeed if relativity theory lost out to quantum mechanics when a new political party took office, but no one is at all surprised when Keynesian economics is abandoned in favor of supply-side economics when a Republican takes over from a Democrat.

Their polemical nature makes the social sciences attractive subjects for general readers. So does their subject matter. Our own behavior—and that of our friends, colleagues, and relatives—is a source of endless fascination. The machinations of politicians, the possibility of reform, or just the workings of governments concern responsible citizens. And what makes the economy tick (or not) matters to everyone. But if the subject matter is of general interest, the methods and prose have become off-putting. In the 1950s, according to Columbia sociologist Todd Gitlin, "even the professional journals were written so that any decently educated person could read them." But "few sociologists today extend their imaginations beyond narrow milieus to the biggest questions of social structures, culture and conflict. Their elders, hellbent on professionalization, do not encourage range."[32] The social sciences have come to rely on statistical methods and mathematical models that rarely capture the imagination of nonspecialists.

The social sciences have become less accessible in part because social scientists have tried to look more like "real" scientists and have ceased to value (or reward) the kind of research that linked them to a wider public. Orlando Patterson, a Harvard sociologist, expressed his dismay in an essay written shortly after the death of David Riesman, whose 1950 book, *The Lonely Crowd*, won a wide popular following. Riesman and his contemporaries

> practiced a sociology different in both style and substance from that of today. It was driven first by the significance of the subject and second by an epistemological emphasis on understanding the nature and meaning of social behavior. . . . These writers, following an earlier tradition, pursued big issues like the cultural contradictions of capitalism, the role of religion in economic life, the problems of America's melting-pot ideology, the nature of civil society and the virtues and dangers of patriotism. But they also painted on small canvases, offering us insights into American rituals of interaction in public and private places.
> . . .
>
> Today, when mainstream sociologists write about culture they disdain as reactionary any attempt to demonstrate how culture explains behavior. And their need to test hypotheses, build models and formulate laws forces them into an emphasis on the organizational aspects of culture, which can be reduced to data suitable for "scientific" analysis. . . .
>
> Mainstream sociology eschews any exploration of human values, meanings and beliefs because ambiguities and judgment are rarely welcomed in the discipline now.[33]

Readers seeking to understand human behavior may find short stories and novels as valuable as psychological treatises, or they may turn to self-help books that translate academic theories into usable advice. Journalists often do a better job of making the government and the economy comprehensible than do academic specialists, and readers may prefer the work of narrative historians to that of economists and political scientists when they become interested in an unfamiliar area of the world.

Some social scientists manage to retain the liveliness of their subject matter without sacrificing the standards of academic study. Certainly

Robert Coles, John Kenneth Galbraith, Lester Thurow, Robert Jay Lifton, Milton Friedman, and Paul Krugman have managed to attract large audiences. Motivated by their commitment to their subjects and the importance of influencing policymakers and the public, they have joined the other two cultures in translating their work and findings into ordinary language.

Scholars in the humanities have often made a point of communicating with nonspecialist readers. Biographers and some historians, within and outside the academy, have long seen general readers as part of their natural audience, and they have written traditional narratives that are well received. But if someone without doctoral training (for example, Barbara Tuchman) can write good, readable history, then is history truly a profession? "History, because of its fluidity and openness, is not an arcane discipline. Although its critical operations are exacting, its fundamental tasks of organizing data into a design and thereby recreating the life of the past does not depend on any systematic methodology. Nor has history a special language of its own. Consequently, professional historians are unable to immure themselves completely within a specialized sphere, and writers unblessed with special training are often capable of doing important historical work. Then the professional faces stiff competition."[34]

In the late nineteenth century, historians newly established in the academy began to view history's accessibility as a threat. If history could be done by "amateurs," then perhaps it was time for the discipline to professionalize itself: to acquire methodologies and language that were not accessible to laypeople and to start being more "scientific":

> [They] demanded . . . that historical study conform to standardized rules of operation centered on objectivity and the scientific pursuit of factual knowledge. In nearly all fields of intellectual endeavor, including theology and science, scholars . . . had been insisting on "evidence" as the measure of accuracy and judgment. Part of the larger professionalization movement sweeping the nation in the 1860s and 1870s in the wake of a new scientific spirit infusing the age, disciples of this new cult of exactitude focused their energies on determining what could be directly observed and verified in Nature. . . . Led by scholars who eventually formed the American Historical Association, these professionals condemned efforts of popularizers to make history more attractive to readers.[35]

Scholars in all humanities disciplines began to look more carefully at questions of theory and methodology, and arguments about the degree of objectivity and veracity that humanistic knowledge could claim became quite loud.

In many ways, humanities scholarship has benefited from the effort to become more scientific. In history, for example, social science historians have used statistical methods to analyze phenomena and groups that had resisted understanding. Statistical analysis of census data, public records, and other evidence about groups of people has allowed us to learn more about the lives of farmers, workers, and other "ordinary" folk. History could for the first time include people who did not write autobiographies, memoirs, or large numbers of letters. But in other ways, quantitative history distanced researchers from a lay audience. Much of this research resulted in monographs heavy on data, statistical analysis, and methodology and light on narrative and human interest. To the extent that becoming scientific meant becoming obscure or difficult, this shift removed historians from their natural public audience. John Higham summarized the situation neatly:

> The security the professional historian enjoyed in a university sheltered him from the daily necessity that disciplined the freelance writer to the utmost clarity and pungency of expression. The increasing number of seminars and professorships in each of the major universities encouraged more and more division of labor and specialization, the reverse of what the layman wanted. Then too, every form of resistance to a general audience was perhaps stiffened by the academic man's general feeling of being unwanted and unappreciated outside his own realm. . . . The failure of the public to appreciate the professional historical expert—as it appreciated both the popular historian and the scientific expert—rankled deeply. This aggravated the professionals' defensiveness.[36]

Similar trends can be seen in other humanities fields. Philosophy in the United States became essentially *analytic* philosophy, which emphasizes logic and linguistic analysis, expressed in highly technical terms, over explorations of what nonspecialists had always considered the basic questions of philosophy: How do we know what is right? What is the meaning of life? What do we mean by "knowledge"? What is reality? Movement toward professionalization and specialization, and away from what ordinary people consider to be the subject matter of philosophy, began in the nineteenth century, but it became dramatic in the mid-twentieth century. By adopting methods and language that were increasingly complex and self-referential, philosophers isolated themselves from the general reader. In his history of philosophy at Harvard, Bruce Kuklick quoted a graduate of the department: "Philosophy, as taught here, is more and more a detailed, isolated, academic discipline. Its role as the overall integrator of other fields of intellectual endeavor is increasingly curtailed." In Kuklick's own view, "When narrow professionals turned to their scholarship, they thought of their work as a game. For a few, professional philosophy had become a way, not of confronting the problem of existence, but of avoiding it."[37]

Some classics scholars see the field withering as a result of deliberate exclusion of students and the public, unlike the more open scientific fields. They contrast their discipline with the sciences, which "have advanced in step with the society that supports them and welcomed new and diverse practitioners. . . . We like to think of our profession as a vocation, distinguished not only by certain traditions but also by the class, background and ideology of its practitioners. Like new methods, newcomers who do not conform to our way of doing this cannot enrich but only disrupt the profession and should not be encouraged to join it."[38]

The most prominent example of a humanities discipline building fortifications against amateur intrusion is literary criticism. Literary studies, like history, aimed at becoming more "scientific" beginning in the late nineteenth century. Research in literature initially meant textual analysis, which requires both access to manuscripts and other archival material and a rigorous, painstaking analytical approach. It has never been a field open, or even attractive, to most professors of literature. Yet faculty members faced new requirements to do research and publish. At first literary history filled this role. In the 1930s, "criticism was secondary to history in courses and lectures, in examinations and dissertations, in appointments and promotions, and in research and publication. Generally speaking, literary historians . . . paid much attention to historical documents and comparatively little attention to poetic texts. Literary critics for their part were concerned with reasoned discourse about literary works themselves and with scrupulous exegeses of texts as aesthetic productions."[39] By the 1950s, with the rise of the

"New Criticism," the positions were reversed. Criticism, with its painstaking "close reading" of texts—and in some formalist variants, statistical analysis—was seen as more rigorous and was accorded higher status. Adherents of subsequent schools of criticism have attacked this approach: "This assimilation of literary works to perceptual objects and the attempt to make meaning a matter of ontology were a desperate (and misguided) attempt to give criticism the certainty of a natural science."[40] Yet New Criticism was nevertheless readable and accessible.

In the 1960s and 1970s, the search for legitimation and a scientific footing led literary critics to emulate the social sciences, "to gain the authority of linguistics or anthropology by adopting their style" as well as their theories and language.[41] Within the profession, the rise of theory can be seen in the creation of the Modern Language Association's subdivision of Literary Criticism and Literary Theory in 1967 and in the appearance of a multitude of new theory-based journals at the same time. What is striking about theory-based criticism is the opacity of its language, its self-referential nature, and its apparently deliberate difficulty of access. Even a writer as sympathetic to the movement as Elizabeth Bruss described the theoretical journals as "almost aggressively extraordinary in their language. The breadth of reference might suggest the rebirth of the encyclopedist or the man of letters, but these new letters were obdurately, forbiddingly opaque." A more neutral analyst, Frank Lentricchia, described "a continuing urge to essentialize literary discourse by making it a unique kind of language—a vast, enclosed textual and semantic preserve."[42]

To a hostile critic such as Harold Perkin, literary criticism was merely the worst of the disciplines in communicating its wares. He saw the academic world as a collection of

> ever more splintered disciplines, each determined to hold its ground against all-comers by means of an exclusive jargon and mind-set or to corner the market in an enclosed and lucrative career. Having rejected communication with one another outside their narrow specialisms, they have totally lost the capacity to reach, educate and persuade the public on whose financial and moral support they depend. An unintelligible intelligentsia, according to [Peter] Scott, retreats from reality into a self-indulgent world of verbal disputation. . . . Academics from different

parts of the "hard–soft" spectrum suspect one another's competence: "Physics is fundamental knowledge; chemistry is only applied physics"; "natural science is science; social science is organized prejudice"; "economists deal in facts; political scientists think the plural of anecdote is data"; "social science produces testable theories; history is mindless empiricism"—and so on down the line.[43]

In this vision, rivalry and what we might call "rigor envy" have turned the ivory tower into the tower of Babel.

Some postmodernist scholars in the humanities have taken another approach toward leveling the playing field. True, they argue, the study of literature is not objective or "scientific"—but then neither are the sciences. Scientists themselves have spent the last several decades analyzing and redefining their ideas about objectivity, but they stop far short of disclaiming it is an ideal. They also see no reason to abandon the practice of experimentation and observation simply because their results may be interpreted variously. The debate over scientific objectivity, when conducted by scientists and philosophers of science, has been rigorous and productive. In the hands of those less well trained in science and logic, it has at times become laughable.

The best joke in the field was played by physicist Alan Sokal, who submitted an article titled "Transgressing the Boundaries: Towards a Transformative Hermeneutics of Quantum Gravity" to the postmodernist journal *Social Text*. His first paragraph summarizes both the worldview and the language of postmodernist critics of science:

> There are many natural scientists, and especially physicists, who continue to reject the notion that the disciplines concerned with social and cultural criticism can have anything to contribute, except perhaps peripherally, to their research. Still less are they receptive to the idea that the very foundations of their worldview must be revised or rebuilt in the light of such criticism. Rather, they cling to the dogma imposed by the long post-Enlightenment hegemony over the Western intellectual outlook, which can be summarized briefly as follows: that there exists an external world, whose properties are independent of any individual human being and indeed of humanity as a whole;

that these properties are encoded in "eternal" physical laws; and that human beings can obtain reliable, albeit imperfect and tentative, knowledge of these laws by hewing to the "objective" procedures and epistemological strictures prescribed by the (so-called) scientific method.[44]

The editors of *Social Text*, without the advantages of hindsight and perhaps blinded by the prospect of publishing an article written by a physicist concordant with their views, accepted the article and its more than one hundred absolutely genuine footnotes. It appeared in the Spring/Summer 1996 issue.

Soon after that, another article by Sokal appeared, this time in the magazine *Lingua Franca*, which described itself as "The Review of Academic Life." There Sokal described the *Social Text* piece as "a modest (though admittedly uncontrolled) experiment: Would a leading North American journal of cultural studies . . . publish an article liberally salted with nonsense if (a) it sounded good and (b) it flattered the editors' ideological preconceptions?"[45] The *Social Text* editors tried to save face with an editorial and responses in other journals; critic Stanley Fish attacked Sokal in the *New York Times*; Sokal responded with a letter to the editor; other scholars from a variety of disciplines chimed in on both sides of the argument. Because many of the founders of postmodernism were French, *Le Monde* took up the cause, outraged by what they viewed as an attack on their homeland. A website dedicated to the Sokal affair was established at the University of Washington, and it quickly became voluminous.

Along with much nonsense, the Sokal affair generated some serious thought and writing about the relationship between science and society, and about the nature of science and the humanities. As the editors of *Nature* pointed out, Sokal's achievement was "to highlight the extent to which the issues transcend simple political ideologies or motivations and reach to the heart of contemporary ideas about science, truth, and reality."[46]

Decades after Snow's lecture, scientists and humanists were still making faces at each other. But instead of glaring across the room at faculty parties, they were airing their differences in national newspapers and on NPR. The academic disciplines—both their content and their disputes—had become matters of interest to a significant segment of the public. This was in some measure inevitable. A higher percentage of the American public had attended college, or had sent their children, and were therefore interested in what was going on in the academy. Government funding of education through student support and research grants entailed public accountability. But it also came about because some members of both cultures had gone public with their work, writing books for general readers and discussing them in popular magazines and on radio and television. The public crossed the walls of the university from outside by enrolling in college in record numbers, and some of the faculty crossed in the opposite direction. Despite its increased complexity and specialization, they managed to make their work attractive and understandable. Why they did so—often in the face of criticism or even ridicule by their peers—is the subject of the next chapter.

5

ACADEMIC PHILANTHROPISTS

John Allen Paulos, a prolific popularizer, once took his colleagues to task: "Mathematicians who don't deign to communicate their subject to a wider audience are a little like multimillionaires who don't contribute anything to charity."[1] His colleagues might defend themselves with a number of explanations: academics are not rewarded for writing popularizations; current scholarship is too complicated to explain to laypeople; it's too *hard* to write for nonspecialists—much harder than writing a check to the food bank. How valid are these defenses? How widely are they believed? And what rewards await those who do share their intellectual wealth?

As we have seen, the distinction between "scholarly" and "popular" writing is relatively new. For generations, those who made scientific discoveries or gained new understanding of history simply wrote books and articles for readers with a solid general education. The authors themselves were rarely professional geographers, anthropologists, historians, or chemists, for these fields were not professionalized until the late nineteenth century. Rather, they were men—almost never women—with the time and money to explore, conduct research, and write. The intelligent but less affluent sought patrons. The people who could afford books and had the leisure to read were sufficiently educated to understand almost everything that was being written. At least through the Victorian era, educated people in the English-speaking world could understand virtually any book published in their language on any subject. Every educated person could, and can, read Locke, Darwin, or Gibbon without specialized training as a philosopher, biologist, or historian.

As learning advanced, and as education and research grew more specialized and professionalized, the Great Schism between scholarship and popular literature emerged. For the past century, and especially since World

War II, scholars have been professional philosophers, biologists, historians, or academics in some other specialization, and they have worked from a base of knowledge far deeper and narrower than that of most educated readers. They have also learned to write in a language shared by their peers, but not necessarily by anyone else. And they have been trained by scholars who value research and its communication to other scholars more highly than they value teaching—whether in the classroom or in popular books.

The rise of academic professionalization and specialization described in the previous chapter has had two contradictory effects. Some scholars have chosen to focus inward, on their own research and on communicating exclusively with others in their subspecialties. Others use the security and status of their academic posts to reach outward, to the public at large. In one study of professionalization, Eliot Freidson offers an economic explanation:

> University professors are granted enough time free from teaching to make it possible for them to do scientific, scholarly, and intellectual research and writing that does not generally have sufficient market value to provide a living by itself. Some can work as extremely specialized scientists or humanistic scholars who report their obscure investigations in academic journals and monographs. By virtue of their sinecures they are free to address only each other rather than the general public, on whose support they would otherwise depend. . . . Others, however, are made similarly free by their sinecures to spend much of their time serving as critical intellectuals in nonscholarly journals of opinion. They can address the general public on broader subjects as "intellectuals" if they so choose but without having to depend on the public's economic support because they gain their living from teaching.[2]

Each of these paths has its own rewards and pitfalls.

Carl Sagan and the National Academy

If we use Paulos's simile, Carl Sagan was extraordinarily philanthropic. Whether he actually said "billions and billions" of stars (he denied doing so), he captured the imaginations of millions and millions of readers and viewers by sharing what he knew and loved about astronomy. His books and television shows, together with NASA's own lobbying and promotional efforts, garnered millions and millions of dollars for the American space program. He was probably the only astronomer besides Galileo whose name was a household word. Yet when Carl Sagan was nominated for membership in the National Academy of Sciences, the nomination was voted down.

Many scientists and journalists attributed Sagan's rejection to academic attitudes toward popularization. Academy member Lynn Margulis, one of Sagan's former wives, wrote to him saying that his fellow scientists were "jealous of your communication skills, charm, good looks and outspoken attitude." Nobel laureate Roald Hoffmann said that Sagan's "exposure to public view, the lingering presence of the Cosmos cinematographer's camera on his visage, all these have served to arouse the *worst*—petty jealousy—in some scientists' reaction." Stanley Miller, who had nominated Sagan, also blamed jealousy: "I can just see them saying it: 'Here's this little punk with all this publicity and Johnny Carson. I'm a ten times better scientist than that punk!' Nobody said this, but I can just see them saying it."[3]

Other scientists thought that more was involved than jealousy. Writing after Sagan's death, Timothy Ferris claimed that "behind such criticism lurks the more serious issue of whether Carl sacrificed a promising scientific career on the altar of celebrity—and whether, more generally, other think-ers blessed with the gift of gab ought to divert their energies to populariza-tion." One of Sagan's biographers, William Poundstone, dismissed jealousy as a motive but suggested a problem more general and—for readers who value serious nonfiction—more ominous: "The near-universal sentiment is not that popularization is bad, but that it is less important than doing origi-nal research."[4] Even authors of popularizations may agree with this assess-ment. Richard Dawkins, the author of a number of popular books on evolu-tion and the Charles Simonyi Professor of Public Understanding of Science at Oxford, is among them: "I'd rather go to my grave having been Watson or Crick than having discovered a wonderful way of explaining things to people. But if the discovery you're talking about is an ordinary, run-of-the-mill discovery of the sort being made in laboratories around the world every day, you feel: Well, if I hadn't done this, somebody else would have, pretty soon. So if you have a gift for reaching hundreds of thousands—millions—of people and enlightening them, I think doing that runs a close second to making a really great discovery like Watson and Crick."[5]

Stephen Jay Gould was aware of the problem. Early in his career he told an interviewer that "anyone who generalizes and writes for the public, *ipso facto*, is going to be an object of great suspicion."[6] Gould clearly valued both original research *and* popular writing. He began and ended his long book-writing career by publishing a major scholarly work and a popular work in the same year (*Ontogeny and Phylogeny* and *Ever Since Darwin* in 1977 and *The Structure of Evolutionary Theory* and *I Have Landed* in 2002). He did so not to preserve his reputation, but because he was active as both a researcher and a popularizer and enjoyed both roles.

The belief that academics do not respect popularization extends beyond the sciences. In a review of John Kenneth Galbraith's *The Age of Uncertainty* (1977), a British economist noted that "Ken Galbraith has always evoked the execration of most of his colleagues. First of all, he can write English." He went on to say that seeing Galbraith on television, wandering all over the world with his expenses paid, "must have aroused real fury," as did the fact that Galbraith was known to be a highly successful forecaster and investor.[7] A *New Yorker* profile of Harold Bloom suggests that professional critics now generally ignore his work, although some of his early books were extremely influential in academe. "When Bloom's colleagues read his recent writing at all, it often appears to them impressionistic and self-indulgently personal. With his best-sellers and his middlebrow, preacherly tone . . . Bloom is thought to have become little more than a popularizer, cooking chicken soup for the literary soul."[8]

Things may be even worse in the Netherlands. One writer said that the Dutch have not produced a body of quality nonfiction because of "the Dutch academic world's aversion to 'the general public'" and cites examples:

> Hans Crombag, a professor at Maastricht, has told me that only now, at the end of his career, is he able to write books for the general public; his academic colleagues would otherwise have made his life miserable. Ivan Wolffers, a professor in Amsterdam, is not taken at all seriously by other medical professionals, because he has been able to make medical science accessible to lay persons, thereby breaking a taboo. The career of Karel van het Reve, a professor at Leiden, has not been made any easier by his ability to write books for the general public, and not at all by his having dared openly to criticize the abuses in the groves of

academia. Piet Vroon, a professor at Utrecht, has been ridiculed by his colleagues, because he dared to write bestsellers about psychology. And Dr. Jan Bor has been blackballed for coming up with a plan to write a history of philosophy that would be accessible to lay readers, and to include pictures in it as well.[9]

It is easy enough to believe that American academics—being human—envy colleagues who are able to write books that are reviewed prominently in the popular press and that win them fame, media attention, and large royalties. It is also easy to believe that many academics have no interest in writing for the general public, preferring to spend their time in the laboratory or the library, advancing their research and writing for their peers. It is less easy to believe that the envy of colleagues is strong enough to prevent successful popularizers from getting tenure and good jobs, or to discourage scholars who wish to broaden their following beyond colleagues and the classroom from trying to do so. In fact, there is no evidence that academics are deterred from writing popularizations by anything except lack of interest or unwillingness to tackle a difficult writing task.

Academics who venture into popularization are, for the most part, at the top of their profession. They are graduates of highly selective colleges who have gone on to earn their doctorates in highly selective graduate programs—in the Ivy League or at equally prestigious universities like the University of Chicago and Stanford. They then get jobs at the same kinds of institutions, where they achieve tenure ahead of schedule and frequently end up in endowed chairs. They win prestigious fellowships from the National Science Foundation, the Guggenheim Foundation, the National Endowment for the Humanities, and the MacArthur Foundation. They win Pulitzer prizes, Bancroft prizes, and occasionally Nobel prizes. They are awarded honorary degrees and are appointed to presidential committees, and they are inducted into the National Academy of Sciences or the National Academy of Arts and Letters. These honors come throughout their careers, but most often *after* they have written books that are reviewed in popular media and sold in large numbers in bookstores.[10]

It is probably impossible for academics to succeed as writers of popular nonfiction unless they are successful scholars in their fields. Because writing for nonspecialists is so challenging, it requires a mastery of the subject matter that is difficult to acquire without substantial scholarly achievement.

Margaret Mead claimed that "if one cannot state a matter clearly enough so that even an intelligent twelve-year-old can understand it, one should remain within the cloistered walls of the university and laboratory until one gets a better grasp of one's subject matter."[11] Each book has different requirements, but generally an author needs a thorough understanding of all the literature—not only the work of colleagues who agree but also that of the dissenters. The author also needs a good sense of what is both intellectually important and interesting to general readers, a host of good examples, an independent point of view, and a distinctive voice. None of these assets is available to the novice or the second-rate.

To attract a publisher, the author needs a reputation and, possibly, a prestigious academic post. Publishers and literary agents are more interested in recruiting established scholars at major institutions than in taking risks on an unknown. Especially since contracts for many nonfiction books are signed before the manuscript is completed, publishers need some confidence that the author will produce a salable book. Publishers also know that book buyers have more confidence in authors with impressive titles at well-known universities than in unknown writers at lesser institutions.

Just as publishers value an author's academic status, university administrators value scholars whose books sell well. Having a well-known author on the faculty attracts students, pleases alumni and donors, gains media attention, and helps recruit other faculty members. Laurel Thatcher Ulrich was an exacting and creative historian before *A Midwife's Tale* won a Pulitzer prize. Before winning, she was an associate professor at the University of New Hampshire. Very soon after the Pulitzer, she became a full professor at Harvard. The prize brought her book to the attention of a wide audience, including the faculty and administration of universities seeking to enhance their image as well as their academic strength.

Even the envy of colleagues is probably exaggerated. Academics may make snide remarks about popular books at parties and in university hallways, but when they review them—whether for mass media magazines or for scholarly journals—they generally praise the books and almost never comment adversely on the fact that they are written for a general audience. These books achieve such wide circulation that scholars must pay attention to them. As one reviewer commented, "Because [Edward O.] Wilson has become a prominent spokesman for biology and conservation to the general public, professionals should take an interest in how he represents scientific issues." Another noted that Simon Schama's *Citizens* "has been received in some quarters as something like the authorized version of the [French] Revolution. Therefore it deserves serious critical consideration."[12]

Academic reviewers point out both the importance and the difficulty of writing for nonspecialists. Not all reviews are positive, however, and the handful of negative reviews almost all assume the impossibility of writing a book that will please both educated general readers and one's own colleagues. Is this a fair assessment, or another manifestation of the green-eyed monster?

Clarity and Complexity

The carefully thought out and varied rhetorical approaches writers use to present the complexities of their specializations to others hint at the practical difficulties they face, but some scholars make the larger claim that serious scholarship *cannot* be presented to a lay audience without oversimplification. Successful authors disagree and make a counterclaim: the absence of clarity in academic writing is simply the verbal re-creation of muddled thinking or deliberate obfuscation. Some analysts reject any firm distinction between scholarly and popular writing in favor of the clearer distinction between good and bad: "There's no point in saying that Bourdieu's writing is 'scholarly' and therefore reserved for specialists in the academy, whereas Hobsbawn's is more accessible and therefore can be safely let out on to a more popular market. The point is that Bourdieu's writing is hideous, and that Hobsbawm's breadth of vision, however popularly expressed, is anything but unscholarly."[13]

A reviewer of *The Coming of Post-Industrial Society* (1973) said that Daniel Bell "has undertaken a grandiose task of great complexity. . . . He believes that he can write simultaneously for the academic specialist and for a much larger, informed readership. While he is convinced that this can be done and that he can do it, I am not at all certain. For me, this goal is a much more problematic issue." Carl Degler's *At Odds* (1980) received a similar reception in *Social Science Quarterly:* "This ambitious effort to produce a book equally salable in popular and academic markets is, to this extent, as much a liability as an asset. Inevitably, many of the features which enhance *At Odds* as popular nonfiction detract from it as scholarship, and vice versa.

. . . This ambiguity over its audience creates a dilemma. He downplays to scholars his noteworthy methodological and theoretical synthesis and risks overestimating the ability of lay readers to fill in knowledge gaps." One analyst of academic writing even suggests that "a text that is written by an academic for a designated academic readership and published by an academic press or journal might well be deemed an academic failure were it to succeed with a popular audience"—a conclusion that university presses would resist.[14]

The alleged impossibility of the task is often attributed to the hopeless ignorance of the audience, which is characterized as unwilling to read a long book, in need of a great deal of handholding and repetition, and generally ill educated. One reviewer of Stephen Jay Gould's *Full House* was particularly unkind to those of us who have let our undergraduate statistical training (if any) lapse: "The book is clearly aimed at a new target for Gould: a readership that needs to be told that living organisms do not disobey the second law of thermodynamics and why; that has yet to be introduced to elementary notions of probability and to the shapes of statistical distribution curves; that must be taught the difference between a mean, a median and a mode, and shown the lack of significance of a mean without its variance; that is more interested in baseball than in evolution, but can be lured by love of the former to take an interest in the latter and so become converted to Gould's creed of contingency. If you don't recognize yourself in this description, don't read the book."[15] Where some would praise Gould's efforts at making material accessible to the statistically challenged, at least one of his colleagues interprets them as pandering to the hopelessly ill informed.

Those who succeed in conveying complex knowledge to nonspecialist readers are adamant about the importance and the feasibility of the task. Gould told an interviewer that "anything, even the conceptually most complex material, can be written for general audiences without any dumbing down. Of course you have to explain things carefully. This goes back to Galileo, who wrote his great books as dialogues in Italian, not as treatises in Latin. And to Darwin, who wrote *The Origin of Species* for general readers. I think a lot of people pick up Darwin's book and assume it must be a popular version of some technical monograph, but there is no technical monograph. That's what he wrote. So what I'm doing is part of a great humanistic tradition."[16]

Archaeologist Geoffrey Bibby argued:

> It has long been customary to start any book that can be included under the comprehensive heading of "popular science" with an apology from the author to his fellow scientists for his desertion of the icy uplands of the research literature for the supposedly lower and supposedly more lush fields of popular representation. This is not an apology, and it is not directed to archaeologists. In our day, when the research literature of one branch of knowledge has become all but incomprehensible to a researcher in another branch, and when the latest advances within any science can revolutionize—or end—our lives within a decade, the task of interpreting every science in language that can be understood by workers in other fields is no longer—if it ever was—a slightly disreputable sideline but a first-priority duty.[17]

John Kenneth Galbraith took the argument one step further and put his colleagues on the defensive. "I have also been much helped in writing on economics by the conviction that there is no idea associated with the subject that cannot, with sufficient effort, be stated in clear English. The obscurity that characterizes professional economic prose does not derive from the difficulty of the subject. It is the result of incomplete thought; or it reflects a priestly desire to differentiate one's self from the plain world of the layman; or it stems from a fear of having one's inadequacies found out. Nothing so protects error as an absence of readers or understanding."[18]

Run-of-the-mill academic writing is rarely transparent to lay readers. Sociologist Donald P. Hayes undertook a statistical study of the difficulty of articles in scientific journals, based only on word choice. He found that between 1930 and 1990, science journals rose dramatically on the scale of lexical difficulty, from at or below 0 (the level of a modern newspaper) to 30 or more (the scale is open-ended, but the most difficult articles register in the 50s). Hayes noted that science and its journals had become more specialized, but he also pointed out that the audience for general science journals such as *Scientific American* had grown. His statistical analysis clarifies the relationship between intelligibility and readership:

> For 125 years, between 1845 and 1970, the use of vocabulary in *Scientific American* was at or slightly below the level of a modern

newspaper (0.0); indeed, *Scientific American,* for its first 75 years, *was* a weekly newspaper of technology and science. Its language began to resemble that used in professional science journals after 1970. Interestingly, when the difficulty of the average article approached 15, there was a decline of over 125,000 subscribers, implying that many readers found texts written at those levels too opaque. When the level of *Scientific American* later dropped towards 10, there was a coincident increase in subscribers.[19]

Scholarship in science as well as in the social sciences and humanities has grown more complex and specialized, and there is no reason why researchers should not communicate with one another in language that lay readers or academics in other disciplines and subspecialties have not mastered. Yet, as Hayes notes, this opacity carries a cost: "Ideas flow less freely across and within the sciences, and the public's access to (and maybe trust in) science is diminished. . . . This erection of higher and higher barriers to the comprehension of scientific affairs must surely diminish science itself. Above all, it is a threat to an essential characteristic of the endeavour—its openness to outside examination and appraisal."[20]

Some question whether much of this opacity is really necessary for, or even conducive to, communication among researchers. Accusations of deliberate obscurity abound, attributed to the full range of motivations listed by Galbraith. Historian Patricia Nelson Limerick offered one explanation:

> In ordinary life, when a listener cannot understand what someone has said, this is the usual exchange:
> LISTENER: I cannot understand what you are saying.
> SPEAKER: Let me try to say it more clearly.
> But in scholarly writing in the late 20th century, other rules apply. This is the implicit exchange:
> READER: I cannot understand what you are saying.
> ACADEMIC WRITER: Too bad. The problem is that you are an unsophisticated and untrained reader. If you were smarter, you would understand me.[21]

Being unintelligible in order to seem superior may be a genuine motivation for some academic writers, but it is certainly a dysfunctional one. Limerick

pointed out that trust in the academy is not very high, especially among
conservative politicians, and the faculty's failure to get its messages across
does not help when it is time to allocate the state budget.

Using language to impress the laity is an ancient professional ploy. For
members of a profession, specialized jargon is what Kenneth Hudson calls
"masonic glue" that at once binds the insiders and distances them from out-
siders. A monopoly on practice—whether medical, legal, or academic—is
thought to require a language that is not accessible to anyone but the initi-
ates. In his history of the medical profession, Paul Starr traced the parallel
enhancement of status and obscurity. In colonial times, ordinary people had
access to domestic medical manuals. "Written in lucid, everyday language,
avoiding Latin or technical terms, the books set forth current knowledge on
disease and attacked, at times explicitly, the conception of medicine as a
high mystery." The author of one of these manuals, John C. Gunn, "main-
tained that Latin names for common medicines and diseases were 'originally made use of to *astonish the people*' and aid the learned in deception and
fraud." In the next century, though, an 1881 manual for doctors by D. W.
Cathell, *The Physician Himself,* offered the following advice: "By employing
the terms ac. phenicum for carbolic acid, secale cornutum for ergot, kalium
for potassium, natrum for sodium, chinin for quinia, etc., you will debar the
average patient from reading your prescriptions."[22]

Lawyers used the same technique. Historian Samuel Haber tells the
story of a minister who had twice lost a legal case. His lawyer, Jeremiah
Gridley, "stood self-confidently before the judges and, calling upon the
elaborate technical distinctions of eighteenth-century special pleading, in a
rapid series of exchanges with the opposing counsel, won the case. When he
told his client, 'You have obtained your cause,' the minister was astonished.
'How, sir?' the minister asked. 'You can never know,' Gridley replied with a
slight smile, 'till you get to Heaven.'"[23]

Scholars who study the way occupations become professions have shown
that less established groups with little knowledge that is not easily available
to others develop specialized language to set themselves apart from outsid-
ers. Kenneth Hudson organized his book *The Jargon of the Professions* around
a hierarchy of knowledge that runs from "The Learned Professions," through
"The Politicians and the Military" and "Literature and the Arts," and ends
with "The Near-Professions" and "The Would-Be Professions." As you slide
down this scale, the level of obscurity and abuse of language rises.[24] To reach

the heights of professional status, academics identified themselves, not as teachers—the one title they could all claim—but as physicists, chemists, historians, literary theorists, sociologists, and so forth. Greater specialization allowed for more esoteric knowledge and made it possible for a given discipline to isolate itself not only from the general public but also from other academics. Thus, the rise of literary theory or analytic philosophy allowed the practitioners of those disciplines to claim the sort of inaccessible expertise previously available only to the theoretical physicist. Judging only by language, one might well believe that literary criticism *is* rocket science.

Obfuscation sometimes also works with colleagues, who may be afraid to admit that they do not understand what they have read. This is the Emperor's New Clothes phenomenon, and it is all too common. On a grand and public scale, it underlies the success of Alan Sokal's hoax. But it is far more widespread in the day-to-day communications of scholars: witness the stiff competition in the annual Bad Writing Contest. Initiated by Denis Dutton, the editor of *Philosophy and Literature*, the contest began in 1995 with a solicitation on the Internet and ended in 1998. Entries were brief passages, no more than two sentences, from published scholarly works. The 1998 winner, a passage from an article by Berkeley professor Judith Butler, reads: "The move from a structuralist account in which capital is understood to structure social relations in relatively homologous ways to a view of hegemony in which power relations are subject to repetition, convergence, and rearticulation brought the question of temporality into the thinking of structure, and marked a shift from a form of Althusserian theory that takes structural totalities as theoretical objects to one in which the insights into the contingent possibility of structure inaugurate a renewed conception of hegemony as bound up with the contingent sites and strategies of the rearticulation of power." As Dutton explains, "To ask what this means is to miss the point. This sentence beats readers into submission and instructs them that they are in the presence of a great and deep mind. Actual communication has nothing to do with it." The winners of his contest "hope to persuade their readers not by argument but by obscurity that they too are the great minds of the age."[25]

Graduate students often complain that they are forced to write incomprehensibly, and studies have validated the anecdotal evidence. One group of researchers analyzed the papers written by a graduate student they called Nate over three successive semesters. The papers grew longer, used less metaphorical language, and eliminated the use of the first-person pronoun. By the end of three semesters, the student's writing had grown more difficult for nonspecialists. "To many readers Nate's meaning would appear to be obfuscated by a thicket of jargon. . . . By Text 3 Nate has assimilated a literature and a lexicon and therefore is more comfortably able to speak in the discourse of his subspecialty."[26] Presumably, Nate got his Ph.D., used his mastery of "the discourse of his subspecialty" to publish articles and perhaps a book, and is now happily indoctrinating new generations of academic writers. Anthropologist Alan Campbell has suggested a way around such counterproductive training:

> If it was *demanded* of academics that, to be taken seriously, every one had to produce a piece of work for the popular market, an introductory textbook, or something in that idiom, the exercise would generally be found enormously challenging, the difficulty being that many people who regard themselves as scholarly are locked in, in a sort of constipated way, to stuffy old conventions—like men in suits. That's all the initial distinction is trying to defend. It's not defending rigorous standards of writing, of presentation, of debate and scrutiny. "Scholarly" over against "popular" is nothing more than a prim vigilance about etiquette. And the main reason why "scholars" don't write popular work is not that they have some sort of conscientious objection to it. It's that they can't do it.[27]

Whatever underlies bad academic writing—a desire to appear smarter, a lack of something to say, an inability to write in any other way, or the more honorable belief that impersonal technical writing is the most efficient way to communicate with one's peers and advance knowledge—the scholar who wishes to communicate with nonspecialists has a hard row to hoe. The writers we are examining have overcome their socialization and peer pressure to write in a very different mode.

Why Bother?

Not all academics like to write. They may enjoy doing research but dislike organizing the results and sitting down in front of the computer screen.

They may find writing, especially longer pieces, extraordinarily difficult, or it may simply be an anticlimax after the excitement of research and discovery. An astonishing number of teaching academics write the bare minimum needed to get tenure and an occasional raise.

Authors of popular books are different. Most successful popularizers write a lot. They write scholarly articles and monographs, textbooks, popular nonfiction, magazine columns, novels, memoirs, and children's books. John Kenneth Galbraith wrote about fifty books (including two novels); Harold Bloom has written thirty or more (depending on how you count); Carolyn Heilbrun wrote literary criticism and (as Amanda Cross) mystery novels. People do not write that much unless they enjoy the task. Paul Fussell recalled, "I loved writing, even writing against deadlines, and . . . I enjoyed as almost nothing else watching the pile of first-draft yellow paper, augmented daily, grow gradually from a fraction of an inch to a full four inches, representing one hundred thousand words. I loved every part of the process. . . . I love being interviewed. I love mail generated by my books. I delight not just in making books and publicizing them but in observing their progress." For Stephen Jay Gould, writing was "the best way to organize thoughts and to try and put things in as perfect and as elegant a way you can. A lot of scientists hate writing. . . . Writing is a chore. It's something they have to do to get the work out. They do it with resentment. But conceptually to them, it is not part of the creative process. I don't look at it that way at all. When I get the results, I can't wait to write them up. That's the synthesis. It's the exploration of the consequences and the meaning." It is not hard to understand why people undertake a job that they enjoy so much.[28]

Writing is never really easy, even for those who write fluently, but academics who write for a general audience seem to have less trouble than many of their peers. Edward O. Wilson found that "writing has come easily to me since grade school—far easier than mathematics," and Gould claimed not to know what writer's block is. Galbraith often thought his work "was writing itself," but he also described deliberate experimentation "with cadence and rhythm" and the extensive revision that added a year to the time it took to complete *The Affluent Society*. Given their productivity, it seems fair to say that writing is at least not painful for any of these authors.[29]

Many authors of popularizations feel an urgency about the message they have to convey, and they want to reach an audience beyond their peers and students. Robert Jay Lifton is a psychiatrist who has written about Hiroshima, genocide, the Vietnam war, and nuclear war. He describes studying these subjects as a "calling." Reading about such difficult topics, interviewing participants and survivors, and dealing with the aftermath of disaster firsthand is disturbing, but for some it is also personally fulfilling. For Lifton, understanding is only the beginning of what he is trying to accomplish. To understanding he adds activism that includes writing for as broad an audience as possible. He is "a very dedicated scholar. I spend a lot of hours in my study, I've written a lot of books and papers, and I try to be as scholarly and as accurate as I can be. But I don't think that precludes taking an active stand in one's own culture in favor of those things that one believes in and against those things that one thinks are dangerous and awful to human beings in general. So I have been an activist in various ways at various times. . . . This is a phase where I'm focusing a lot on writing, but on issues that are related to these moral and political questions on which I have been active."[30]

A similar activism underlies Edward O. Wilson's writing on the environment and the preservation of biological diversity, and he makes the connection between advocacy and writing popular works:

> Scientists in many disciplines have a dual responsibility. They have to continue functioning as scientists, and that means that when they present evidence in the scientific journals they have to subject what they are claiming to peer review, and have all of the protocols of scientific research. . . . The second role is that of activist. And I believe that most scientists should be activists at least to the extent of making the work in their field more transparent, and the willingness to speak to an issue with the backup of the information that they obtain as scientists. . . .
>
> My hope is that the more people hear and learn, the more they have a strong background in *why* it matters. They don't have to have a strong background in the science. But [understanding] why it matters, why certain parts of the world are these hot spots, and what's happening to the world, and that it's a creation, and that it's disappearing and we can save it . . . I think they'll get involved.[31]

Writers may be equally passionate about subjects that do not threaten the planet or humanity when they feel the public misunderstands or is being misled. Biologists are moved to write about evolution when state school boards mandate teaching about creationism, and Stephen Jay Gould stepped outside his field of expertise to write about the misuse of intelligence testing, an issue he felt strongly about. John Allen Paulos's books explaining mathematics and statistics read like manifestoes in a crusade against innumeracy and statistical stupidity. Steven Pinker wrote *The Language Instinct* for two audiences: other scientists and "educated laypeople" whose curiosity about language was not being satisfied. And one impetus came from impatience with inaccurate descriptions of language in the media. "Mavens like William Safire or John Simon purvey a serious misunderstanding to the public. They think language is something you have to learn in school, and are so patronizing about the speech of the man in the street. Well, I think they're quacks, literally ignorant of the basic facts. The self-appointed experts are mainly self-taught and don't bother to read academics like me. Most of them focus on obscure words, slang, etymologies, but I try to show that everyday figures of speech have a richness from the point of view of the psychologist that is much more interesting."[32]

Writing for a general audience is also an extension of teaching. One way to think about the readers of popularization is that they are the same people who were learning in the college classroom ten or twenty years earlier. They have the same intellectual ability but probably have a better idea of what they are interested in. And, of course, they can *choose* what to read rather than having books assigned. It is reasonable to think that the kind of material and presentation that appeals to students will also attract alumni.

Many books that succeed in bookstores also are assigned in college classrooms. C. W. Ceram's *Gods, Graves, and Scholars* was an early success in both settings. Daniel Bell's *The End of Ideology,* Oscar Handlin's *The Uprooted,* B. F. Skinner's *Walden Two,* and David Riesman's *The Lonely Crowd* continued this tradition in the 1950s and 1960s. In the following decades, John Rawls's *A Theory of Justice,* Robert Nozick's *Anarchy, State, and Utopia,* Lester Thurow's *Zero-Sum Society,* and several of Jonathan Spence's histories of China could be found in classrooms as well as living rooms. More recently, Laurel Thatcher Ulrich's *A Midwife's Tale,* Paul Kennedy's *The Rise and Fall of the Great Powers,* and Steven Pinker's books about language have joined the list. One of the unsung virtues of popularization is that college students returning home for holidays are astonished to find their parents reading the same books they are, giving them something to talk about together.

Publishers see the connection as well. Edwin Barber, who edited nonfiction at Harcourt Brace Jovanovich and W. W. Norton, described the division between textbooks and trade books as "totally artificial. . . . If you take the intellectual spectrum, what is a textbook and what is a trade book? Look on the reading list of any college, and you are going to find three-quarters of the books weren't initially pegged to be textbooks."[33] Internal correspondence at some publishing houses reveals turf battles over whether a book would be published as a trade paperback or as a textbook, while in other cases the same book would be given two different covers: one stodgy enough to be a textbook and one flashy enough to stand out on bookstore shelves. Since the 1970s, paperbacks for both textbook and trade markets have been published in identical formats.

Some writers make the connection between teaching and popular writing explicit. Carleton Coon, who wrote several successful popular anthropology books in the 1960s, began his first book with his lecture notes from the introductory anthropology course he taught. Galbraith used *The Affluent Society* in manuscript in his classes and felt that this raised enrollment, and his Harvard colleagues used *The New Industrial State* as a textbook. Many other popular books probably began their lives in a classroom. Edward O. Wilson explained the connection between teaching and writing as a way to influence similar people at different times in their lives: "There are no prerequisites for reading *Consilience*. For 40 years I taught basic biology at Harvard University to non-science majors, to future business executives, doctors, lawyers, humanities scholars, and the like. I did this voluntarily because I thought I would do the world more good by introducing scientific ideas to this audience than by teaching science to scientists, who would get it somewhere else anyway. I learned from this how to present very complex ideas in simple ways, without condescending. I learned, too, how to present such ideas in books that nonscientists would be able to read."[34]

Reaching a larger audience than the author of a scholarly monograph brings greater financial rewards as well. A genuine bestseller will earn its author hundreds of thousands of dollars and bring a measure of celebrity that may include television and radio appearances as well as the possibility of lecture fees and other lucrative writing opportunities. Sagan, Gould, Schlesinger, Galbraith, and Stephen Ambrose are among the few academic authors who have reached these heights of fame and fortune. Most books, of course, are not bestsellers. Nonetheless, a trade book that sells reasonably well can supplement an academic salary significantly.

The definition of "reasonably well" has changed as publishing houses have been acquired at high prices by conglomerates that expect a return on their investment greater than the industry has traditionally demanded. In the 1950s, a Knopf editor called the sale of 60,000 copies of *Gods, Graves, and Scholars* "phenomenal."[35] Today that figure would be very good but would barely repay the kinds of advances that some academic authors have been able to demand. (An advance is a payment given to an author before publication in anticipation of the royalties a book is expected to earn. Royalties on trade books are generally paid at a rate of 10 to 15 percent of retail price or net revenue.) Scientific authors with the right credentials (and the right literary agent) have gotten advances in the $200,000 range, which can be earned back only with six-figure sales. (To put these figures into perspective, Bill Clinton was paid an advance of $10 to $12 million for his memoirs.) Most academic authors of trade books, though, must be content with four- or five-figure advances anticipating sales of under 100,000 copies.

A philosophy professor once told me that he wrote textbooks so that he could buy boats. He started with an advanced logic text that paid for a small sailboat. He wanted a bigger boat, so he wrote an intermediate text. Finally, he wrote an introductory text and bought a really big sailboat. That is a handy way to think about how much money academic authors can actually make. A scholarly monograph may not even pay for a bathtub toy; in some cases, presses do not offer royalties for books with very small sales possibilities. The royalties on most monographs, though, cover a dinner cruise for two on the nearest large body of water, with little left over. An academic book with occasional textbook adoptions might allow an author to buy and maintain a rowboat or canoe.

To upgrade to a sailboat, an author needs to reach beyond the academic community. Authors and publishers do not make an author's earnings public because they are really nobody's business, but it is sometimes possible to get sales figures or print runs from trade magazines and publishers' archives. One can extrapolate from those to a very rough estimate of an author's royalties—very rough because a print run tells only how many copies are printed, not how many are sold; sales figures are sometimes inflated to encourage booksellers to stock a title; contracts vary, so we do not know what percentage each author is receiving of the sales price; and there are other uncertainties.

Peter Gay's *Education of the Senses* (1984), the first volume in his work about bourgeois society, had a first printing of 26,000 copies, of which 16,000 were destined for the History Book Club. He was therefore being paid full royalties on 10,000 copies and at a lower rate for the others. This sounds like an enormous number of copies to a university press author, but it is certainly not enough (especially after taxes) to buy a very large boat. There were later printings, but they would have provided only a pleasant supplement to Gay's university salary. Paul Fussell's early books had sold no more than 8,000 copies apiece, so the sales of *The Great War and Modern Memory* were a welcome change. Published in 1975, it had sold 40,000 copies in cloth and paper by 1980 and a total of 53,000 by 2000, when a twenty-fifth-anniversary edition was issued. Although 53,000 copies is a lot of books, those sales were spread out over 25 years, hardly providing a reliable primary income. Similarly, Elaine Pagels's first popular book, *The Gnostic Gospels* (1979), sold very well. The hardcover edition, priced at $10, sold 43,000 copies, and in 1978 she received an advance of $37,000 for the paper edition, of which nearly 400,000 copies had been sold by 1995. Her gross income from the book would have been about $75,000 over fifteen years. Of course, all of these authors published more books, so that they were earning two or three times this amount, but over several more years.[36] In other words, although substantial sums of money are involved, we are still talking about sailboats and marina rents—supplements to income rather than substitutes.

Authors whose tastes run to yachts—or to becoming full-time writers— need not just one bestseller, but several. No single nonfiction book is likely to provide an adequate continuing income, and royalties alone are rarely enough. A book needs other media tie-ins—a movie or a television series— to bring in really large revenues. Stephen Ambrose's works sold well enough that he did not need to teach and could, in fact, employ family members as researchers and agents. He left teaching only in the last decade of his life, though, when his writing and related activities began to generate enormous revenues—as much as $3 million a year. *Undaunted Courage* (1996), his book about Lewis and Clark, was probably less profitable than his World War II books, but it sold over a million copies. Ambrose was able to command million-dollar book advances and five-figure speaking fees. He also had significant income from movie rights and from consulting on films and television projects.[37] The ability to live independently as a writer, at least on a grand scale, is achieved only by a few.

We can end this chapter where we began, with Carl Sagan. His books were all profitable. *Dragons of Eden* sold 179,000 copies in cloth and about a million in paper. Sagan eventually earned around $200,000 in royalties for it. He had additional income of over $200,000 from subsidiary rights (foreign rights, book club revenues, and so forth). The first printing of his *Broca's Brain* was 75,000 copies, and the book brought Sagan around $200,000 in royalties. Paperback royalties were around $35,000. *The Cosmic Connection* sold 35,000 in hardcover and half a million in paper. These are impressive numbers, but *Cosmos*, with its television series, makes them look run of the mill. By January 1982, *Cosmos* had sold more than 825,000 copies in hardback, earning Sagan over $2 million in royalties and Random House about $8 million in gross revenue. Additional book club royalties were in excess of $350,000. Books by other authors tied into PBS series also performed well. Kenneth Clark's *Civilisation* sold 360,000 cloth copies and 150,000 in paper, for revenues to the publisher of over $7 million plus more than $3 million in book club sales. The figures for Jacob Bronowski's *The Ascent of Man* were almost identical. Alistair Cooke's *America* sold more than half a million copies in hardback, for gross revenues of $10 million, plus book club sales of $7.5 million.[38]

Earnings like these would allow an author to give up an academic post and write full time. Sagan certainly could have done so: the figures just cited do not include what he earned from PBS, paid lectures, or other sources. Yet he did not give up his post at Cornell, where he continued to teach until his death. John Kenneth Galbraith, too, continued to teach, as did Stephen Jay Gould and other bestselling authors. Many successful nonfiction writers do not have university ties: literary journalists sometimes have appointments in creative writing departments, but they are the exception. Successful authors of popular history have frequently been independent scholars: Barbara Tuchman and David McCullough are well-known examples. But for many authors, the link to students and colleagues—even jealous ones—is critical. These writers might find it difficult to say whether teaching or writing is their day job. Their popular writing enriches their teaching and research, while communicating with colleagues and students enhances their ability to reach an audience eager to be taught and challenged. It also requires them to master narrative techniques not required in traditional scholarly writing, as we will see in the next chapter.

6

WRITING TO BE READ

It's eight o'clock in the evening, and you have just settled into a comfortable chair with a paperback:

> In the early-morning hours of May 16, 1968, Ivy Hodge awoke in her flat on the eighteenth floor of Ronan Point Tower. She had moved into the newly constructed block of apartments in Canning Town, east of London, almost a month to the day earlier. She put on her slippers and dressing gown and went to the kitchen. Her apartment in the southeast corner of the tower consisted of a living room, a bedroom, a kitchen, and a bath, in a compact layout typical of postwar construction. She filled the kettle with water, placed it on the stove and, at exactly five forty-five, lit a match to light the burner. . . . She had disconnected the pilot light some weeks earlier for fear of explosion and had not smelled gas. . . . One witness described a blue flash; another, a vivid red flame.

You know what will happen next: the arrival of the emergency team, followed by Scotland Yard, the multiplication of suspects and motives, possibly another victim or two, and in a couple hundred pages, the culprit under arrest. But you have committed the "capital mistake" Sherlock Holmes warned against in *A Study in Scarlet*, theorizing "before you have all the evidence." The quotation comes, not from a mystery novel, but from a book called *Why Buildings Fall Down* (1992) by Matthys Levy and Mario Salvadori, two engineers specializing in structural failure.[1]

Now that I've told you, of course, you can see the clues. There is a little too much detail about the layout of the apartment, "typical of postwar construction" isn't very literary, and we haven't been told much about Ivy. But on a quick reading, you could be fooled. The authors had learned their lessons about writing for people who are not engineers: they gave the story a human face, provided details, and had a narrative fiction model in mind. (By the way, Ivy survived—along with all but four of the residents of the building. The perpetrators were a lack of continuity in joints and insufficient redundancy.)

Most academic writers who turn their hands to popular nonfiction receive similar advice from their editors and agents: The book they are undertaking is completely different from the scholarly monographs and journal articles they are used to turning out. Most writers focus first on avoiding or simplifying technical language, a necessary but insufficient step. In fact, language is the least of the writer's problems. Far more important are helping readers relate to the subject, finding the right voice, choosing a structure for the book (preferably one with continuous joints and sufficient but not excessive redundancy), and providing context. Authors have found a multitude of ways to solve these problems.

Biography and Beyond

Biography is the most popular form of serious (as well as tabloid) nonfiction, and the earliest successful books popularizing science in the twentieth century took a biographical approach to their subjects. The first was *The Microbe Hunters* (1926), by Paul de Kruif, an account of the lives and discoveries of microbiologists from Anton Leeuwenhoek to Walter Reed and Paul Ehrlich. De Kruif managed to pack a fair amount of what was then an unfamiliar science into a series of biographical essays. He provided biographical information about each researcher, some historical context, and accounts of their experiments and what they proved. He also described the scientific community of each researcher's time. He depicted science as an intense competition between scientists and microbes and, at a more personal level, between rival researchers. De Kruif's book is informative and entertaining, but to make it so he used techniques that later nonfiction writers would be criticized for. He melodramatically turned microbes into humans ("Beings these were, more terrible than fire-spitting dragons or hydra-headed monsters. They were silent assassins that murdered babes in warm cradles" [11]), and he created dialogue and thoughts from thin air. Thus, when a young Louis Pasteur was working on his fermentation studies, fuming at Justus von Liebig's denial of his discoveries, de Kruif reported on his thoughts:

> He would show this Liebig! Then a trick to beat Liebig flashed into his head, a crafty trick, a simple clear experiment that would smash Liebig and all other pooh-bahs of chemistry who scorned the important work that his precious microscopic creatures might do.
>
> "What I have to do is. . . ."
>
> That night he turned over and over in his bed. He whispered his hopes and fears to Madame Pasteur—she couldn't advise him but she comforted him. She understood everything but couldn't explain away his worries. She was his perfect assistant. (11–12)

This approach has not disappeared: Michael Guillen used it in *Five Equations that Changed the World* (1995) when he reconstructed the emotions and thoughts of Isaac Newton, Daniel Bernouilli, Michael Faraday, Rudolf Clausius, and Albert Einstein as they worked through the mathematical challenges of their careers and the personal challenges of their family relationships. Historians would not approve, but he did make the physics and math understandable.

Despite its faults, *The Microbe Hunters* offered a model in which biography provided a framework to explain science. One of his admirers, C. W. Ceram, called de Kruif the first who set out to

> trace the development of a highly specialized science so that one could read about it with genuine excitement, with the sort of response too often produced, in our times, only by detective thrillers. De Kruif found that even the most highly involved scientific problems can be quite simply and understandably presented if their working out is described as a dramatic process. That means, in effect, leading the reader by the hand along the same road that the scientists themselves have traversed from the moment truth was first glimpsed until the goal was gained. De Kruif found that an account of the detours, crossways, and blind alleys that had confused the scientists . . . could achieve a dynamic and dramatic quality capable of evoking an uncanny tension in the reader.[2]

Ceram used de Kruif's book as the model for *Gods, Graves, and Scholars*

(1951), a series of true adventure stories that described the archaeological discoveries of Heinrich Schliemann, Howard Carter, Austen Henry Layard, and other pioneers in the field. Ceram (the pen name of Kurt Marek) explained that his "aim was to portray the dramatic qualities of archaeology, its human side. I was not afraid to digress now and then and to intrude my own personal reflections on the course of events. Nor have I shied away from prying into purely personal relationships. . . . Romantic excursions go hand in hand with scholarly self-discipline and moderation" (v). Most chapters of the book focus on an individual archaeologist and describe his early years, discoveries, setbacks, and personal life. They also provide insight into the nature of the archaeologists' discoveries, what they deduced from their findings, how they decoded extinct languages, and their ways of working. The language is straightforward, and the index even provides phonetic spellings for some of the names.

Ceram's book was an instant and long-lasting success. It was a bestseller and a Book-of-the-Month Club selection, and it has been in print for more than fifty years, outliving dozens of competitors. His editor at Alfred A. Knopf, Harold Strauss, latched on to the formula and began commissioning books that applied it to other fields. He summarized the "De Kruif–Ceram method" very simply: "All the scientific material is dealt with, but it is organized in the framework of individual adventures in discovery, and told in a biographical and narrative manner."[3]

Strauss was unable to influence Ceram's writing very much. *Gods, Graves, and Scholars*, like Ceram's other books, was translated from the German. At Strauss's request the translator, novelist E. B. Garside, cut about twenty-five thousand words from the text, over Ceram's objections, and removed some of the awkwardness from the original. The general approach and tone, however, were fixed. In working with other authors, Strauss was more directive, and his suggestions to one of them tell us what he thought made the book work: "It tells how a man decided to become an anthropologist, how he was trained, what first roused his curiosity, his luck or bad luck in seeking his objectives, the climactic discovery that established his reputation, and finally the reception of his discoveries or theories by his scientific peers and the world at large. Within this capacious formula you can incorporate a huge amount of information." He later advised the same author, Ruth Moore, to "drive home in a little more human and immediate terms the popular meaning of the work done in the last few years. . . . [T]he approach to the scientific material [must] be humanized by an attempt to get at what made the particular scientist click." He told her that in some places she had "tacked the basic biographical information on near the end, almost as an afterthought. . . . I think you ought to go a little further than this and speculate, where you have any evidence at all, regarding the temperament and psychology of the man in question. . . . [T]his is a somewhat different thing than merely including the biographical facts."[4]

Science is not the only field that can be popularized through biography. In 1953, Robert Heilbroner wrote *The Worldly Philosophers*, biographical accounts of Thomas Malthus, David Ricardo, Robert Owen, Karl Marx, Thorstein Veblen, John Maynard Keynes, Joseph Schumpeter, and other economists. For each, he provided a brief biography, described the economist's personality, set the work into historical context, summarized the works, and assessed both their immediate impact and their permanent influence. Heilbroner's writing is far more sophisticated than de Kruif's or Ceram's, but the framework of his book is the same as theirs. And perhaps because Heilbroner—unlike Ceram—had an academic reputation to maintain, he was careful to defend himself in advance against criticism from his peers: "My purpose has been to illustrate great flowerings of thought and not to document them, to rouse the interest of the curious reader and not to drown it, and therefore my selection of material may dismay a scholar. . . . But I must ask the scholar to recognize that many great economic ideas are interesting only to a professional" (353).

This episodic, biographic approach worked well, but it was a formula, and formulas quickly grow predictable and boring. The authors Strauss worked with during the 1950s and 1960s outgrew the model, and more recent authors have found very different ways to use biography. In *Wonderful Life* (1989), Stephen Jay Gould used the intellectual biographies of two paleontologists, Charles D. Walcott and H. B. Whittington, to explain both a puzzling fossil record and the way science works. The two men are important because they looked at the same evidence and came to opposite conclusions. We need to know something about their lives, especially their education and the prevailing scientific theories, in order to understand why this happened. Gould's purpose was to convey "the most important message taught by the history of science: the subtle and inevitable hold that theory exerts upon data and observation. Reality does not speak to us objectively, and no scientist can be free from constraints of psyche and society. The greatest impediment to scientific innovation is usually a conceptual lock, not a factual lack" (276). Biography is merely the hook on which Gould hangs science, history, and philosophy.

The historian Simon Schama did something similar in *Dead Certainties (Unwarranted Speculations)* (1991), a "work of the imagination that chronicles historical events" (327). The book combines two slightly related biographical essays that instruct the reader in the problems of writing history rather than solving the mysteries they narrate. In fact, they simply make the mysteries more mysterious. In the first essay, Schama uses a variety of texts about the death of General James Wolfe in the battle of Quebec: Benjamin West's painting, *The Death of General Wolfe,* which is reproduced in a foldout color plate in the book; various contemporary accounts of the battle; and the account written by nineteenth-century historian Francis Parkman.

The second essay is an account of the murder of Francis Parkman's uncle, George, in 1849. Again, Schama provides a variety of contemporary accounts, including trial records, letters, and newspaper clippings. Like the first essay, this piece forces the reader to contemplate the discrepancies and contradictions found in the documents, replicating what Schama calls "the habitually insoluble quandary of the historian: how to live in two worlds at once; how to take the broken, mutilated remains of something or someone from the 'enemy lines' of the documented past and restore it to life or give it a decent interment in our own time and place" (319). Writing such a narrative allows Schama to illustrate "that even in the most austere scholarly report from the archives, the inventive faculty—selecting, pruning, editing, commenting, interpreting, delivering judgements—is in full play" (322).

In an interview conducted shortly after the book was published, Schama explained his purpose:

> I really wanted to drop people into the history more directly. I did not want some sort of theoretical framing before [the text] started. That seemed to me to ruin the storytelling voice. And I wanted to reproduce the experience of stumbling around in an archive. The archive could be just one's own attic or photograph album, where the narrative line is not polished. . . . I wanted a very staccato sense of bumping into things, which one often has when one's trying to piece something together—like an archeologist on a dig. Historical reconstruction is full of hunches and

guesses and speculations, and finding the document you were looking for is worthless and ineloquent and dumb but the one that's underneath it is unbelievably eloquent and surprising and strange—fruitfully strange.[5]

In these two books we see the transformation of biography as a tool for explanation—from the "great man" version of science promoted by de Kruif and Ceram to biography as a curtain-raiser, inviting the viewer/reader to participate in the process of discovery and interpretation. The emphasis has shifted from fact to evidence, from conclusion to process.

Biography can also be used, not to illustrate the development or methods of a discipline, but to illustrate and advance the author's own thesis. In *The New Radicalism in America* (1966), Christopher Lasch used the lives of figures as varied as Jane Addams and Norman Mailer to enunciate a theory of radicalism as a revolt against patriarchal bourgeois society that is unlike liberal, progressive notions of reform. Barbara Tuchman used the life of a single nobleman, Enguerrand de Coucy VII, as the basis for the detailed description and interpretation of the fourteenth century she presented in *A Distant Mirror* (1978).

Making Your Subject Human

The subject of biography is usually human, although there have been biographies of lions, race horses, and other animals. But when writing about black holes, tiny prehistoric creatures, or numbers, the author may need to be very creative to follow the editor's advice to "humanize your subject."

One of Harold Strauss's authors in the 1960s, anthropologist Geoffrey Bibby, chose human beings as his subject in *The Testimony of the Spade* (1956), but their experience was so remote from ours that readers would have had great difficulty identifying with them as individuals. Therefore, in writing about a prehistoric settlement in northern Europe, Bibby brought the pile villages to life. Readers

> could see the party of two or three hundred settlers in their first arrival on the lake shore; the womenfolk keeping the cattle and sheep and goats and children from straying too far from the vulnerable beach encampment, while the men, with keen-eyed

outposts in the treetops and on the surrounding hill summits, set to work with their polished-flint axes to cut the forest back. . . . The felled trees can be seen, topped and rolled down to the beach, where the older men burn the ends to a point before quenching the charred ends with leather buckets of lake water. . . . The thud of stone ax on standing timber, and the hollower sound of piles being hammered home with blows from large stones, must have formed the constant background to the early days of the settlement. (214)

Bibby also wrote about the history and techniques of archaeology, but he abandoned the great man approach, emphasizing the nineteenth-century amateur tradition and the participation of farmers and other working people in excavations. Rather than viewing archaeology as a series of vaguely connected individual adventures, he showed how the work of scientists all over Europe could be brought together to create an overview of human movement and settlement. For Bibby, making the story human meant bringing to life both subjects and investigators.

When writing about disasters, authors can make the experience immediate by individualizing the experience. In *Why Buildings Fall Down*, Levy and Salvadori nearly always found an individual like Ivy Hodge to draw the reader into the story. Their account of the collapse of the Kemper Arena roof begins with an arena employee who was the only person in the building at the time, who "heard strange noises emanating from the great hall" and "barely had time to run out of the building" (59). The Hartford Civic Center Arena roof collapse is seen through the eyes of Horace Becker, a guest in the Sheraton Hotel that faced the building. Becker "was awakened by what sounded like a 'loud cracking noise.' . . . Within seconds the windows of his room had started to shake" (68). In telling the story of the B-25 bomber that struck the Empire State Building in 1945, they began by recreating the pilot's experience, "weaving through the maze of skyscrapers over Manhattan" in clouds and fog that severely reduced visibility, and went on to describe what happened to people in the building, including "two women in another elevator [that] fell seventy-five stories when the cable holding their cab snapped, cut by flying shrapnel" (28). The reader, intrigued by the effect on individuals, is then willing to read on to see why the buildings collapsed (or, in the case of the Empire State Building, survived) and to absorb a fair amount of engineering and physics.

An author whose subject predates people by millions of years is bound to have some problems humanizing his subject. Richard Fortey, author of *Trilobite! Eyewitness to Evolution* (2000), almost managed this feat. Even if he didn't quite make readers identify with his extinct, fossilized creatures, he found other ways to bring their story closer to us. One of the striking features of trilobites, marine arthropods whose bodies were divided into three segments, was their eyes. Fortey consequently set out to have the reader "see the world through the eyes of trilobites, to help you to make a journey back through hundreds of millions of years. . . . This will be an unabashedly trilobito-centric view of the world" (22). He painted vivid pictures of these creatures, which existed in an enormous variety of fantastic shapes, of the seas in which they lived, and of the other animals they lived among. But it remains very difficult for most readers to imagine themselves into the shells of a long-extinct ancestor of the horseshoe crab peering up through the depths of a prehistoric sea. What Fortey did manage to do, very entertainingly, was to convince his readers that trilobites are important and interesting enough that we do not find it at all peculiar that he would happily devote his life to studying them.

More than most authors, Fortey told his readers a great deal about himself—not all of it flattering. What he humanized was himself and, in passing, many of his colleagues, so that even if we cannot identify with the trilobites we can identify with the trilobite experts. He begins by telling us about how he decided to become a paleontologist: "If you can have love at first sight, then I fell in love with trilobites at the age of fourteen. . . . This was the time I explored with a coal hammer at a period of my life when my voice had just turned unreliably falsetto and baritone by turns. While others discovered girls, I discovered trilobites" (19–20). Carl Sagan, not known for modesty or self-deprecation, made a similar confession from adolescence in an essay in *Broca's Brain:* "In rereading L. Ron Hubbard's *The End Is Not Yet*, which I had first read at age fourteen, I was so amazed at how much worse it was than I had remembered that I seriously considered the possibility that there were two novels of the same name and by the same author but of vastly differing quality" (139). Both authors used their own foibles to make themselves more human and to put the reader at ease.

Fortey also managed to make readers appreciate the value of systematic classification and nomenclature, two aspects of the life sciences that beginners find most deadly and pointless. "The sign that the beginner has joined the hidden club of experts is when he can trade technical descriptions with confidence" (29); a shared vocabulary makes communication possible. He gradually introduced readers to the technical terms they need by explaining how he learned them, again allowing the reader to identify with the author and—not incidentally—to learn the mnemonic tricks that he worked out for himself. And rather than pretend that this is a totally serious business, he gave an example: "I named a trilobite with a singularly hourglass-shaped glabella *monroeae* (after Marilyn), and a friend of mine named a hunchback-looking fossil *quasimodo*. These little diversions actually help to make names more memorable" (154). Throughout the book, Fortey shared puns and jokes (often groan-inspiring) that make readers feel that they know him and might even enjoy sharing in some of his fieldwork. Finally, he allowed the reader to see why scientists are willing to do so much work that seems tedious. Looking for fossils for the most part "consisted of bashing hard rocks with a geological hammer, until they were in small pieces on which fragments of trilobite could be seen. Hardened criminals used to be required to do the same thing before it was banned as inhumane. I loved it. . . . You never knew what the next hammer blow might bring" (35).

Like Stephen Jay Gould and Simon Schama, Fortey wanted readers to learn not just about trilobites but also about how science works. After describing other views of scientific pursuits—as a race for glory or a journey into uncharted territory—he presented his own metaphor: "The way science works might be a series of interconnecting paths. . . . [T]here may be a crucial conjunction of circumstances which changes everything, and something as small and ancient as a trilobite may be the catalyst for this transformation" (25). And moving as far as possible from the "great man" version of science, he stressed the contribution of "the regular footsoldiers" (25).

Michael Pollan turned the principle of humanizing on its head by showing that humans play a role in evolution that is not usually recognized. In *The Botany of Desire: A Plant's-Eye View of the World* (2001), he described the relationship between plants and humans as parallel to the relationship between plants and bees: through the process of coevolution, plants have developed features (such as the sweetness of apples and the beauty of tulips) that attract both bees and people, who benefit from the plants and in turn help the plant species to survive. Pollan did not anthropomorphize and made it very clear that the plants are not doing this consciously or purposefully. Yet the principles of evolution, as played out in the presence of humans, ensure that the plants that develop human-pleasing qualities will benefit from conscious, purposeful human behavior. Anyone whose household includes a cat knows that animals influence human behavior, and endangered species such as the panda and tiger are more likely to attract attention and preservation funds than the less cuddly or striking species. Pollan pointed out that plants, too, seduce humans into acting on their behalf.

Reassurance

Almost every writer of serious nonfiction tries to reassure readers and potential readers that what they are about to read is not rocket science, even when the subject is in fact rocket science. It sometimes seems that they may be reassuring themselves as well. After all, they are translating material it has taken them a lifetime to master into a few hundred pages of accessible prose, and they may not be sure they can do it. In any case most writers make an effort to tell readers that (a) they *can* understand this and (b) even if they can't understand all of it, they can understand the important parts. Some writers even physically separate the really hard stuff from the rest, just in case, placing the most technical material in boxes or printing it in italics. In *A Theory of Justice* (1971), John Rawls noted that his book is extremely long and then provided advice to the nonspecialist reader:

> The fundamental intuitive ideas of the theory of justice are presented in §§1–4 of chapter I. From here it is possible to go directly to the discussion of the two principles of justice for institutions in §§11–17 of Chapter II, and then to the account of the original position in Chapter III, the whole chapter. A glance at §8 on the priority problem may prove necessary if this notion is unfamiliar. Next, parts of Chapter IV, §§33–35 on equal liberty and §§39–40 on the meaning of the priority of liberty and the Kantian interpretation, give the best picture of the doctrine. So far this is about a third of the whole and comprises most of the essentials of the theory. (viii–ix)

The book is still not easy going, but it is encouraging to know that one may skip the *really* hard parts and still get the main message of an extremely important and influential work.

Mathematics is most often the topic of such authorial reassurance, which makes sense, given the prevalence of math phobia among Americans. As the twentieth century progressed, authors gained confidence in their readers' intellectual (and even mathematical) abilities. In response they continued to offer reassurance but offered more difficult material. In the acknowledgments to *A Brief History of Time*, Stephen Hawking repeated the advice he had received: "Each equation that I included in the book would halve the sales. I therefore resolved not to have any equations at all. In the end, however, I *did* put in one equation, Einstein's famous equation, $E = mc^2$. I hope that this will not scare off half of my potential readers" (vi–vii). He thus managed both to let us know that there will not be a lot of math and to tell us that we know enough math to get the joke. Henry Petroski, an engineer who has written many books for nonengineers, cautiously included his reassurances in the subtitle of his 1986 book, *Beyond Engineering: Essays and Other Attempts to Figure without Equations*. To explain the solution to the puzzle at the heart of *Fermat's Enigma* (1997), Simon Singh provided fairly simple descriptions of problems and solutions in the text, placing proofs in appendixes "for those readers with a slightly deeper knowledge of the subject" (xvi).

At least one author demonstrated his increasing confidence in readers' mathematical literacy in the course of his own career. Michael Guillen has been both an instructor in mathematics and physics and a television science editor. He is the author of two books about math and physics for general readers—*Bridges to Infinity* (1983) and *Five Equations That Changed the World* (1995)—and he explained the relationship between the two books in the introduction to the second:

> This is not so much an offspring of my last book, *Bridges to Infinity: The Human Side of Mathematics*, as it is its evolutionary descendant. I wrote *Bridges* with the intention of giving readers a sense of how mathematicians think and what they think about . . . without sub-jecting the reader to a single equation.
>
> It was like sweet-tasting medicine offered to all those who are afflicted with math anxiety. . . . In short, *Bridges to Infinity* was a dose of mathematical literacy designed to go down easily.
>
> Now . . . I have dared to go that one step further. . . . One might say I am offering the public a stronger dose of numeracy, an oppor-tunity to become comfortably acquainted with five remarkable for-

mulas in their original, undisguised forms. Readers will be able to comprehend *for themselves* the meaning of the equations. (5)

One can trace a similar growth of confidence in the reading public among writers and publishers over the course of the postwar decades.

Harold Strauss and his Knopf authors in the 1950s and 1960s were careful not to scare off readers. In a letter to Ruth Moore, Strauss worried about three of the chapters that were "theoretical and, to an extent, mathematical. They seem to me to be somewhat less effective than the rest of the book." It was not only math that worried him, though. In choosing illustrations, he wrote, "I have come down rather hard on teeth and skulls. . . . They are the raw material from which experts work, and not of very great interest to the general reader. I think I have included enough of them to do justice to the scientific basis of your book, but not so many that the general reader will be deterred."[6]

Even without Strauss's urging, Moore had soft-pedaled technical details, attaching the following footnote to a very simple equation in *Man, Time, and Fossils* (1953): "Only a part of Fisher's equation is noted. I shall not attempt to explain it other than to say that the whole equation shows that a race which multiplies too fast will outrun its food supply. It is included only to give the non-mathematical a glimpse of what such mathematics looks like, and in the hope that it may be interesting in much the same way as a picture of some undecipherable hieroglyphics" (197 n. 2). Five years later, when Moore was at work on her fourth book, Strauss had changed his tune (or at least the key he was singing in): "Times have changed a bit, and it is now possible to publish trade books in the field of science for the general reader with a *slightly*—I repeat—slightly—increased seriousness, and a corresponding slight decrease in sugar coating."[7]

Writers of the 1970s and later are much more generous, or at least more subtle, and are willing to present more difficult material. In *Innumeracy* (1988), John Allen Paulos, the mathematician whose books aim to show that anyone can understand math at least well enough not to be duped by journalists, politicians, and statisticians, described his approach as "gently mathematical, using some elementary ideas from probability and statistics which, though deep in a sense, will require nothing more than common sense and arithmetic. . . . The occasional difficult passage can be ignored with impunity" (5). His 1995 book, *A Mathematician Reads the Newspaper*, tells us: "Don't worry about the mathematics itself. It is either elementary or else is explained briefly in self-contained portions as needed. If you can find the continuation of a story on page B16, column 5, you'll be okay" (4). In fact, Paulos's explanations are both clear and complex, so that he can write—with full confidence that readers are following him—a sentence like this: "To reiterate, the conditional probability that you test positive given that you have D is 99 percent, yet only 9 percent of those with positive tests will have D" (137).

An astronomer writing about mathematics, John D. Barrow described his *Pi in the Sky* (1992) as "a book about mathematics without being a book of mathematics. . . . I have tried to avoid writing a history of mathematics and I have assiduously avoided doing any mathematics." To humanize his subject, he promised "our journey will take us first to the most ancient and diverse anthropological evidences of counting, and the origins of mathematical intuitions. . . . And in our story we shall meet many strange characters and unexpected events that make plain the humanity of those engaged in the search for number and its meaning" (vii–viii). He kept his promise, writing entertainingly and clearly, offering few computations or equations, and providing comprehensible examples that make it possible for even the nonmathematical to understand complex abstract arguments.

Stephen Jay Gould warned readers of *Wonderful Life* (1989) that he was presenting difficult material but assured them that it would be worth the trouble: "I am asking some investment here from readers with little knowledge of invertebrate biology. But the story is not difficult to follow, the conceptual rewards are great, and I shall try my best to provide the necessary background and guidance. The material is not at all conceptually difficult, and the details are both beautiful and fascinating. Moreover, you can easily retain the thread of argument without completely following the intricacies of classification" (108–9). Gould presented an enormous amount of detail in the text, diagrams, and italicized insets. By the middle of the book he was confident enough in his audience to start a paragraph "But was *Aysheaia* an anychophoran?" Readers may not know the answer, but they can understand the question and why it matters (171).

John Kenneth Galbraith similarly challenged his readers, but in his case the challenge was clearly meant to flatter. In *The Affluent Society* (1958), which was a bestseller, Galbraith invited the reader to join him in rejecting the "conventional wisdom," an expression that he coined:

These are the days when men of all social disciplines and all political faiths seek the comfortable and the accepted; when the man of controversy is looked upon as a disturbing influence; when originality is taken to be a mark of irritability; and when, in minor modification of the scriptural parable, the bland lead the bland. Those who esteem this world will not enjoy this essay. Perhaps they should return it to the shelf unread. For there are negative thoughts here, and they cannot but strike an uncouth note in the world of positive thinking. (15–16)

It's a safe bet that few people put the book back on the shelf. Galbraith also flattered his readers' intelligence by assuming not only that they could follow his argument but that they would find it easy to follow. Indeed, he assumed that they would have an easier time of it than a professional economist would. "The businessman and the lay reader will be puzzled over the emphasis which I give to a seemingly obvious point. The point is indeed obvious. But it is one which, to a singular degree, economists have resisted. They have sensed, as the layman does not, the damage to established ideas which lurks in these relationships. As a result, incredibly, they have closed their eyes (and ears) to the most obtrusive of all economic phenomena" (127). Galbraith brought the reader over to his side, against his professional opponents.

Metaphors and Analogies

Metaphors and analogies are essential to nonfiction. John D. Barrow, the author of several popular science books, views comparisons as essential not only to writing about science but to actually doing science:

> When scientists attempt to explain their work to the general public they are urged to simplify the ideas with which they work, to remove unnecessary technical language and generally make contact with the fund of everyday concepts and experience that the average layperson shares with them. Invariably this leads to an attempt to explain esoteric ideas by means of analogies. Thus, to explain how elementary particles of matter interact with one another, we might describe them in terms of billiard balls colliding

with each other. . . . If we look more closely at what scientists do, it is possible to see their descriptions as the search for analogies that differ from those used as a popularizing device only by the degree of sophistication and precision with which they can be endowed.[8]

Analogies can take you only so far—either in thinking or in writing—but they are an extremely useful tool for scientists, social scientists, and humanities scholars.

Engineering is a tough sell. Most people aren't sure exactly what engineers do—applied science is about as close as most definitions come—but whatever it is, it sounds boring. Henry Petroski clearly knows his field's reputation. His 1986 book of essays, *Beyond Engineering*, begins with a section titled "Writing as Bridge-Building," which evokes the most poetic example of the engineer's art. It also calls to mind a metaphorical meaning of bridge-building as communication, something he believes engineers need to do better. He then explores the analogy:

> Whatever the engineer does, he must anticipate how the thing he is constructing, whether in concrete or abstract terms, can fail to meet its objectives. This is little different from writing an essay or story, for the writer must anticipate the questions his reader will ask of the work, and to accomplish its end is to answer beforehand those questions. Just as the engineer must demonstrate to himself and to his colleagues the soundness of a bridge, so must the writer demonstrate to himself and his reader-critics the soundness of his metaphorical bridge. (5–6)

Petroski's best-known book, *The Pencil: A History of Design and Circumstance* (1990), is not only a history of pencil design and manufacture; pencil making is used as an extended metaphor for engineering. "To reflect on the pencil is to reflect on engineering; a study of the pencil is a study of engineering" (xi). The book is more than four hundred pages long and looks as much like a pencil as a book can if it is to be readable. (It is tall and thin, with a yellow spine.) To sustain a metaphor for that many pages is no small feat, and Petroski carefully chose an everyday object that would fit his purpose well. It had to be something that every reader would be familiar with and understand—or rather believe that there was nothing about it to understand. True, most of us have wondered from time to time how they get the lead in, but a pencil is nowhere near as mysterious as, say, television or the kitchen faucet. But it also had to be an object with a history that would allow Petroski to develop the ideas he wanted to impress upon the reader. The pencil, with its links to education, art, and literature, serves very well. It also benefits from the varieties of materials it comprises: wood, graphite, rubber, and metal. The choice of metaphor is what makes the book work.

As Petroski told the story of the pencil's invention and development, he repeatedly brought out specific themes. The pencil could not be created without the basic raw materials: something to make a mark and something to make the marking substance easy to hold and write or draw with. The marking substance was initially a black lead found in substantial quantities (and of high quality) only in one place in England. Hence, Petroski could write about the roles of supply, international trade, protectionism, substitution, price, and quality. Pencils also require woodworking skill, and the role of carpenters and cabinet makers in their development brings out the influence of trade guilds and the nature of craftsmanship. Developing an alternative to the rare black lead required knowledge of chemistry; maintaining a supply of the best kind of wood required knowledge of botany and forestry. In addition to wooden pencils, we have mechanical pencils; and we have colored pencils as well as black ones. And pencils need to be sharpened, so there is reason to examine the ancillary technologies of knives and pencil sharpeners.

After telling the story of William Munroe, the first pencil maker in America (whose successors included Henry David Thoreau), Petroski showed the human side of the analogy: "This story of initial enthusiasm, early discouragement, repeated frustration, constant distraction, prolonged determination, total isolation, and, finally, a serviceable but far from perfect product has all the ring of an honest recollection of a real engineering endeavor, an odyssey from idea to crude prototype to artifact to improved artifact as full of adventure as Ulysses' travels. And this is a story of research and development that can be repeated, *mutatis mutandis*, with 'lead pencil' erased and 'light bulb,' 'steam engine,' or 'iron bridge' written in its place" (98). Even if the story lacks Sirens, Cyclops, and Circe (to say nothing of Penelope and the suitors), it is far more exciting than one would expect. By the end of the book, in addition to knowing more about pencils than seemed possible, readers understand what engineers do, how they work, what materials science is, the conventions of drafting and technical illustration, and how engineering and technology interact with markets, advertising, world politics, labor conditions, tariffs, and other types of legislation.

Most writers use metaphor in a more limited way—to raise the reader's comfort level, create an image or impression, or help readers understand a specific point. One of Richard Fortey's problems in writing *Trilobite!* was to give the reader an accurate picture of the creatures' appearance. Photographs of fossils show the shape, and drawings enhance them, but fossils and drawings have no color. We do not know what colors trilobites came in, but according to Fortey, the fact that they could see means that colors could be used to attract mates and for camouflage, so that they likely came in a variety of hues. And we know from the fossil record that they came in a variety of bizarre shapes and sizes. Fortey repeatedly used the metaphors of carnival and parade to suggest this array. Rather than leaving it as a superficial metaphor, he used it to show the creative leap required for a researcher to get from fossil to image: "Carnival floats flaunt colourful and extravagant paraphernalia, and it comes as a surprise when the dressing is removed—beneath is a humdrum Ford. We have laid bare the workings of the trilobite: what lies under the chassis is no longer mysterious. We are ready to envisage a parade of trilobites walking past on their paired limbs: and it will be as odd a parade as any carnival could offer. Some smooth as eggs, others spiky as mines; giants and dwarfs; goggling popeyed popinjays; blind grovellers; many flat as pancakes, yet others puffy as profiteroles" (73). When he later explained how he figured out the method of locomotion from the fossil of an eye, we can see this as an example of how a scientist would move from form to function:

> There were lenses gawping, every which way. . . .
>
> Surely this trilobite needed to see all around, but what could it possibly be for? Where in the ocean is it necessary to have an all-encompassing view of the watery world? Perhaps it was my customary view of trilobites as bottom dwellers that prevented me from seeing the obvious. It must, of course, have been a swimmer! A leap of the imagination had the trilobite leaping off the sea-floor. . . . Suddenly there was a different vision of the lives of trilobites: from groveling on the sea-bed, they filled the seas as well. (111)

The parade metaphor thus does more than simply create a picture. It becomes part of the reader's understanding of the way a paleontologist works, moving from fossil to anatomy and anatomy to motion.

Sometimes a writer develops and expands a metaphor already widely in use. In *A Midwife's Tale* (1990), Laurel Thatcher Ulrich reminded readers that "historians sometimes refer to the structure of relations in a community as a 'social web'" (75). She took this vague and malleable image (is it a spider's web? a net of some kind?) and made it visually precise and rich with interpretive value:

> Imagine a breadth of checkered linen of the sort Dolly "warpt & drawd in" on September 12, 1788, half the threads of bleached linen, the other half "coloured Blue." If Dolly alternated bands of dyed and undyed yarn on the warp in a regular pattern, white stripe following blue stripe, then filled in the weft in the same way, alternately spooling both bleached yarn and blue, the resulting pattern would be a checkerboard of three distinct hues. Where white thread crossed white thread, the squares would be uncolored, where blue crossed blue the squares would be a deep indigo, where white crossed blue or blue crossed white the result would be a lighter, mixed tone, the whole forming the familiar pattern of plain woven 'check' even today. Think of the white threads as women's activities, the blue as men's, then imagine the resulting social web. Clearly, some activities in an eighteenth-century town brought men and women together. Others defined their separateness. (75–76)

Ulrich returned to this metaphor several times throughout the book, each time recalling both the image and the historical interpretation.

Most often, though, a metaphor or comparison simply helps get a specific idea across clearly. Thus, John D. Barrow, in *The Origin of the Universe* (1994), suggested that the reader think of space as a balloon or an elastic sheet, explained entropy as what happens in children's bedrooms, and said of one theory that "it's like invoking the tooth fairy." When he tried to explain how time becomes a dimension of space, he pointed out that one reason this idea is so hard to convey is that there are no apparent physical analogies for it (6, 23, 17, 105). In *Words and Rules* (1999), Steven Pinker compared the elements of grammar in a combinatorial system to the chemical elements that compose molecules or the bases in DNA that compose proteins—as well as the books in the library in a story by Jorge Luis Borges (7–8). Richard Fortey described the rules of nomenclature as "a set of 'thou shalts' and 'thou shalt nots' for the naming of animals" (154). Edward O. Wilson, in *The Diversity of Life* (1992), compared the unfolding of evolution to "a succession of dynasties. Organisms possessing common ancestry rise to dominance, expand their geographic ranges and split into multiple species" (94). He used a military metaphor to illustrate extinctions: "Imagine advance infantrymen walking forward in eighteenth-century manner, posting arms in one serried rank into a field of fire. Each man represents a species, belonging to a platoon (genus), which is a unit of a company (family), in turn a unit of a battalion (order), and so on up to the corps (phylum)" (191–92).

Sometimes writers use analogies that researchers themselves use in their descriptions or explanations. In *The Beak of the Finch* (1994), Jonathan Weiner repeated the commonly used comparisons of birds' beaks to pliers and tweezers, not simply as tools but as highly varied tools ideally suited to specific tasks. He also explained the ecological use of the term *guild* as analogous to the historian's use of the term in describing organizations of artisans, a use with which readers are more likely to be familiar. Like other scientific authors, Weiner also used metaphors that rely on the reader's knowledge of literature, comparing the finches "trying to keep their budget in balance" to Dickens's Mr. Micawber (18, 65, 63).

Telling a Story

The discipline of history has a long tradition of accessibility and popularity that is periodically interrupted by attempts to become scientific or objective, to use statistical or psychological methods, or to emphasize theory (whether Marxist, colonialist, postcolonialist, deconstructionist, or something else).[9] Historians who write for general readers remain tied to the narrative tradition, although much of their work is informed by other approaches. Every work of history is an interpretation of the past, and interpretations grow necessarily out of the historian's training, ideology, and theories about the subject. Modern historical narratives do not purport to tell the Truth about the Past; they admit to other possibilities and to gaps in the record. As a result the narrative is less seamless but more nuanced and interesting, and readers get a better sense of the process of researching, interpreting, and writing history.

Telling history as a story poses problems. The most popular subjects—

biographies of famous people and accounts of wars and major political events—are difficult to infuse with suspense: readers already know the ending. Authors must find other ways to hold attention. One way is to offer new, preferably dramatic, insights into well-known characters or events. Fawn Brodie's *Thomas Jefferson: An Intimate History* (1974), along with subsequent biographies emphasizing Jefferson's relationship with Sally Hemings, marked a dramatic departure from political and intellectual biographies. David McCullough's *Mornings on Horseback* (2001) showed Theodore Roosevelt's character developing in response to his ill health in childhood.

Another approach is to provide a more detailed, nuanced view of events made possible by the availability of new sources. The success of this approach may derive from the failure to teach history in an interesting way to high school students. Textbooks and teachers, pressed to fit too many facts and dates into too little time, generally oversimplify and leave little room for alternative accounts and explanations. Popular history, with interested readers and no standardized tests looming, can take the scenic route, with detours as warranted. One example is *Undaunted Courage: Meriwether Lewis, Thomas Jefferson, and the Opening of the American West* (1996). Stephen Ambrose went well beyond the basic story of Lewis and Clark, covering the political motivations behind the expedition and adding the physical detail that brings to life the beauty, daily miseries, and occasional terror of the journey. Ambrose used a great variety of documentary sources, benefiting from the availability of a superb modern edition of the journals of members of the expedition. He had also traveled the route himself. In keeping with current historical interests, he paid more attention than previous accounts had to women and to Native Americans, although—as the subtitle suggests—the book is written from the point of view of white explorers. Lewis's death has been the subject of debate, and while Ambrose was convinced that he was a suicide he provided evidence for the opposing view. Readers know how the story ends, but the drama of individual episodes, descriptions of the environment, and details of daily progress make up for the lack of suspense.

Authors who choose subjects not previously treated face a different challenge. Even if they have an exciting story to tell, they must attract readers with something other than name recognition. Dava Sobel told the story of an unknown English clockmaker who solved a scientific and navigational puzzle: how to determine longitude at sea. She made the story of this obscure character gripping by describing his quest—accurately—as a race for a prize. Fortunately, too, her protagonist was eccentric, and the other characters were at least interesting. Readers thus find no difficulty in attending to the scientific problems and technical details of *Longitude* (1995).

Dramatic events are not the only subjects that capture an audience. Psychological drama can also hold attention. When Jean Strouse wrote *Alice James: A Biography* (1980), she was writing about someone whose life was both unknown and nearly devoid of public event. Alice was the younger sister of William and Henry, both subjects of other biographies. Strouse used the documents of the entire family to bring Alice memorably to life. The book is a biography, but it is also a study of family dynamics—fitting for the story of a woman whose life was shaped almost entirely by the family into which she was born and in which she struggled to find an identity.

The main task of the popular historian is rarely to explain the technically difficult material that the physicist or biologist must make clear. Rather it is finding a subject, or an approach to a subject, that will appeal to a lay audience and then to write like a good storyteller. What differentiates modern popular history from the work of earlier popularizers is the authors' willingness to share their professional secrets: to discuss sources and methods and to admit to disagreements and uncertainty.

Writers in other fields recognize the value of a sustained narrative with settings, characters, and action—if not an actual plot. Gould's *Wonderful Life* is a narrative history of scientific discovery and interpretation, interspersed with the scientific facts and theories that the reader needs to understand it. *The Beak of the Finch* is a narrative of evolution, with science. *Why Buildings Fall Down* is a series of short stories of detection. *Pi in the Sky* is a narrative history of counting.

The Right Place at the Right Time

Some books find a large readership not because of the writing style (though they must be written clearly enough to be understood) or any well thought out rhetorical approach, but simply because they strike a nerve. The *New York Times* obituary of David Riesman described how *The Lonely Crowd* (1950) made "other-directed" and "inner-directed" watchwords of educated Americans:

The intention of "The Lonely Crowd" was primarily to analyze American life rather than to point with anxiety to its deficiencies, but as the sociologist Dennis H. Wrong observed, "it was widely read as deploring the rise of the psychological disposition it called 'other-direction' at the expense of 'inner-direction.'" Professor Wrong said the combination of urgent warning, however misinterpreted, and manifest learning "came across as a trumpet call to some sort of remedial action" and helped to account for the book's phenomenal success.

"The Lonely Crowd" was among the first of the postwar classics written by academics who gained unanticipated fame and fortune because an anxious public believed that their works had uncovered some deteriorating and alarming condition in American society.[10]

Although these authors were undoubtedly pleased by their books' success, neither they nor their first publishers anticipated reaching a wide audience. Riesman's book was published by Yale University Press, and they printed only 3,000 copies. The book was reprinted many times in cloth and was then made accessible to a wider audience in a revised, shorter volume as an Anchor paperback. This popularization sold around 600,000 copies. When Riesman died in 2002, the book in all its U.S. editions had sold nearly one and a half million copies and was still in print.[11] The success of Allan Bloom's *The Closing of the American Mind* (1987) was similarly unexpected: the first printing was only 10,000 copies.

It is not accurate to call these books accidental bestsellers. They succeed because the authors' research is in tune with the concerns of the public and because they are able to explain their work in a way that makes sense to lay readers. We can expect sociologists to be aware of the undercurrents of social anxiety, so their choice of subject is likely to reflect popular concerns. The 1950s were certainly an era when conformity was much on American minds. Riesman provided a way to understand the need to conform but also expressed his own discomfort with the tendency and gave readers reason to be alarmed by a phenomenon that they were likely to see in themselves and others. William H. Whyte's *The Organization Man* (1956) succeeded for much the same reasons: it helped readers to understand something that was very much on their minds but not satisfactorily analyzed. Such books sometimes succeed because they generate controversy. *The Lonely Crowd* was not terribly controversial, but *The Greening of America*, by Charles Reich (1970), sent both academics and policymakers rushing for the op-ed pages, as did *The Bell Curve* (1994) two decades later. In 1960 Daniel Bell started a war of words with *The End of Ideology*, and in 1990 Francis Fukuyama capitalized on Bell's title and generated similar dissent with *The End of History*.

Some nonacademic writers have sought and found such attention deliberately by focusing on urgent issues. The best examples are Rachel Carson's *Silent Spring* (1962) and Ralph Nader's *Unsafe at Any Speed* (1965), which sold at bestseller levels and launched major social movements for environmental preservation and consumer safety. Both inspired controversy, congressional interest, and industrial hostility. *Silent Spring*'s success may be attributed in part to the quality of the writing, but for both books it was the subject matter—and timeliness—that made the difference.[12]

Books on foreign affairs sometimes achieve overnight success, even years after publication, because they are available when conflict flares in a little-known region. In September 2001, Yale University Press had one of the few books written about the Taliban (by Ahmed Rashid), and they rushed it back to press in time to sell several thousand copies in a few weeks. Books about scientific topics that attract congressional hearings, such as cloning, benefit from the publicity. Their success may not have been predictable at the time of publication, but clearly the authors knew that their topics were important and hoped that readers and opinion makers would share their enthusiasm.

A topic of public concern may become the subject of popular books by academics and journalists, of sensational accounts, and of fiction. In the 1990s, the possibility of an outbreak of highly contagious, deadly viral diseases such as Ebola fever motivated several writers to address the issue. *Virus Hunter* (1997), by physician C. J. Peters and Mark Olshaker, is a dramatic but not sensational narrative. *Level 4: Virus Hunters of the CDC* (1996), by Joseph B. McCormick, Susan Fisher-Hoch, and Leslie Alan Horwitz, is similar in tone but more biographical. Physician Frank Ryan's *Virus X* and journalist Robin Marantz Henig's *A Dancing Matrix* (1993) focus more on how viruses develop than on the medical sleuthing aspect of the story. Another journalist, Laurie Garrett, wrote *The Coming Plague* (1994) and *Betrayal of Trust* (2000) to alert readers to the dangers of emerging viruses. Ed Regis, another journalist, disagreed in *Virus Ground Zero* (1996), dismissing fears of viruses as "foaming viral paranoia." The best-selling account of Ebola was Richard Preston's *The Hot Zone* (1994), a sensational, vivid (if occasionally exaggerated) account. Robin Cook, Tom Clancy, and other novelists provided fictional accounts. The Preston, Cook, and Clancy books (and movies) generated not so much an exchange of ideas as widespread interest and anxiety. Possibly, though, the appearance and success of the terrifying Preston book encouraged the authors of its more thoughtful successors to sit down and write, and created an audience for them as well.[13]

Fairness

Books may become controversial because they are opinionated rather than evenhanded. The publisher in search of a bestseller is like the litigant in search of a one-armed lawyer: neither wants a litany of *on the other hand*s. But below the bestseller level, where most successful popularization finds its place, balance and fairness carry the day. Often the material that an author is presenting—the facts, data, and so forth—is not particularly difficult, but the argument being advanced is complex. The author's goal (usually) is to convince the reader that the interpretation being offered is correct and preferable to the alternatives. For intelligent, critical readers, acceptance of an argument requires genuine understanding. Authors must therefore explain their own theories as well as competing ones clearly, help readers keep the different views distinct in their minds, and explain them in a way that makes them comparable. Equally important, they must convince readers that they are playing fair: either they must be almost superhumanly evenhanded or they must be open and good-natured about their biases.

Clarity has always been a necessity; fairness is a more recent requirement. Popularizations published in the 1940s and 1950s often succeeded because they presented new discoveries, new theories, and new ideas with little attention to where they fit into the discipline and without admitting that other scholars disagreed with them. The writers with the highest prestige in the marketplace might not be the scholars with the highest prestige in the academy. This was certainly true of the journalists-turned-authors, like de Kruif and Ceram. But it was also true of academic popularizers such as Margaret Mead and Ruth Benedict. Clifford Geertz argued that one-sidedness was what made Ruth Benedict's work popular among nonexperts in the 1940s and 1950s. "This hedgehog air of hers of being a truth-teller with only one truth to tell, but that one fundamental . . . is what so divides Benedict's professional readers into those who regard her work as magisterial and those who find it monomaniac. It is also what brought her such an enormous popular audience. . . . Benedict found herself a public by sticking determinedly to the point."[14] But what worked fifty years ago is less likely to work now. Today's readers—better educated and more sophisticated about the politics of academe and the nature of research and scholarship—respond more enthusiastically to even-handed treatments. They expect to be given all sides of the story and to be allowed to make up their minds. Also, modern academic authors who introduce controversial material to the public rather than to peers—especially if they do so without putting readers on notice that they are in the minority—often come under attack in professional journals, review media, and competing books. The controversy over cold fusion is the most extreme example.

To help readers understand complex arguments, authors must post directional signs in the form of memorable examples and reminders of how the discussion is moving and where it is going. These authors are essentially drawing illustrated maps, with plenty of arrows, "You Are Here" dots, and pictures of places being visited en route to the destination.

John Kenneth Galbraith was a master cartographer of economic ideas. His 1958 bestseller, *The Affluent Society,* guided the reader through what was then a new argument, using new terms, such as the now-indispensable "conventional wisdom," with such grace that one is unlikely to challenge it unless strongly committed to an opposing ideology and well up on economic theory. Galbraith constructed the book geographically. He began with the conventional wisdom of the center and then moved to the right and left. He noted how the periphery had influenced the center. Throughout the book, when he presented new information or ideas, he placed them clearly within this spectrum. Transitional passages help the reader figure out where the argument had been and was going. For example, at the end of chapter 8, he noted:

> The reader scarcely needs to be reminded of the point at which this essay has arrived. The ancient preoccupations of economic life—with equality, security, and productivity—have now narrowed down to a preoccupation with productivity and production. Production has become the solvent of the tensions once associated with inequality, and it has become the indispensable remedy for the discomforts, anxieties, and privations associated

with economic insecurity. . . . The nature of the present preoccupation with production and the devices by which this preoccupation is sustained are the next order of business. (99–100)

Every step of his argument was similarly placed among the ideas already presented so that the reader could move on confidently to the next stage.

In describing the writing of his fellow anthropologists, Clifford Geertz noted the success of Sir Edward Evan Evans-Pritchard in building upon the assumptions and understandings he shared with readers. Evans-Pritchard's "strategy rests most fundamentally on the existence of a very strictly drawn and very carefully observed narrative contract between writer and reader. The presumptions that connect the author and his audience, presumptions that are social, cultural, and literary at once, are so strong and so pervasive, so deeply institutionalized, that very small signals can carry very big messages." Evans-Pritchard conveyed his self-assurance to his readers through what Geertz describes as his "of course" discourse.[15] Galbraith, writing for a larger, more diverse audience, had to establish the social, cultural, and literary connections that Evans-Pritchard could assume, but his skills were more than adequate to the task.

Galbraith also had a flair for the telling example. In explaining the decline of ostentatious display of wealth as a result of spreading affluence, he mentioned mansions and yachts in passing, but the image that remains with the reader is a striking visual one: "Once a sufficiently impressive display of diamonds could create attention even for the most obese and repellent body, for they signified membership in a highly privileged caste. Now the same diamonds are afforded by a television star or a talented harlot" (79).

Telling examples may come easier to economists than to other academic writers. In *The Zero-Sum Society* (1980), Lester Thurow illustrated the political problems of inducing people to make economic sacrifices voluntarily:

Recently I was asked to address a Harvard alumni reunion on the problem of accelerating economic growth. I suggested that we were all in favor of more investment, but that the heart of the problem was deciding whose income should fall to make room for more investment. Who would they take income away from if they were given the task of raising our investment in plant and equipment from 10 to 15 percent of the GNP? One hand was quickly raised, and the suggestion was made to eliminate welfare payments. Not surprisingly, the person was suggesting that someone else's income be lowered, but I pointed out that welfare constitutes only 1.2 percent of the GNP. Where were they going to get the remaining funds—3.8 percent of GNP? Whose income were they willing to cut after they had eliminated government programs for the poor? Not a hand went up. (10–11)

No one would accuse Galbraith or Thurow of being evenhanded, but they are totally open about their biases. They criticize their opponents tellingly but in a civilized way. And, in fairness to the reader, they make it perfectly clear that many economists disagree with them. (In Galbraith's case, isolation seems to be a point of pride.) Readers who come to these books without preconceptions are likely to be convinced. Readers whose politics and ideologies are at the opposite pole from Galbraith's and Thurow's can read their work with enjoyment, even if they are unlikely to change their minds.

Psychologist Steven Pinker took on a psycholinguistic controversy in *Words and Rules* with admirable fairness to all. "This book tries to illuminate the nature of language and mind by choosing a single phenomenon and examining it from every angle imaginable. That phenomenon is regular and irregular verbs, the bane of every language student" (ix). His approach is clearest in chapter 4, where he pitted two theories of irregular verbs against each other. After laying out the two explanations in detail, with abundant examples, and showing the strengths and weaknesses of each, he concluded, "One phenomenon, two models, both explaining too much to be completely wrong, both too flawed to be completely right." He then described a "hybrid" that he and a colleague had proposed, noting that others had also tried to bring the two theories together. He admitted that "the modified words-and-rules theory may sound like a sappy attempt to get everyone to make nice and play together, but it makes a strong prediction. . . . If the modified words-and-rules theory is correct, it would have a pleasing implication for the centuries-old debate between associationism and rationalism. Both theories are right, but they are right about different parts of the mind" (117–19). Pinker was fair to his opponents, fair to his allies, fair to his own theory, and fair to his readers.

Richard Leakey took a similar tack in *The Origin of Humankind* (1994), written for a series designed to "present cutting-edge ideas in a format that will enable a broad audience to attain scientific literacy." Few subjects are more controversial among anthropologists and interested lay readers than the origins and genealogy of modern humans. But Leakey managed to present both the controversy and his own point of view so openly and fairly that readers feel free to agree with him: their agreement seems like a choice that is informed and voluntary, rather than coerced. For example, he presented a dispute between Owen Lovejoy, on the one hand, and Jack Stern and Randall Susman, on the other, over the extent to which Lucy, an early hominid, walked the way modern humans do. Lovejoy "concluded that the species' bipedal locomotion would have been indistinguishable from the way you and I walk. Not everyone agreed, however." Leakey then discussed the way the two groups interpreted various pieces of physical evidence, making his own sympathies clear. He concluded: "Lovejoy seems to want to make hominids fully human from the beginning. . . . But I see no problem with imagining that an ancestor of ours exhibited apelike behavior and that trees were important in their lives. We are bipedal apes, and it should not be surprising to see that fact reflected in the way our ancestors lived" (35–36). In other words, Lovejoy's interpretation was reasonable, based on the evidence he had; Leakey thought his own interpretation was preferable; the reader can take either side. Equally important, the reader is motivated to read on, to see what other evidence can be brought to bear on the argument that might strengthen either interpretation.

The Quest

Most research is a form of quest. Some researchers are looking for artifacts—if not the Holy Grail or the Ark of the Covenant, then fossil remains of dinosaurs or hominids, documents and manuscripts, or pots and stone tools. Others are looking for the structures of proteins, for plants with pharmaceutical promise, or for invisible particles of matter. Still others are looking for theories that will explain the workings of the economy, international relations, or human behavior. It is not surprising, then, that a very general version of the quest motif is common to many popularizations. We find the quest story at the heart of many books even if we refine our definition, as Clifford Geertz did in discussing the work of Claude Lévi-Strauss: "The departure from familiar, boring, oddly threatening shores; the journey, with adventures, into another, darker world, full of various phantasms

and odd revelations; the culminating mystery, the absolute other, seques-
tered and opaque, confronted deep down in the sertão; the return home to
tell tales, a bit wistfully, a bit wearily, to the uncomprehending who have
stayed unadventurously behind."[16]

Some books include an actual journey. The researchers whose work is
described in *The Beak of the Finch* traveled to a remote island among the
Galapagos where simply getting from boat to shore to camp was an adventure. They lived alone in a hostile environment among species of birds that
are found nowhere else. The success of their research depended on the dramatic changes in climate that lead to rapid evolution, at the cost of the
deaths of large numbers of the birds they study. When they returned to
Princeton, they were both wistful and weary. Though their close colleagues
were not uncomprehending, most others did not quite see the charm of
spending months in a remote, hot, arid, unforgiving place without electric-
ity or running water. Edward O. Wilson began *The Diversity of Life* with an
evening in Brazil, where he was doing fieldwork. He was, however, ambivalent about finding the grail. A thunderstorm was moving in, and he described
the violence, darkness, "noise and stink" that created a strong sense of oth-
erness, of being surrounded by "unsolved mysteries . . . like unnamed
islands." Far from being repelled by this experience, he was inspired: "The
unknown and prodigious are drugs to the scientific imagination, stirring
insatiable hunger with a single taste. In our heart we hope we will never
discover everything. We pray there will always be a world like this one at
whose edge I sat in darkness" (3–7).

Other authors evoke aspects of the quest metaphorically. In *Pi in the Sky*,
Barrow promised, "Our journey will take us first to the most ancient and diverse
anthropological evidences of counting. . . . And in our story we shall meet many
strange characters and unexpected events" (vii–viii). Matthys Levy and Mario
Salvadori described their book as a "voyage of discovery" (14).

Richard Fortey, too, portrayed his trilobite research as a quest, sometimes
real, sometimes metaphorical. He began with a journey that does not sound
terribly dangerous or exotic: to a pub in North Cornwall from which he was
going to explore the Beeny Cliff, even though its slate contains no trilobite
fossils. The path was narrow and slippery but required no special equipment
or clothing; Fortey was not climbing Mount Everest. In some places there are
even stairs. Once at Beeny Cliff, though, Fortey exoticized it by bringing in
Thomas Hardy's fictional account of the same climb in *A Pair of Blue Eyes*. In

this case, fiction is stranger than truth, for unlike Fortey, who retained his footing, Hardy's Stephen Knight slipped and ended up "dangling desperately at the edge of the cliff-face." In Hardy's account, "Opposite Knight's eyes was an imbedded fossil, standing forth in low relief from the rock. It was a creature with eyes. The eyes, dead and turned to stone, were even now regarding him. It was one of the early crustaceans called Trilobites. Separated by millions of years in their lives, Knight and this underling seem to have met in their place of death. It was the single instance within reach of anything that had been alive and had had a body to save, as he himself had now" (14–15). Fortey noted that, aside from the fact that there are no trilobites, Hardy's account of the geology and history of the area was factual. Hardy needed the trilobite's eyes as a symbol; the fossils of the creatures actually embedded in the cliff would not serve. "A scientist would be appalled if one of his colleagues invented such an occurrence, for science trades on the truth—nothing but the objective fact. The truth of the artist can recombine the facts of the world in the service of creation, but the scientist has a different duty, to discover the truth lying behind the façade of appearance. Both processes may be equally imaginative" (18). (As we have seen, when it comes to historical rather than scientific fact, scientists can also play fast and loose.)

Fortey, like Hardy, needed the trilobite: it is the subject of his book. But he also needed Hardy's account, for it established the link that Fortey would use to interest us in the trilobite—the eyes—and admitted us into Fortey's own quest for fossils, understanding, and meaning. Fortey was on that cliff in a symbolic search for trilobites, not a real one, for he knew there were none to be found. He wanted to see the place as Hardy had *imagined* it. For both Fortey and his readers, part of getting to know trilobites is exercising the imagination to understand how others, including novelists as well as scientists, have seen them.

A variation on the quest motif is the race for the prize. In romantic fiction, the prize might be great wealth, the throne, or the hand of the princess. In science it is generally the Nobel. The best-known example of this variant is James D. Watson's account of the race to find the structure of DNA in *The Double Helix* (1968). Watson's book was a bestseller not because it explained the science of the discovery but because it described the very human activities of the discoverers. Indeed, Watson made no effort at all to explain the science. The unfortunate college student depending on this easy read to make it through an hour exam in biochemistry would be in deep trouble.

Watson had something else in mind: "There remains general ignorance about how science is 'done.' That is not to say that all science is done in the manner described here. . . . On the other hand, I do not believe that the way DNA came out constitutes an odd exception to a scientific world complicated by the contradictory pulls of ambition and the sense of fair play" (ix–x). The same tension characterizes sports, and the race is a reasonable metaphor.

Watson wrote a memoir, not a treatise on the philosophy of science. His notion of the workings of science must be deduced from the details of his account of his own work with Francis Crick and others at Cambridge. They were competing with Linus Pauling in California and sometimes competing and sometimes cooperating with Maurice Wilkins and Rosalind Franklin in London. The competitive side of the tension dominated the book until the point where it became clear that the Cambridge team had won, at which point Watson graciously gave at least partial credit to all. Until that point, he was capable of joy at a colossal blunder by Pauling (though concerned that once Pauling discovered it he would redouble his efforts and reach the finish line first) and not above interrogating Pauling's son, then a student at Cambridge, about his father's work. He was also quite nasty about Rosalind Franklin and given to wondering how she would look if she wore lipstick. Once Crick and Watson had disclosed their discovery of the double helix, however, everyone rallied round and acted like good sports. We will never know whether Watson would have been so gracious had Pauling or Franklin won the race.

Along the way, Watson tells us a lot about how scientists work—the importance of reading outside one's narrow field, the reasons biologists must study physics and chemistry, the different approaches various scientists take to the same problem, the value of letting one's mind stray superficially to tennis or movies while a scientific problem simmers underneath, and the necessity of cooperating with other scientists on any problem of consequence. At the same time, he makes it very clear that scientists are human, sharing his rather immature views about women (he was a very young twenty-five at the time of the discovery), the personality conflicts within and between various laboratories, his enjoyment of creature comforts when they were available and his discomfort when they were absent. (He was particularly unhappy with English food, which upset his stomach, and with the lack of central heating.)

Finally, he teaches one memorable lesson about science: that the solutions to important problems are elegant once discovered, though they may be extremely elusive. That quest for the elegant solution is what drove Watson, and being the first to find it was crucial. Throughout the book he refers to the discovery of the structure of DNA not as a solution or an answer but as "the prize."

The Shared Voyage

The authors of the best postwar nonfiction collaborate with the reader. The author is recounting a voyage of discovery and has invited readers on board. But the ship is a good deal more egalitarian than most. True, the author is the captain who has undertaken the journey before, and the readers are the crew and are expected to do some work. But the captain does not merely give orders. In exchange for their labor, readers are made privy to the discoveries the author has made and the way in which the knowledge has been won. Unlike the early writers in this genre, these authors do not simply impart information and expect to be believed. They seek readers' support and understanding by sharing the process of discovery and interpretation. They are doing what Ceram rather generously claimed for de Kruif: "leading the reader by the hand along the same road that the scientists themselves have traversed." But instead of beginning "at the moment truth was first glimpsed," they begin at the moment the question was asked, and they go far more deeply into the knowledge and techniques needed to approach the question. The shift reflects changes in perception of how research is done and of how sophisticated readers have become. As examples, we can look at three books I have mentioned, two from the humanities, by the researchers, and one from the sciences, by a science writer. All won Pulitzer prizes.

IN THE ARCHIVES

A Midwife's Tale: The Life of Martha Ballard, Based on Her Diary, 1785–1812 (1990) is at once a biography, a social history, a documentary history, and an introduction to the way historians think and do research. Laurel Thatcher Ulrich uses Ballard's diary—so sketchy and mundane that other historians had considered it unworthy of publication—to build a picture of Ballard, her town, her household, and her time. Ulrich found the value of the diary "in the very dailiness, the exhaustive, repetitive dailiness" (9).

The book is chronological, and each section begins with several diary passages. Thus, the reader begins where the researcher begins, with the documents. Ulrich describes the diary as a physical object, and the book includes some pages reproduced in facsimile, giving the reader a visual sense of the document. After each set of diary excerpts, Ulrich fills in the blanks, providing readers with the information and thoughts hidden between the lines. Rather than simply tell readers what is meant, she tells us how she knows.

For example, historians often want to know what people read, but this is very difficult information to ferret out. Wills sometimes included the titles of books owned, but few Americans in the Revolutionary era owned books, and few women left wills. Besides, books might be borrowed. Books that were not valuable rarely survived, lost in moves or to floods, fires, or insect predations. The most popular books simply wore out after being passed from hand to hand. Yet Ulrich is able to deduce that Ballard's family was familiar with the popular novels of the day: two of her nieces were named Pamela and Clarissa Harlowe Barton, after the heroines of two of Samuel Richardson's novels (10).

In several places, Ulrich demonstrates how short, apparently straight-forward, records of economic transactions can be used to work out the complex economic relations of the times. In one case, she pieces together several one-sentence entries spaced over three years to show how a visiting cousin paid for his stay with shingles sent to a merchant in Boston, who supplied fabric for a dress made for Ballard by a local seamstress whose child she had delivered (90–91).

In other places, Ulrich untangles family disputes, professional rivalries, and court cases in which Ballard was involved directly or tangentially. In addition to the diary—which in most cases acts purely as a signal that there is a story to be found somewhere—she uses legal documents (wills, deeds, the minutes of town meetings, court records), local histories, the papers of other citizens of the area, and books of the time (religious tracts and medical texts, as well as popular novels). Although she records the details of these sources in the endnotes, she discusses them in the text as she recounts her unraveling of the story, allowing readers to feel that they are participating in the solution of the mystery.

Of course, Ulrich brings more to her work than research skills. Her education and reading provide a background that translates into the context as well as the interpretation of the documents. A midwife is central to the social fabric of her community, interacts with physicians and other mid-wives, is privy to the secrets of other families, and participates in the local and regional economy. To gain an understanding of her life from her diary requires a background in the history of the area's medical and professional community, its economy, theology, and society. Ulrich brings this to the diary, and she imparts it to the reader gradually, as needed to understand the text. For example, when Ballard reports an encounter with a physician during a difficult childbirth, this is an opportunity for Ulrich to describe not only the changing relationship between doctors and midwives but also the economic and medical developments that affected it. When the diary refers to friction between Ballard and her grown children, Ulrich shows us the economic friction as well as the personal disagreements that underlay the angry, unpleasant scenes referred to obliquely in the document.

Ulrich also admits readers into an area central to historical interpreta-tion: gender relations. Being female is central to all of Ballard's activities: delivering babies, raising a family, participating in the domestic economy, and attending church. But the meaning of being female is complex. Although not legally equal to male citizens of the town, Ballard was not restricted to the domestic sphere. She was a social, legal, and economic actor in the larger world. The centrality of her relationship with her husband and family rose and fell with the fortunes of its members and the prosperity of her practice. Ulrich includes accounts from men's papers covering the same events that Ballard witnessed to show the differences in what they deemed noteworthy, but she also imparts her consciousness of how important gender is in read-ing the diary, so that readers can join her in a more nuanced understanding of Revolutionary society and economics.

Because she develops a *collaborative* relationship with the reader, Ulrich makes the experience of reading active and challenging. Not incidentally, every reader will notice how closely Ulrich reads the diary, the attention she focuses on every word. How many would have thought that nieces' names could tell you what family members read? Readers not only under-stand the diary and its writer; they appreciate the process by which it was deciphered and developed as a historical study.

HUMANITY AND THEORY

The relationship between Sally Hemings and Thomas Jefferson has been known, though not universally believed, nearly since it began. First used as anti-Jefferson propaganda, it later became the subject of historical debate and in 1974 reentered popular consciousness as the subject of Fawn Brodie's *Thomas Jefferson: An Intimate History*. In 2008 Annette Gordon-Reed took up the story again, recentering it on the Hemings clan, in *The Hemingses of Monticello: An American Family*. Gordon-Reed brings new life to the Hemings story by expanding outward from the Hemings–Jefferson dyad to the larger families they shared, not only their children but her mother, her siblings, and the family of Jefferson's wife, who was Sally Hemings's half-sister.

Gordon-Reed used sources that other historians had not tapped, and all the tools of social history, to restore full historical citizenship to people whose very humanity was denied during their lifetime and who had been relegated to minor status by earlier historians. She also employed—selectively and skeptically—theories of race and gender, allowing her to move beyond the history of "ordinary people" as groups to the history of individuals, who are never ordinary. Her frank discussion of theory and its limits brings readers directly into the mainstream of current historical thought.

To begin, Gordon-Reed justifies her efforts to understand the family as individuals by taking on historians' warnings against "essentializing," assuming that all people at all times share a common human nature: "Warnings notwithstanding, there are, in fact, some elements of the human condition that have existed forever, transcending time and place. If there were none, and if historians did not try to connect to these elements . . . , historical writing would be simply incomprehensible" (31–32). She applies this insight in imagining the feelings of Jefferson's daughter Patsy and Sally Hemings when they attended balls in Paris:

> Just as these evenings in the beau monde had a deep meaning for Patsy Jefferson that she carried with her throughout her life, and helped to make her the woman she became, they had a deep meaning for Sally Hemings and shaped the woman she became. They were both young females, around one year apart, who probably looked forward to and enjoyed very much dressing up and making themselves look attractive, thinking of how they compared to other females in the room . . . and of what effect they were having on the males. Not one of the feelings, thoughts, and yearnings of a young person was foreclosed to Sally Hemings; not a hair on her head or wish in her heart was less important than Patsy Jefferson's. She had the misfortune to be

born into a society where the people in power chose not to recognize that reality. (263)

Similarly, Gordon-Reed considers and rejects the notion that the cohort
into which Sally Hemings was born—"eighteenth-century enslaved black
women"—defines her: "While the experiences typical to that cohort are
highly relevant as a starting point for looking at Hemings, they can never
be an end in themselves. For Hemings lived in her own skin, and cannot
simply be defined through the enumerated experiences of the group" (290).

The relationship between Sally Hemings—a young enslaved black
woman—and Thomas Jefferson—a middle-aged, powerful white male slave
owner—calls into play a range of theories about race and gender. Gordon-
Reed spells them out and discusses their relevance to her subject. For example, she examines the theory underlying many of the behavioral codes on
campuses and in workplaces, that when power is distributed unequally
between two individuals consensual sex is not possible: "The no-possible-
consent rule . . . suggests that the individual personalities, life stories, and
dignity of enslaved women are meaningless or, in the case of 'dignity' even
nonexistent" (315). "These shorthand formulations, beneficial . . . as easy-
to-apply tools for setting uniform standards on important matters, hinder
historical inquiry. They make it unnecessary to pay attention to details,
discern patterns, and note sometimes even sharp distinctions between given
situations, putting one on a more comforting voyage of reiteration rather
than one of potentially disconcerting discovery" (319).

Gordon-Reed's account also enhances Jefferson's humanity, reconstruct-
ing his feelings toward Sally Hemings as carefully as she analyzes Sally's
feelings toward him. She imagines the complications of a household that
included his and Sally's children alongside his white grandchildren, as well as
the influence Jefferson's other Hemings relatives had on his behavior. "His
extreme forbearance [when one of the Hemingses ran away] gave the family
who ran his household, including his mistress and children, and his favored
artisans, one more reason to have a sense of gratitude toward him while deep-
ening any affection they may have had for him. . . . If it was manipulation, it
was the type of manipulation that all human beings engage in as we try to
keep order in our existence by pleasing the people closest to us and maintaining our own internal sense of ourselves as just and fair actors" (582).

The Hemingses of Monticello ends with Jefferson's death and the disposition of his estate. Because Gordon-Reed has made each member of the fam-

ily fully human, we care about the fate of every one. Sally Hemings and her children were freed, as Jefferson had promised, when he died. Yet this is not a happy ending. The Hemingses,

> whom he had sentimentalized as having the best hearts of any people in the world, had given their lives to him. . . . He had held them as chattel, trying . . . to soften a reality that could never be made soft. While he claimed to know and respect the quality of their hearts, he could never truly see them as human beings separate from him and his own needs, desires, and fears. In the end, all he really knew of their hearts was what they were willing to show him, and they carried enough knowledge in their heads to know his limitations and the perils of giving too much of themselves. . . . The world they shared twisted and perverted practically everything it touched, made entirely human feelings and connections difficult, suspect, and compromised. What could have been in the hearts of any human beings living under the power of that system was inevitably complicated, inevitably tragic. (650–51)

"A PARTNER IN THE PROCESS"

The Beak of the Finch (1994) is an extraordinarily complex narrative. Science writer Jonathan Weiner holds the text together by focusing on the work of Peter and Rosemary Grant, evolutionary biologists who study the Galapagos finches. But he must support the framework with the underlying evolutionary theories and flesh it out with studies on other species. He must also show how the Grants and other scientists work, and how observation, analysis, and theory interact.

Weiner begins and ends his book on Daphne Major, the small island that is the home of several of Darwin's finches and the focus of the Grants' research. He describes the way they live on the island (definitely roughing it) and the processes of data gathering: trapping, banding, weighing, measuring, photographing, and taking blood samples. Later in the book he adds descriptions of the ways the Grants measure the food supply and observe finch behavior. He also describes what they do when they are not in the field: data analysis, further theorizing, comparing notes with students and other researchers, and simply reviewing with each other what they have observed.

The Grants arrive at the island equipped with more than calipers and bands. They bring a deep understanding of evolutionary theory as well as their own more specific questions and ideas. They know a great deal about Darwin's finches from their own work and from reading the reports of researchers between Darwin's time and their own. They know about parallel studies being done on other islands and with other species. As a science writer rather than a researcher, Weiner had to acquire enough of this background and approach to the research to understand what the Grants are doing, appreciate its importance, and ask the right questions. Perhaps most important, he had to have sufficient control over all this material to convey it, in all its complexity, to readers who know little or nothing about evolution or finches. Weiner's solution is to teach readers what they need to know as they need to know it in order to understand what the Grants are learning. What the Grants knew before they began, readers learn as they go along. This experience roughly duplicates the thought processes of the researchers themselves. When they observe a phenomenon in the field or during data analysis, they call to mind the knowledge they already have that bears upon it. Weiner provides the reader with a summary of that knowledge at the same moment. And when an idea sends the Grants to the literature, the reader goes along: "Thoughts like these send Peter back to a paper that two evolutionists, Richard Lewontin and L. C. Birch, published in 1966" (193). Weiner then provides a summary of the paper and explains its relevance to the problem that the Grants are studying.

The book moves continuously between Darwin and the Grants, Daphne Major and Princeton, observation and theory, finches and guppies. Rather than seeming disjointed or leaving the reader confused, the motion itself re-creates at least one intellectual process of coming to grips with the material. The result is a coherent explanation of evolutionary theory and the origin of species. It roughly replicates the thought processes of the researchers and the author, leading readers through a way of understanding rather than simply delivering information.

Weiner's research took him into the scientific literature, which is carefully listed in the bibliography, but it also took him into the Grants' laboratory and into the work and lives of other researchers, and he invites readers to come along. Unlike the traditional "new journalism" narrative, however, this book is not a chronological account of Weiner's travels. Readers learn about research on fruit flies in the laboratory, moths in specimen boxes, guppies in artificial streams, and sticklebacks in artificial ponds when that research is relevant to a problem the Grants are tackling. Mathematical modeling and DNA extraction are brought in when the Grants use them to analyze their data. The history of pigeon breeding is recounted when it is needed to understand selection.

The organization of the book creates a "you are there" quality, enhanced by the inclusion of vivid descriptions of the island and its occupants (as well as the settings of other work), drawings, and reproductions of conversations with the Grants and other researchers. But readers are "there" more than physically: they are there intellectually, listening, seeing, thinking, interpreting, and anticipating. Weiner makes this possible by digesting, explaining, and carefully placing what he has learned into the interpretive geography that underlies his book.

Writing as Teaching

When academics write for one another, they write as researchers, using the language, shorthand, and assumptions of shared knowledge that are appropriate to the technical literature. When they write for nonspecialists, they are writing more as teachers in an ideal classroom: all the students are there of their own volition, they are interested, the class is not broken arbitrarily into 50-minute segments, and there are no exams or departmental requirements. Authors are thus free to choose and shape their topics as they like, and to indulge in the humor, anecdotes, literary allusions, and other devices that they hope will attract and keep readers' attention. It is a very attractive alternative to writing the usual journal article or research monograph.

Yet, as we have seen, it is a tremendously challenging endeavor. A casual reader will simply enjoy the books I have described. In reading them as *writing*, rather than for the ideas and information they impart, one is struck by the difficulty of the task these authors have undertaken. The very best books are absolute marvels of ingenuity and craft, and all reflect months if not years of solid work. To make this labor worthwhile, there has to be an eager audience, ready to buy and read the books.

7

FROM AUTHOR TO READER

Editors and publishers are often described as gatekeepers, and to aspiring authors this metaphor evokes images of the troll under the bridge who will not let you pass unless you know the magic word, or perhaps the bouncer at a trendy club. To an editor, though, the word has a different meaning. Editors do control the quality of what they publish, but they must open the gates wide to let enough good books through to keep their companies afloat and their jobs secure. Editors are always on the lookout for good manuscripts, promising authors, interesting ideas, and public demand.

Presents for Authors

Max Schuster, one of the founders of Simon & Schuster, "rose early every morning and breakfasted alone at the Oak Room of the Plaza, and during these hours he devoted himself to clipping articles from the morning papers with a pair of folding scissors. These clippings usually represented ideas for books, which he would send to one or more of the editors, with cryptic instructions scrawled at the top of the clipping." Other editors and publishers get their inspiration from magazine articles, sometimes writing to the authors to ask whether they had considered writing a book on the topic, or calling the agent of another author with expertise in the same subject. One trade editor explained, "If I want to publish in cutting edge political issues then I better be reading the periodicals that are the places where the definition of cutting edge is made." Sometimes the idea takes many twists and turns between the magazine article and the final manuscript. Knopf editor Harold Strauss, intrigued by an article about radiocarbon dating written by a journalist named Ruth Moore, wrote to her about the possibility of writing "a book that would more systematically attempt to recheck archaeological and anthropological dates as they are found in high school textbooks." The book, *Man, Time, and Fossils*, was nothing like what he had imagined. It included material about carbon dating but developed into an account of human evolution of far greater scope and interest.[1]

Articles from certain magazines are a good source of book ideas because the audiences for the two media are the same. In the nineteenth and early twentieth centuries, in fact, some book publishers, including Scribner's and Harper's, had their own magazines, which cultivated new authors and publicized the houses' books. Although these formal connections are long gone (or in some cases replaced by the less visible multiple holdings of conglomerates), books are still excerpted or even published entirely in magazines before appearing in book form. For example, in addition to presenting distinguished short fiction and nonfiction, the *New Yorker* has published several complete books, including John Hersey's *Hiroshima*, Rachel Carson's *Silent Spring*, and Hannah Arendt's *Eichmann in Jerusalem.*[2] Publishers advertise books in magazines whose readers are likely to be interested in their titles, and they talk with magazine editors about the stories they are planning and about the possibility of placing excerpts from books in the magazines. In 1952, Jason Epstein, then an editor at Doubleday, had given some thought to issuing a trade version of David Riesman's book *The Lonely Crowd*, which had been published initially by Yale University Press. "The idea of preparing a layman's version of *The Lonely Crowd* came up one day at lunch with Lee Schryver of the *Woman's Home Companion* who said that he would like to have someone adapt a part of the book for the *Companion*. It occurred to both of us that if it was a good idea as a *Companion* one shot, it was an even better idea as a trade book."[3] Jacques Cousteau's career as a book author began when Cass Canfield, an editor at Harper & Row, was reading *Life*. "My attention was caught by a stunning photograph of a shark coming at a man equipped with a device he had invented. . . . With the thought that the man in the picture might possibly write an interesting book, I cabled our agent in Paris."[4] An editor at Doubleday invited Witold Rybczynski to write his first trade book after reading his first magazine article, and Robert Coles's first published article, in the *Atlantic Monthly*, led to a grant from the Atlantic Monthly Press to write his first book.[5] Edwin Barber, an editor at W. W. Norton, ran across an essay by a young paleontologist in a magazine: "I never had read *Natural History*, but I got that magazine out, and there was the first piece [Stephen Jay Gould] ever wrote, called 'Size and Shape,' about why things look the way they do. I just fell in love with that piece and wrote him a little letter. Luck favors the prepared mind."[6]

Editors are never completely on leave from their manuscript scouting duties. Ken McCormick, an editor at Doubleday, met the cellist Gregor Piatigorsky at a party in the late 1950s and discovered that he was a wonderful storyteller who had led an interesting life. He convinced the reluctant musician to write his autobiography—a process that took five years and a great deal of work by author and editor alike.[7] All publishers' memoirs contain stories of people met at parties or weddings, on vacation, or living in the same building who eventually became authors. Canfield got the idea for one book in a taxi. The cabdriver "was exhausted, having spent some hours at home trying to keep his large brood of young children amused. And as we chugged along a country road, he told me about his wearing experience and exclaimed, 'I wish someone would write a book describing a thousand ways to amuse a child!'" Canfield paid him $100 for the idea and "in due course, Harper's published *838 Ways to Amuse a Child*," apparently falling 162 amusements short.[8]

The ideas for some books come from the success of other books. These include a lot of copycat books of dubious worth, but some of these ideas result in work of lasting value. Harold Strauss, at Knopf, developed about a dozen books inspired by *Gods, Graves, and Scholars*.[9] Cass Canfield noticed that the Harper series The Rise of Modern Europe had sold extremely well and commissioned Henry Steele Commager to undertake a similar series on U.S. history.[10]

When editors meet people with interesting stories, they do not usually encourage them to write novels. Novels almost always begin in their authors' minds, although an editor or agent may sometimes suggest a general subject, the expansion of a short story, or the development of a character from another book. But editors frequently suggest that someone write nonfiction—an autobiography, a book about the work they have been doing professionally or avocationally, or a book about a subject related to their expertise but not growing directly out of their research. Canfield described this role best:

The publisher needs an acquisitive instinct, although he should not let this appear on the surface. If he has an idea he believes in, or if he thinks someone can produce a first-rate book, he should continue to press for it, just short of making himself a nuisance. . . . He should take an interest in almost any subject and be content to remain anonymous, letting the author take center stage, being the creative person. The publisher, in his capacity as editor, must be the catalyst and draw people out as does an effective reporter. He should also be an attentive listener and, if he has a valid idea for a book, should make a present of it to the author, laying no claim to it himself.[11]

Although an author's first trade book may be written at the suggestion of an author or agent, authors who succeed in the genre seem to be bitten by the bug and keep writing for their newfound audiences. But even when good manuscripts arrive on an editor's desk without any previous discussion with the author, the editor still has work to do. Books cannot go from author to reader without help from editors, designers, and marketers.

From Catalyst to Gatekeeper

Ideas are the beginning of books, but you cannot copyright ideas or sell them in bookstores. The ideas must take form as words painstakingly worked into sentences, paragraphs, and chapters. Although authors do the writing, they are often guided—and goaded—by editors. Editors do not only acquire books; they also develop them, evaluate them, and suggest revisions, often with the help of experts. Some manuscripts never become publishable, despite the author's best efforts and the editor's hard work. One of Jason Epstein's Random House files contains eleven single-spaced pages of comments on a manuscript by an English historian for which he had purchased U.S. rights. The author either could not revise to meet Epstein's standards or preferred not to. Random House eventually canceled the contract.[12] An editor at John Wiley explained: "One of the mistakes you can make is thinking you have something when you are not going to be able to depend on it because the writer has got to be able to deliver it. You can tell them all you want, 'Do it this way. Do it that way.' You can come up with all the ideas you want. You can come up with all the concepts, book plans, a description. You can talk about what you want it to be all day, but in the end the author has to be capable of producing it, and a lot of times they really are not. And there are a lot of books that are bought on the basis of concepts that the author is not capable of producing and the manuscript bears that out."[13]

Some editorial work is done outside the publishing house, by the author's agent. As publishing houses have become larger, the agent's role has expanded. Editors are far less likely than they were fifty years ago to read unsolicited manuscripts, and they have less time to spend helping authors to improve their books. Agents have taken on both aspects of the gatekeeper's role, winnowing the heap of manuscripts to find the few that have potential and working with promising authors to get their manuscripts into publishable condition. Although their loyalty is to the author, they also serve publishers by acting as a preliminary filter and as developmental editors. The agent's role has also expanded because publishers are now willing to pay more for books. Agents receive a percentage of the author's royalties and other income (15 percent is the norm). They earn their living by representing authors who can demand respectable advances, and by convincing publishers that their clients are worth a large investment. As popularizations have become more profitable, their authors are more likely to be represented by literary agents. One agent, John Brockman, specializes in popular science books and has represented many of the best-known authors.[14]

Editors of fiction often rely on their own tastes and those of a few trusted colleagues and literary agents. Editors of nonfiction rarely rely on taste alone. They must either have some expertise in the subject or call on people who do, whether their other authors or independent reviewers. The most elaborate evaluation procedure is the peer review system employed by university presses and other scholarly publishers. These presses send promising proposals and completed manuscripts to two or more experts in the field for confidential, anonymous evaluations. Peer reviewers are asked about the quality and originality of the research, the clarity of the writing, and the importance of the subject. The audience for scholarly books is other scholars, and the prepublication peer reviews anticipate the responses of academic book reviewers and readers. If the evaluations are positive, the manuscript is passed along to a committee of scholars at the press's home institution. Sometimes manuscripts with conflicting evaluations are sent on to the committee as well, especially if the topic is controversial and the controversy will generate interest. Only when that committee approves the manuscript is a final contract issued.

Trade publishers do not generally go to the same lengths, but they usually ask the opinion of at least one expert to ensure that the book is accurate and up to date. They are more likely than scholarly publishers to be concerned about the author's ability to communicate with nonexpert readers, and they are likely to devote the time of a developmental editor to working on this problem. A reader for Doubleday sent extensive comments on one book: "There is far too much material here. Its sheer bulk is overwhelming. I should recommend cutting at least half. . . . The organization of the chapters and sections tends to be conceptual and academic, too often based on abstract categories rather than on live problems. . . . The introductory notes . . . fail to put in human terms the practical problems."[15] Editors of trade books, with a lay audience in mind, want to be sure that their authors have provided enough background and context to make the book understandable. They encourage their authors to use the simplest possible language and explain unavoidable technical terms. They look for ways to organize material more logically. And, of course, they encourage their authors to use the rhetorical approaches that help books succeed with the audience they are seeking.

Editors' files are full of handwritten notes and single-spaced typed comments to authors that run on for several pages. Harold Strauss's letters to his authors at Knopf were full of advice: "The approach to the scientific material [must] be humanized by an attempt to get at what made the particular scientist click"; "Nothing should be done which damages the scholarship and the authority of an important book; but within that limitation, everything should be done which will make that book more accessible to the intelligent general reader"; "I know that you will not hide behind professional jargon, since there is always a way to put the weightiest scientific material in the common language"; "Possibly the single most important step . . . is to insert at the beginning of each chapter and at the beginning of some of the more important sections, a clear statement of what you are setting out to prove in the chapter or section."[16] One of his authors described another Knopf editor going "through the manuscript once like an ice storm, breaking off rotten limbs with loud crashes."[17] Editors suggest, or insist on, changes ranging from shortening a text considerably (or adding a chapter when necessary) to grammatical changes. An entire letter to Carl Sagan from Anne Freedgood, an editor at Random House, was dedicated to a discussion of a single comma.[18]

The Paratext

Book historians use the term *paratext* to denote the material in a book that precedes, accompanies, and follows the text: front matter such as the title page, copyright page, and table of contents; accompaniments to the text such as headings, illustrations, and marginal glosses; and back matter such as notes, bibliography, appendixes, and indexes.[19] The paratext of fiction is usually minimal—sometimes no more than a title page, copyright page, and page numbers. Especially if chapters have no titles (or the book is not divided into chapters), there is little reason to have a table of contents. Fiction rarely has notes, and when it does—as in Sterne's *Tristram Shandy*, Swift's *Tale of a Tub*, or Nabokov's *Pale Fire*—the notes are themselves generally fictional.[20] And although fiction readers might find an index useful, there is no tradition of providing this feature for novels. (Critical editions of fiction, of course, include extensive paratexts of many varieties.) Nonfiction, however, may be significantly enhanced by paratext that introduces and amplifies the text and makes it more accessible. Author, editor, and designer share decisions about how much of this material a book will contain and how it will be presented.

Some material in the front of the book, such as the opening half-title, represents longstanding publishing conventions. Beyond the standard elements, a publisher may add material that helps sell this book and others, such as a list of the author's other works. Some mass-market paperback editions now begin with several pages of excerpts from reviews. Other front matter, such as the table of contents and lists of maps, tables, and illustrations, is designed to help the reader navigate the book.

The back of a nonfiction book may provide extensive information and tools that make the text more accessible. If notes are not placed at the bottom of the page, they usually appear at the end of the book. The bibliography provides a list of sources for readers to consult and sometimes amplifies the information in the notes. (Occasionally novelists provide bibliographies.)[21] The index provides access to the text in a different way than the table of contents and headings do. A glossary (which may appear in front of the text instead of at the back) defines terms used in the book.

Appendixes can solve a number of structural or narrative problems. They can provide more depth or detail than most readers will want or provide information that would interrupt the story. In some cases, such as Stephen Jay Gould's *Wonderful Life*, material that could have appeared in appendixes was placed within the text, but set off typographically to minimize the interruption. Appendixes may provide facsimiles or transcriptions of literary or historical texts discussed in the book, additional data, genealogical tables, chronologies, or other information that assists the reader's understanding. Sometimes they are used to add material that editors fear would deter readers, such as equations and formulas. For example, in *Why Buildings Fall Down*, the authors provide appendixes, replete with diagrams, on load, stress and strain, structural materials, and structural systems. They note at the beginning that "the reader even rudimentarily familiar with the basic principles of structural theory may want to skip this section of the book" (267–314). Stephen Hawking provides a glossary for *A Brief History of Time*, but he also offers readers brief biographical sketches of Einstein, Galileo, and Newton that somehow did not find a place in the text. And Henry Petroski uses an appendix to *The Book on the Bookshelf* to suggest twenty-one different systems for arranging one's library, with additional notes on what to do with dust jackets, how two people can merge their libraries without destroying their relationship, and other book-related problems (233–52). Within the book, running heads and page numbers help the reader take advantage of the table of contents and the index, while part titles, chapter titles, and section headings highlight the book's structure and organization. What readers are most likely to notice, though, are larger additions to the text—illustrations, tables, and graphs.

Illustrations are the subject of much discussion between author and editor. Harold Strauss worried about too many pictures of skulls and jaws, while Bruce Catton and his editor exchanged half a dozen letters about the maps in *Mr. Lincoln's Army*. Catton argued for maps with a lot of text—"something that would give the reader an idea of what happened where, so that he wouldn't have to keep going back to the map while he reads the account of the fighting and make little check marks with his pencil to keep himself straight." The editor accepted some of the suggestions but did pare the annotations a bit.[22]

Editors usually discourage authors from including equations, tables, and graphs in trade books on the theory that most readers are phobic about mathematics. When such material is vital, though, editors and designers take great pains to make it attractive and accessible. For example, Simon Singh illustrated Fermat's enigma with two diagrams. The first, which is two-dimensional, shows how two squares can be added together to create a third square by picturing a square of 9 (3^2) gray tiles and 16 (4^2) white tiles being combined to form a square of 25 (5^2) tiles. The second, which is three-dimensional, shows a cube of 216 (6^3) gray blocks, a cube of 512 (8^3) white blocks, and a larger cube of both colors comprising 728 blocks—9^3-1. The minus 1 is the symptom of the problem (29–31).

Illustrations—maps, photographs, and drawings—are thought to encourage general readers, and readers do comment favorably on these additions or complain about their absence. Every nonfiction book, regardless of audience, will include illustrations that are vital to the reader's understanding. (Adult fiction is rarely illustrated, except for maps and house plans in mysteries and, occasionally, decorative pen-and-ink sketches.) Trade books, however, are more likely than scholarly books to include optional illustrations—pictures that make an argument or example clearer or are simply decorative. Thus, a trade book will include more photographs or drawings of people mentioned in the book, places where events occurred, and equipment, experimental subjects, and the like. Jonathan Weiner provides many technical drawings in *The Beak of the Finch* that help the reader understand how different beaks allow birds to eat different seeds, but he also includes historical drawings that are not strictly necessary for understanding as well as drawings by the researchers' daughter, Thalia Grant, that give a clearer picture of the islands and add a human dimension but that probably would not have been included in a book for evolutionary scientists.

One area in which editors frequently intervene is footnotes—a matter that seems at first glance to be mechanical and simple but in fact provokes extensive debate between editor and author, and among reviewers. This debate sheds a surprising amount of light on what publishers and reviewers think about popularization and about its readers. For some, footnotes are the touchstone—the element that tells you whether you are reading serious scholarship or something less rigorous. According to Kevin Jackson, "they are the invention, the speciality, the particular art form, the home or homeland, the badge of office, the *forte*, the signifier, the *sine qua non* and maybe even the *ne plus ultra* or, who knows, the *e pluribus unum* of scholars and scholarship."[23]

Footnotes (or endnotes, if they appear at the end of the book rather than at the foot of the page) tell the reader the sources on which the author has based the findings in the text. All scholarship is based on the work of others, and notes both credit that work and tell readers where to go to learn more. But the form those notes take really should not matter. The substance is what is important: the fact that the author has both consulted and credited the relevant sources and can document the assertions and observations made in the book. Nevertheless, the form of the documentation has its own mystique. Some publishers believe that readers who are not scholars will be frightened away by superscripts and footnotes; some reviewers believe that, unless there are superscripts and footnotes—which provide, in the words of one reviewer, "scholarly caste"—the work cannot be taken seriously.[24] Both are wrong.

Footnotes do not scare readers. Many of the books I have described, including some of the bestsellers, have footnotes or endnotes indicated by superscripts. *A Midwife's Tale* has between twenty-five and eighty endnotes for most chapters, and many of the notes are detailed and lengthy. Steven Pinker's endnotes in *Words and Rules* are brief but just as numerous. Some of Elaine Pagels's chapters include more than a hundred endnotes. And in *Undaunted Courage*, a major bestseller, Stephen Ambrose employed a dual system of footnotes signaled by asterisks and daggers and endnotes keyed to superscript numbers. No one appears to have been frightened by these. Indeed, why would they be? Most readers of popularizations are college graduates and have survived reading many books chock full of footnotes and endnotes. One reader—a pipefitter who had attended college but had not graduated—commented, "I do *not* like footnotes in the back of the book. Put them on the same page. I'm going to read them anyway."[25] Many people probably do not read most of the notes, but they have learned not to be distracted by the presence of superscripts (which are, after all, pretty tiny).

Nevertheless, authors and editors worry about notes. Bruce Catton described his travails over the footnotes in *Glory Road* in a series of letters to his editor. In one he wrote, "If I had had any idea that these damn footnotes were going to be this extensive, or that the job of making them up would be half as arduous as it proved to be, I would have gone out and hanged myself decently long ago." (By "making them up" he meant pulling them into order, not fabricating them.) The next day he explained why he had gone to all this trouble:

> In "Mr. Lincoln's Army," as you doubtless remember, the foot-notes were pretty sketchy. I had the notion that since I was not pretending to be a genuine historian I could just hit the high spots, give people a general idea where I got my material, and let it go at that. But evidently that was not a good system. If you recall Commager's review, lush and fruitful though it was, he felt impelled to take a paragraph down near the end to say in effect that the system of references, footnotes and so on was beneath contempt, and the professional historians whom I know in the flesh seem to have the same idea: they smile rather pity-ingly when the subject comes up. Also, I got quite a few letters from readers wanting to know on just what page of that book I based certain statements.
>
> So, as I got into this one, I figure we'd better give the custom-ers more substantial footnotes. I was genuinely appalled, how-ever, when I came to put them together, to see how extensive they became. . . . And now you are getting a rather horrifying bale of material which neither of us had originally counted on. I don't quite see anything else to do about it, and I hope this may lead a few of our historian-critics to deal more gently with us, but I am free to admit that you are getting a lot more in the way of footnotes than you had any reason to expect. I feel a profound sympathy for your copy editor.[26]

Despite the increasing use of alternative documentation systems, some reviewers still think that only traditional notes can provide the assurance they and other readers need. Reviewers criticized Peter Gay for using end-notes without superscripts in his biography of Sigmund Freud. One wrote that "the scholarly apparatus in this book, to which succeeding students of Freud and the history of psychoanalysis should have recourse, is seriously defective." A review of Henry Petroski's *Invention by Design*, which provides brief bibliographical essays, criticized the author for not providing "a better critical apparatus." At the same time, however, both reviewers praised the quality of the books.[27]

And we have all learned time and again that the presence of copious notes is no guarantee of meticulous scholarship. (Why anyone should think it would be is a bit of a mystery. If you can fabricate text, you can fabricate notes.) In a much-publicized case, a historian at Emory University, Michael Bellesiles, was the subject of extensive debate for the claims he made about the history of American attitudes toward guns in *Arming America: The Origins of a National Gun Culture*. The book was published by Knopf in 2000 and won the Bancroft prize. It contains more than a hundred pages of footnotes, amounting to about 20 percent of the book. Yet Bellesiles was accused of misusing and misrepresenting sources and even fabricating some of them. The *William and Mary Quarterly*, a prestigious journal of American history, commissioned a forum on the subject, with four articles evaluating the claims against Bellesiles along with his response. Emory University formed a special panel to review his work, Bellesiles resigned from his post, the Bancroft prize was rescinded, and Knopf announced that they had halted sales of the book and would pulp any unsold copies returned by retailers.[28] Superscripts do not guarantee the quality of scholarship, and their absence does not mean that the author has not done superb research. It is time to put the footnote mystique to rest.[29]

Although the editor may have had extraordinary influence on the content, organization, style, and mechanics of a book, the editor's work is invisible. A reader cannot tell whether the author got it right the first time or went through multiple drafts commented on by a series of reviewers and editors. Even the correspondence in the publisher's files tells only part of the story. The manuscripts themselves, when available, are heavily marked, cut, pasted, and revised. Elaine Pagels, whose books read as though they flowed effortlessly from her keyboard, gives her editor, Jason Epstein, credit for the quality of her writing: "Jason is quite brilliant at seeing how the intellectual argument fits in with the story. We have worked over every chapter maybe 10 to 15 times."[30] In 1955, Arthur A. Knopf decided to copyedit Samuel Flagg Bemis's biography of John Quincy Adams himself, rather than assigning it to a copy editor. As he worked, he wrote to historian Lyman Butterfield: "If I ever undertake copyediting of a manuscript like this again, I truly hope the good Lord will strike me dead. It's a dreadful job and it is hard for me to understand how Sam could have written the books he has written and achieve the place he has achieved in the world of historical scholarship without learning to write moderately competent English. . . . I'll be curious to see his reactions to my suggestions, which are radical, but

I am inclined to put up rather a fight." Bemis adopted Knopf's suggestions without a whimper, and the book won a Pulitzer prize.[31]

Editors' interventions have a single goal: to reduce the distance between author and reader. Editors of books written by scholars for other scholars have an easier job, because the distance is not great to begin with. But trade book editors, especially when they are working on an author's first book for general readers, may have to do a lot of coaching, urging, prodding, and reminding. Fortunately, most of these editors share the educational level and interests of the prospective readers, so it is easy to put themselves into the reader's place and work with the author. As more Americans attended college, the "educated general reader" began to look more like the educated general book publisher. As a Doubleday marketer explained, "The kind of books I work on are the books that appeal to me, basically. And that's the easiest way for me to approach marketing a book: how is it going to get through to me? What media am I drawn to? What do I watch? What do I read? What kinds of things am I interested in?" An editor at John Wiley argued that "there's got to be some correlation in what kind of reading experience you find enjoyable as an editor and the kind of reading experience the readers of your books will have."[32]

A Book by Its Cover

A book designer's work is parallel to that of the book editor: just as the editor seeks to remove barriers of language that obstruct communication between author and reader, the designer seeks to remove visual barriers by creating a readable page. Book designer Hugh Williamson summarizes the designer's goals as serving four purposes of the book: "A book is to be sold"; "a book is to be laid open, held, and carried"; "a book is to be seen"; and "a book is to be kept."[33] This means that the designer must consider practical questions such as size and cost, mechanical solutions that allow the book to function as an object, material selections that ensure the volume's longevity, aesthetic questions that make the book an attractive and valued object, and marketing concerns that make the book stand out from others and attract buyers. The designer addresses marketing issues primarily in the design of the dust jacket or paperback cover, but the design of the interior must serve all four purposes. One marketing executive summarized the importance of design for trade nonfiction: "For 90 percent of the books that we do, this is the marketing plan: the physical object and what it says and what it looks like and what it communicates."[34]

The very existence of a dust jacket or a paperback edition distinguishes trade books from those scholarly monographs meant for a library and specialist market. Because research libraries typically discard dust jackets, the publishers of scholarly monographs may simply omit them. And publishers will not risk a paperback edition unless they expect either trade or textbook sales. University presses often use variations on generic internal designs as well, with all basic design decisions programmed into a computer. The designer can vary typefaces and make other changes, but no full-scale design effort is required. These savings on design decisions are appropriate for scholarly books, because readers usually find them through reviews and buy them from catalogs or online. They are rarely found in bookstores and therefore do not need to attract the reader's eye. The internal design matters, because the book must be readable and usable, but it must also meet the economic limits set by the small audience and consequent small print run. The careful choice of typeface, type size, page size, and other design elements can measurably reduce the length and therefore the cost of a scholarly book.

Trade books are designed individually, with dust jackets chosen to attract the reader's eye in the bookstore. It is not unusual for the publisher to solicit designs from several artists, or to have a single artist submit several alternatives. Jacket design reflects the publisher's view of the audience. Readers of mass-market genre fiction are apparently drawn to bright-colored foils, die-cut patterns, embossing, and other flashy gimmicks. The names of best-selling authors appear in extremely large type; check out the Stephen King and Danielle Steel selections in your bookstore. Some genre fiction declares its identity with its paperback covers. Not only are the covers of certain lines of romance novels all similar in layout, ornaments, and typography, providing brand identity, but the amount of cleavage the heroine displays and the definition of the hero's muscles tell readers exactly what they are getting. Serious nonfiction, like serious literature, conveys its identity equally clearly, but with more subtlety.

Paperback covers on serious nonfiction may be varnished with a matte finish rather than a high gloss. Art is often *fine* art: reproductions of paintings or photographs of friezes or sculpture. Elaine Pagels's *The Gnostic*

Gospels has a very simple cover: the author's name is given in capital letters at the top; the rest of the cover reproduces a Holbein engraving of the Crucifixion in beige, as a background; and the title is printed over it in dark green; a blurb from a *New Yorker* review appears in the same green, in much smaller type at the bottom; and all the type is centered, line by line. The cover conveys very clearly that this is a serious book, on a serious topic, that has been given the imprimatur of a serious magazine.

When the topic of the book requires a great deal of explanation beyond the title, a purely typographic cover may be used, or the type may dominate the artwork or photography that accompanies it. The paperback cover of Laurel Thatcher Ulrich's *A Midwife's Tale* is printed in three colors on a white background, and the design is purely typographic. The white background is the paper on which part of the diary is reproduced in facsimile, in beige. The title appears at the top, in dark blue ink within a beige box bordered in blue and dark red. The subtitle, "The Life of Martha Ballard, Based on Her Diary, 1785–1812," appears in the center, in dark blue ink, in a hand imitating handwriting of the period. The author's name appears in a beige band at the bottom, in dark red ink, in the same typeface as the title. In addition, "Winner of the Pulitzer Prize" appears in red below the title box, and a blurb from the *New York Times Book Review* appears at the bottom, in blue. All the type is centered. The designer has managed to put a large number of words on display, some as decoration but most for content.

The dust jacket of John Allen Paulos's *Once Upon a Number* uses numbers instead of type as a decorative element. The jacket is occupied mostly by a red box, but a black band wraps around it, extending beyond the white border. Over the band and about half an inch of the red box above and below are rows of numbers printed in gray. The author's name appears in white on the top part of the red box, and the subtitle (*The Hidden Mathematical Logic of Stories*) is similarly printed in the bottom part. The title itself also appears in white, in the middle of the black band. Two lines identifying Paulos as "Bestselling Author of *Innumeracy* and *A Mathematician Reads the Newspaper*" appear below his name. All the type is centered.

Some paperback covers impart an astonishing amount of information. Even though more than a third of the cover of Stephen Ambrose's *Undaunted Courage* is devoted to a reproduction of Edgar Paxson's painting *Lewis and Clark at Three Forks*, the designer still found room for the longish subtitle (*Meriwether Lewis, Thomas Jefferson, and the Opening of the American West*), the author's name and his identification as the "author of *D-Day*," a fairly lengthy blurb from the *Chicago Tribune*, and a line pointing out that the book is a *New York Times* bestseller.

All of these covers contrast with the covers and jackets of novels, which rarely have subtitles beyond "a novel" or "a romance" and therefore leave room for more artwork. But they share with literary novels certain assumptions about the kind of design that appeals to the expected audience: it is subtle, sophisticated, elegant, and understated. It is meant to catch the reader's eye with a seductive whisper, not a crass shout. No metallic foil, no Day-Glo colors, no starbursts—although a Pulitzer gold seal is always permitted. Most of all, the covers must convey the nature and content of the book *accurately*. A book that treats difficult material in depth needs a serious cover. Even the covers of John Allen Paulos's books, which use a great deal of humor and are relatively lighthearted, convey the seriousness of their purpose. Reflecting the content accurately serves Williamson's first and fourth reminders: a book is to be sold *and* kept. As one editor points out:

> The first object is to make someone pick up the book, but it's useless if someone picks up the book unless they're willing to put down $22.95 at the cash register for it. As a marketer, my ultimate object is to have all of our package, including the typeface inside, and how it's used and how the book is designed, communicate to the right person, to the person who is going to buy it. It's like an ad; it's about communicating properly with people who want this book, who want what's inside of it. . . . If the packaging makes me buy the book, and then I read it, and I thought it was a serious book that was going to tell me what is going on in the Supreme Court, but it's a joke book inside, what have we accomplished?[35]

Similarly, if the book looks frivolous, readers looking for a serious treatment of the subject will not pick it up in the first place.

Readers are far less likely to notice internal design, but it contributes to readability, usability, attractiveness, cost, and value. Book designers must decide how large the pages will be, how much of the page the text will occupy, the color and texture of the paper, the typeface and type sizes to be used for all typographical elements, and the design of chapter openings, notes, and front and back matter. Trade books sometimes use slightly larger type than scholarly books and still more often are set with extra leading, or white space, between the lines, which gives the page a more open feeling. Designers can be generous with white space only when the book is short enough that visual economy is not needed to make the book a manageable and affordable size, so editorial intervention works toward this end as well.

Book design, though rarely noticed consciously by readers, is a complex practical art. Hugh Williamson touches on the complexity in his explication of the importance of a book's being seen:

> If it fails to attract more than a glance, it may not be read at all. Then it must be capable of being read with ease, speed, and accuracy, by the reader for whom and in the conditions for which it is intended. This can be achieved only by the precise adjustment to each other of all the variables of the text page, and is a matter of paper and presswork as well as of the arrangement of printing images. Illustrations no less than composition need to be planned by the designer. The well-made book presents an appearance of pattern and purpose: all its parts are planned to suit each other. The designer must concern himself with the intellectual as with the optical process of reading, arranging the text and illustrations with their headings, captions, notes, reference systems, and other accessories in a clear and convenient manner.[36]

A book like Simon Schama's *Dead Certainties*, short and devoid of typographical complexities such as subheadings and footnotes, is nevertheless notable for its design: it is small and of unusual dimensions, suggesting visually the unusual nature of the text itself. (For all its simplicity, the book nevertheless required the designer to incorporate a foldout color plate.) Gould's *Wonderful Life*, full of practical challenges for the designer, demonstrates the creativity and knowledge required to accommodate drawings, tables, subheadings, captions, discursive footnotes, and textual material outside the body of the text. By using a simple design element—a thin line, or rule—the designer provided unity and prevented the book from disintegrating into visual miscellany.

To Market

Author, editor, and designer must all consider a book's audience, but the publisher's marketing staff is responsible for informing that audience of a book's existence and convincing them of its desirability. Books are marketed directly to consumers through advertising, but the most important marketing is done through intermediaries, including reviewers, booksellers, and readers themselves as they recommend books to friends and colleagues.

Marketing begins with the book's title. Trade titles are generally direct and informative: they tell the reader exactly what the book is about and what makes it different from other books on the subject. You can't get much more direct than *A Brief History of Time.* While scholarly books use current academic jargon, trade books avoid it. Compare the titles of two books that Deborah Tannen wrote about communication between men and women: *Gender and Discourse* (Oxford University Press) and *You Just Don't Understand* (William Morrow and Ballantine).When trade books have subtitles, they are generally explanatory: *Innumeracy: Mathematical Illiteracy and Its Consequences* or *The Zero Sum Society: Distribution and the Possibilities for Economic Change.* Both titles are newly coined or unfamiliar words that attract attention, and the subtitles explain what they are about. The subtitles of academic books are more likely to narrow the scope of a broader-sounding title: *Creating American Civilization: A Genealogy of American Literature as an Academic Discipline.* Scholar Wendy Doniger has described some of the more extreme versions of this phenomenon as the "post-colonic letdown."[37]

As in any marketing effort, advertising is important. Popularizations are advertised and publicized in the media that their likely audience reads and listens to. The magazines that are a resource for book editors are the same ones that marketers seek out for advertisements, reviews, excerpts, interviews, and feature articles. Major book review media—the *New York Times Book Review, Washington Post Book World,* and the *New York Review of Books*—are appropriate for books in most subjects, as are upscale general interest magazines like *Harper's* and the *New Yorker.* Such magazines are often sent prepublication proof in hopes of early reviews. Beyond those magazines, though, the subject of the book provides direction. *Scientific American* is a good vehicle for advertising books in the natural sciences, but

Foreign Affairs makes more sense for political science. *Smithsonian* covers both science and history.

The advertising copy, based on descriptions of the book written by author and editor, is written by the marketing staff and reviewed by the author and editor. It may be the subject of extensive debate. The advertisements must appeal to a wide range of intelligent readers, including those who are already familiar with the topic. Ads, catalog copy, and jacket copy for popularizations frequently emphasize the novelty of the material ("the first complete study of . . . ," "the birth of a new science," "dramatic story of groundbreaking scientific research"), the qualifications of the author ("one of the nation's leading economists," "one of the world's leading cognitive scientists"), and the readability of the text ("radical yet accessible," "brilliantly entertaining"). The language tends to be understated, a soft rather than a hard sell. Angus Cameron, an editor at Knopf, was unhappy with the initial version of copy advertising *Science in the Cause of Man* that was to appear in *Scientific American* (author Gerard Piel was the magazine's publisher): "The tone in this copy, in the headline, and in the theme . . . will seem not too fresh to the level of readers of this particular magazine. . . . They are apt to know every name associated with the quotes, and, in my opinion, likely to heed such opinion more than they would the approach in the head and subhead. . . . To resort to life and death headlines with this audience is the height of futileville. It will only put the audience off a book whose content would actually interest them. My own feeling is that the copywriter has to find a way to move this particular audience into action without taking a hortatory tone for which the audience would have nothing but contempt."[38] In other words, the advertising must be written at the same level as the book. If it is too elementary, the audience will be put off. Yet, if it makes the book sound academic and dull, it won't serve the book well either. On a smaller scale, the copywriter must perform the same balancing act as the author.

Many publishers believe that, for serious books, reviews are more important than advertisements. Favorable reviews written by well-known and respected scholars provide reasonably independent endorsements that readers trust more than an advertisement. Excerpts from reviews can be used to promote the book in advertisements and on the cover of the paperback edition. Publishers send prepublication copies (sometimes specially bound sets of page proof) to people likely to endorse the book, as well as to influential booksellers and to magazines that print prepublication reviews (such as

Publishers Weekly, Library Journal, Booklist, and *Kirkus Reviews*) to garner blurbs for the hardcover's dust jacket. A favorable reaction to such a prepublication campaign may lead to a larger first printing; a negative reaction is likely to reduce the marketing budget and the publisher's hopes.

The content and source of these blurbs are critical: some potential readers respond to recommendations from scholars, while others value the opinions of public figures. Marketers try to get a variety of endorsements, so that a book by an academic is recommended not only by other academics but also by public figures, journalists, and other writers. One publisher describes an imaginary reader picking up a book about the U.S. Supreme Court: "Say there are two books on the Supreme Court next to each other. I'm a book buyer who is really interested in the Supreme Court. I would go and pick up *Turning Right* and look through it—sounds interesting, looks interesting, who wrote it? Do I believe what they have to say? OK, court reporter for *The Los Angeles Times.* Well, what do other people have to say; who wrote the blurbs on the back cover? And do I care, are these people I care about what they have to say?"[39] Although blurbs for mass-market books may give only the name of the publication in which the review appeared, the blurbs for serious nonfiction almost always provide the reviewer's name.

Radio advertising for books is unusual, and television advertising nearly unheard of, but both media can be used to publicize nonfiction. An author interview or a review on NPR or on C-SPAN's *Book TV* generates a great deal of interest and sales, and radio appearances on local stations can also help to promote a book. Local publicity matters because booksellers and readers talk to one another. Word of mouth can travel from one community to another as booksellers exchange news, or as readers talk or e-mail friends. An appearance on *The Daily Show* or *The Colbert Report* is the most coveted television slot for nonfiction authors.

Online retailers like Barnes & Noble and Amazon.com promote books on their websites, attempting to duplicate or improve upon the experience of shopping in a bricks-and-mortar store. Amazon posts reviews from some review media and allows publishers to post other reviews, descriptive material, dust jackets, tables of contents, and sample chapters for potential buyers to browse. The site generates word-of-mouth by allowing readers to rate books and to post their own reviews; these reviews in turn can be rated for usefulness. Software generates sales rankings, which may influence purchasers. The site's search functions can also find alternative titles, other books by the same author, used copies, and related material in other media. Amazon advertises books before publication as well, allowing purchasers to place advance orders. Like prepublication reviews and orders from retail stores, these may influence the publisher's decisions about advertising and print runs. Amazon's latest venture into bookselling, the e-book reader Kindle, brings the impulse purchase online: a Kindle owner who hears a recommendation from a friend or reviewer, or hears the author on NPR, can order the book instantly and have it delivered in a minute or two. Kindle owners can also get a chapter or two of many books free before deciding whether to purchase.

Some advertising is directed at booksellers rather than readers. *Publishers Weekly* is the magazine of the book trade, and publishers advertise in it regularly. Ads in *PW* tell booksellers which books the publisher is planning to promote heavily; sometimes the advertising budget and the extent of the author's tour are included in the copy. The brief reviews in each issue help booksellers evaluate the suitability of a book for their clientele. This advertising supplements the person-to-person selling done by publishers' sales representatives, who visit booksellers regularly to promote the season's new books, and the intensive courting that goes on at the annual booksellers' convention. Booksellers determine not only which books they will stock, and how many copies, but also how prominently they will display them and whether they will promote them in their own newsletters.

Booksellers strongly influence the fate of popularizations. The staff in the large chain stores may not know their customers as well as those in the independent bookstores, but they still influence customers' choices through their initial selections (or those of the central buying office) and the prominence with which they display and promote them. If several publishers offer books on the same subject, they probably will not order all of them, and if they do, they will not promote them all equally. They will choose the one or two that they think will most appeal to their customers and place them in special racks or affix "staff recommendation" tags. Publishers expend a great deal of effort in keeping the booksellers informed of what is new and exciting on their lists. In fact, one way to think of the marketing effort is to visualize editors trying to pass along their enthusiasm for a book to the marketing staff, which in turn tries to pass it along to the sales staff, which joins them in passing it along to the booksellers, who then pass it along to their customers.[40]

The last—and perhaps most vital—link in this chain is that customer, the reader. Publishers have claimed for decades that books are sold by word of mouth, and the mouth that matters is that of the friend or fellow book club member or colleague who recommends a favorite book. Radio personalities, book reviewers, and booksellers are effective salespeople if they are trusted in the same way as genuine acquaintances. If online readers' reviews actually sell books it is probably because they sound like the recommendations of trusted friends. No one knows a guaranteed way to generate word-of-mouth enthusiasm. In fact, most publishers go out of their way to say that there is no guaranteed way.

I suspect, though, that the mystery is somewhat less profound in the world of popularization than is generally believed. The solution lies in some of the things that editors and marketers themselves say about their books. First, unlike editors who work in some other genres, nonfiction editors identify closely with the audience for their books. They have the same background and interests, so what appeals to them is likely to appeal to readers. If their enthusiasm is genuine, they will be able to pass it down the chain. Also, they have some objective evidence of the quality of their books. A fiction editor may believe wholeheartedly in a first novel, but only experience and faith in one's own judgment lies behind that belief. With nonfiction, the author's credentials and the review process bolster the editor's confidence. These same factors, along with the civilized packaging and the reasonable-sounding claims of the advertising copy, give the reader confidence in the book being offered. When both author and publisher have done their jobs well, good books get to the right readers.

8

WHY WE READ

Reading is a mystery. Sales figures, opinion polls, and library circulation statistics collectively tell us something about who reads and what they read, but they shed little light on *why* people read or what they experience as they read. Theories abound, offered by disciplines ranging from literary theory to clinical psychology, each supported by credible evidence and most consistent with all of the others, but none of them really answers these central questions. The mystery has many sources. Reading is not a single, straightforward act but rather a variety of very different activities, each with its own motivation and rewards, so we are investigating a complex of phenomena. We rightly believe that our choices of what to read are loaded with implications about our intellectual abilities and character, making us reluctant to disclose our preferences to people with questionnaires in hand. Even when we want to answer questions honestly, we may not be aware of why we choose what we do. So we are investigating a complex of activities with multiple meanings, some conscious and some not. And, to some extent, reading is a *genuine* mystery: it may yield up some of its secrets to sociologists' polling techniques, psychologists' PET scans, and historians' archival probings, but in the end there always seem to be motivations and responses we cannot account for completely.

The Varieties of Reading Experience

Reading may be compulsive, compulsory, mesmerizing, boring, exciting, relaxing, inspiring, depressing, or matter-of-fact and devoid of emotional content—all in the course of a single day for a single reader. You get up early one morning, and the paper hasn't arrived. You know it will be here soon, and you don't want to get absorbed in a book, so you read the cereal box and the milk carton, an experience without intellectual or emotional content, bordering on the compulsive. Later you read the newspaper and experience a range of emotions: anger on the front page, sorrow on the obituary page, amusement at the comics. You drive to work and read billboards, or ride the bus or subway and read the ads as well as the rest of your newspaper. At work, you read your e-mail plus the ads, letters, and other routine trivia in your mailbox. You read a request for a proposal, or a budget revision, or something else that requires you to think and respond. If you are a teacher, you read what you have assigned to your students or grade their papers. You may read over your own lecture notes. At lunch, you read the menu and perhaps a magazine if you are dining alone. In the afternoon, you spend some time reading a professional journal, which requires concentration, note-taking, and research on the Web or in one of your reference books. Your printer needs a new toner cartridge, so you get out the manual and read the instructions. When you get home, you read a recipe or at least the heating instructions on a package so that you can prepare dinner. Later you may read a mystery or romance novel that takes you out of your own world—even to the extent that when the telephone rings you are momentarily disoriented. Or you may read the book that your reading group will discuss next week. Or you may choose nonfiction—a biography or a history book that may be as transporting as a novel, or a book on the latest theory in cosmology or neuroscience. You may have selected the book for any number of reasons; possibly you forgot to return the postcard to the History Book Club. If you have young children, you read to them—anything from *Goodnight Moon* to *Harry Potter*. You may consult a television schedule to see whether there's anything worth watching. Before going to bed, you may read your personal e-mail, perhaps a note from a college-age child. As you brush your teeth, you may resort to reading the toothpaste label.

All these experiences are reading, but they are all very different, and we engage in them for very different reasons, some conscious and some not. Let's begin with the compulsive kind of reading—the cereal box, subway posters, and toothpaste tube. This is the Mount Everest reading experience: you read it because it is there. For most of us, this practice is harmless enough and probably something we don't even notice until it is pointed out. For some, though, it is an irritating habit to be broken. Irnerio, the

Nonreader, a character in Italo Calvino's *If on a Winter's Night a Traveler*, is so troubled by the tyranny of text that he teaches himself not to read: "It's not easy: they teach us to read as children, and for the rest of our lives we remain the slaves of all the written stuff they fling in front of us. I may have had to make some effort myself, at first, to learn not to read, but now it comes quite naturally to me." He is an artist who uses books as his raw materials, gluing their pages together and then carving them.[1]

For some, however, reading becomes an addiction. In the course of his research, Victor Nell, a clinical psychologist who studied the psychology of reading for pleasure, discovered one family among whom reading was pathological. The father told Nell, "The more I enjoy a book the quicker I want to forget it so that I can read it again. Like *Fallon* [by Louis L'Amour], for example, I've already read it ten times, and I enjoy it almost exactly the same each time." Nell classifies him as a "gluttonous reader, a text gobbler who swallows books whole, achieving that pinnacle of gluttonous security, the ability to eat the same dish endlessly, passing it through his system whole and miraculously wholesome, ready to be re-eaten again and again." His wife and children also read a great deal, and the father notes: "I think in the long run it becomes a kind of disease because all we do is read. Life passes us by. Normal people go to Fountains Valley [a park in Pretoria], just get into their car and go. But we just sit at home. . . . We don't want to own a TV set. I think it's a waste of time. We wouldn't have enough time for reading. . . . I always want to be able to go back and read the book again. I just want more books all the time." A daughter who lives on her own describes withdrawing from the habit, recovering from "reading fever": "If I don't read for a week or so, I get terribly restless. I'm irritable, it's a type of hunger, not to eat but to read. As soon as I touch a book, I feel better and it gets better as I read on."[2] Their description of their experience suggests that the act of reading—holding the book, scanning the text, turning the pages—matters far more than the content. Reading the same books ensures that there will be no surprises, challenges, or disturbances—the very things that others seek from books.

Many readers use books for a healthier kind of escape—an escape that is temporary, refreshing, and reversible. This was the phenomenon that Nell set out to investigate, the kind of reading that allows us to step into another person's life, into ideas that fully occupy our minds, or into adventures that we might not dare undertake in real life or that simply do not occur in anyone's real life. *Jurassic Park*, *Rosemary's Baby*, and *The Exorcist* are great escapes that are all the more fun because we know they won't actually happen to us. If we believed in cloned dinosaurs, impregnating demons, and possession, they might not be nearly as enjoyable, or they might be enjoyable in a different way. Of course, books need not be fantastic to provide this kind of absorption and escape. I began reading Margaret Atwood's *The Blind Assassin* while on vacation, on my first night in a lovely eighteenth-century home in Cornwall. The book begins in rural Canada between the two world wars, and I became so absorbed in the setting that when I was disturbed by a sound I was for a few seconds completely confused about what country and what century I was in. It was not the first time I have had that experience, and I am sure that others have shared it. That kind of total immersion is one of the reasons we read.

Nonfiction rarely provides an emotional escape, healthy or otherwise. It may provide a diversion from the real world—or it may intensify our concerns about the real world by telling us that it is an even more dangerous place than we believed. It may take us to faraway places—or it may enhance our understanding of our own immediate surroundings. Nevertheless, nonfiction can provide its own kind of escape by totally engaging the reader's mind intellectually. If you are trying to follow a complex argument about evolution, linguistics, theology, or economics, you cannot simultaneously be thinking about what is going on at the office or where your teenager and the current significant other might have taken your new car. The two kinds of escape have an analogy in music. If you play the piano, you can sit down and play for fun—easy pieces or popular music that you can noodle around with—or you can work at a Bach fugue. Both provide escape, one through diversion and the other through concentration.

Some reading is completely practical. Rather than diverting us from a current concern, it helps us resolve it. This is the kind of reading that user manuals, how-to books, reference books, and airline or television schedules provide: answers to questions and guides to action. When we do this kind of reading, we are not seeking escape, and we are unlikely to fall under a spell. We are simply solving a problem. Self-help books are a more complex variant of this phenomenon. When the problem is fixing a relationship rather than a clogged sink, or improving career prospects, the solution is going to take more words. Nonetheless, many of these books are framed as to-do lists or step-by-step solutions (*The Five Pillars of Investing*, *The Six*

Sigma Way, The Seven Principles for Making Marriage Work, Eight Habits of the Heart, Transcend: Nine Steps to Living Well Forever, Ten Stupid Things Couples Do to Mess Up Their Relationships). Booksellers and the "readers who bought this book also bought" lists on Amazon.com tell us, though, that a single book rarely solves the reader's problems. A reader who buys one volume of advice on any given problem is likely to buy several, suggesting that what is being sought is not an immediate, practical solution but general advice and reassurance.[3]

Professional reading is also practical, leading to immediate changes in the way we work, food for thought, or ideas for new projects. Medical journals provide doctors with evaluations of new treatments; reports of court cases give lawyers information that affects the way they advise clients; scientific journals offer updates on what other researchers are doing. But in addition to browsing current literature, practitioners and researchers also use older journals and reference books to get information on specific topics and answers to questions, or to investigate a new topic. For example, a historian may become interested in eighteenth-century agricultural practices when reading a current issue of a journal but will then seek out older books and articles to learn more about the subject. The same media can be read and used in very different ways.

Popularizations, too, are read for many personal or professional reasons: for background knowledge, current information, and entertainment, and to keep up with current political events or scientific advances. They may also be read for social reasons, because readers want to be able to hold their own in conversation. Serious nonfiction ranks very high in the social pecking order of reading.

Mass, Class, and Brows

The way people decorate their homes, dress, and entertain themselves often reveals much about their preferences and backgrounds. The choices we make about what to read may also tell others about our tastes and education, although decoding any of these decisions is not straightforward, and reading is among the most difficult clues to decipher. Neighborhood gossips, political columnists, sociologists, and cultural critics have all attempted to classify people by what they read, but with limited success.

Why does anyone worry about this? Can't we just adopt a laissez-faire attitude toward reading? Apparently not. Cultural critics have been trying to classify books, as well as music and art, since the late nineteenth century. As the concept of class fell from favor in American society, the notion of brow to some extent took its place. Long after essayists ceased to feel comfortable describing their neighbors as lower-class or even bourgeois, they went to great lengths to figure out whether they were highbrow, lowbrow, or middlebrow. As *Harper's* editor Russell Lynes wrote in 1949, "You may not be known by which fork you use for the fish these days, but you will be known by which key you use for your *Finnegan's Wake*"—assuming, of course, that you are not sufficiently highbrow to navigate it without help.[4]

As soon as critics begin classifying people and what they read in this way, readers naturally become self-conscious about how they will be seen. Thus, people who are concerned about making an impression may try to manipulate others' opinions of them by displaying the sort of books that would be owned by the sort of people they wish to seem. This practice dates to ancient times: Seneca the Younger complained nearly two millennia ago that the great library at Alexandria "had collected the books not for scholarship but for display. In the same way you will find that many people who lack even elementary culture keep books not as tools of learning but as decoration for their dining-rooms. . . . Nowadays an elegant library too has joined hot and cold baths as an essential adornment for a house." Jay Gatsby, one of America's legendary pretenders, knew this when he furnished his mansion. In his "high Gothic library, panelled with carved English oak" the guests find a large collection of books. "You needn't bother to ascertain. I ascertained. They're real," one guest announces. "Absolutely real—have pages and everything. I thought they'd be a nice durable cardboard. Matter of fact, they're absolutely real." He takes a volume from the shelf: "It's a bona-fide piece of printed matter. It fooled me. This fella's a regular Belasco. It's a triumph. What thoroughness! What realism! Knew when to stop, too—didn't cut the pages."[5]

Writing about Gatsby's era, book historian Megan Benton describes "one of the decade's pervasive tools of cultural assessment, the assumption that one's books say a great deal about one's self." She argues that for centuries the ownership of books—any books—testified that the owner of the library had not only the wealth to buy books but also the education and the leisure time needed to read them. But as literacy became more general, and books more affordable, ownership of books ceased to be an adequate cultural indicator. Instead, one had to examine more closely *which* books people owned and how they used them before making judgments about their background and education. By the 1990s, when Nicholson Baker analyzed the use of books in upscale mail-order catalogs, the nature of the books on display was critical: "There isn't a self-help book or a current best-seller to be seen, because the men and women who live in the rooms of the mail-order catalogues never read best-sellers. In fact, they never read paperbacks."[6]

Advertisers are on to something, but they are presenting only the surface of a more complex phenomenon. People make statements about who they are by what they read and don't read, by what they admit to reading and what they deny, what they show and what they hide. The hoped-for customers of the Pottery Barn catalog who do not read bestsellers are making a very clear statement about themselves: I am too discerning to read what *everyone* is reading. I make my own choices, and those choices are idiosyncratic, reflecting my extensive reading and better judgment. As Baker puts it, choosing more esoteric reading matter suggests "wealths of patriarchal, or matriarchal, learnedness."[7] One's taste in books, like one's furniture, should be not only distinctive but inherited. The catalogue dwellers do not read self-help books, because that would be an admission of failure in some aspect of life. Readers told a sociologist that "they would not read certain self-help books in public, especially at work"; one remarked that "carrying a book like *Smart Women, Foolish Choices* around" would be "'making a statement' that she would prefer not to make." The researcher concluded that readers "don't want other people deciding that they are maladjusted or stupid for reading these books."[8]

Both Jay Gatsby and the self-help book readers remind us that there is a difference between what is bought and displayed and what is actually read. The pages of Gatsby's books were never cut: they were on display but unread. The self-help books were read, but hidden. Some books are bought to be displayed rather than read, and some books are read—or at least skimmed—simply for appearances. The perception that reading is a virtue, and that certain kinds of reading are more valued than others, complicates the task of getting good information about reading from readers themselves—something like the problem that sex researchers face. The novelist and critic Robert Escarpit suggests that it is even more difficult: "The likelihood of lucid and sincere answers is extremely reduced as soon as someone's reading habits are examined. While the confession of one's sexual peculiarities may flatter a latent exhibitionist, the avowal of literary or anti-literary tastes (whether too undiscriminating or too refined) which lower one's position in society can only be painful. Most people find great difficulty in confessing to themselves the nature of their taste."[9]

Because reading is perceived as a sign of intellectual prowess, people are likely to exaggerate how much they read or to brag about their reading. One touching example is that of Rose Cohen, a Russian Jewish immigrant who published a memoir in 1918. When she learned to read English, she wrote, "I felt so proud that I could read an English book that I carried it about with me in the street. I took it along to the shop. I became quite vain."[10]

Reading to make an impression on others is common among teenagers. One student reported: "I joined the Classics Club just so I could have some neat books on my shelf and pretend I was well read," while another explained: "I didn't want to be a conversational drop-out when it came to reading material, so instead of reading the complete book, I would go to the library and read the book reviews. I would also listen to other people speak about books and make use of their remarks about books as my own first hand reading experience."[11] This kind of behavior does not end with adolescence, of course. Editor and writer Gerald Howard points out that one of the less legitimate functions of book reviews is to act as "marvelous guides to up-to-the-minute intellectual décor for people looking to appear *au courant* with minimum time and effort." The comic strip "Boox," in the *New York Times Book Review*, shows several people discussing the novel *Everything Is Illuminated* and then turns into an advertisement for "Slapdash Notes": "Why spend **long, dreary hours all alone** reading the books that everybody is talking about when all that really matters socially and professionally is talking the talk itself?" There is even a how-to-book for those who wish to perfect the art: *How to Talk About Books You Haven't Read*. Although dishonest, this practice is not entirely harmful. Reviews and articles about important books spread their message to those who have not read them, allowing their influence to be far more widespread than sales would indicate.[12]

Reading any book is socially more acceptable than reading nothing at all, but all books are not equal in conferring prestige. Since the late nineteenth century, American cultural critics have debated the meaning and significance of highbrow and lowbrow, with the adjective applied both to people and to cultural products. The highbrow citizen participated in the

culture of fine art and literature, and—at least until the advent of modernism—the refined and genteel. The lowbrow, by contrast, was uncultivated,
unread, and perhaps unwashed. Highbrow literature was cultural; the lowbrow, commercial.

In his analysis of brow distinctions in the nineteenth century, historian
Lawrence Levine shows how American elites tried to deal with the omnipresence of "strangers"—immigrants and African Americans—in a variety
of ways, including education and training to make them more like the elites
themselves, to reduce the distance between the two groups. But, as Levine
repeatedly emphasizes, this leveling effort was ambivalent, fraught with
tension between preserving high culture and trying to "sow the seeds of
culture among [the masses] in order to ensure civilized order." The ambivalence came from the elite's desire to preserve its own status: "Despite all of
the rhetoric to the contrary, despite all of the laments about the low state of
mass culture, there were comforts to be derived from the situation as well.
Lift the people out of their cultural milieu, wipe them clean, elevate their
tastes, and where in this world of burgeoning democracy was one to locate
distinctiveness?"[13]

As the century progressed, some Americans persisted in the effort to
erase the cultural gap by creating institutions that would extend the reach
of quality literature, art, and music. The "middlebrow" thus arose as a place
where new audiences might be exposed to high culture. Contemporaries
who wrote about the subject—notably Russell Lynes in 1949 and Dwight
Macdonald a decade later—tended to be highbrow and to set the middlebrow citizen apart, "a pretentious and frivolous man or woman who uses
culture to satisfy social or business ambitions." Middlebrow culture was "a
corruption of High Culture," "tepid ooze"; "it pretends to respect the standards of High Culture while in fact it waters them down and vulgarizes
them."[14]

Critics differed over precisely who belonged to the middlebrow, but they
agreed that certain institutions represented it: the Book-of-the-Month
Club, adult education classes, public lectures (even those given by highbrows), *Horizon Magazine*, the postwar *Atlantic*, the television program
"Omnibus," and books like Will and Ariel Durant's interpretations of history and philosophy.[15] Reading these attacks forty or fifty years later, it
seems clear that the objections were less intellectual than social. It is fair
enough to declare the Cliff's Notes version of Shakespeare inferior to the

original, but that is not what we are talking about. Although the Durants were not Plato, they were learned and literate people who wrote intelligently. Their books provided insight into their subjects that at least enhanced readers' understanding and often inspired them to turn to the originals. Rebecca Goldstein, a novelist who holds a doctorate in philosophy from Princeton, credits her adolescent reading of Will Durant's *Story of Philosophy* with her ambition to become a philosopher, and she is not alone.[16] According to an executive of the Book-of-the-Month Club, intellectuals' disdain for the organization was ill founded: "Dr. Gallup found another interesting thing. He asked some of those educators and professors of English if they liked the Book-of-the-Month Club and the books it sent out. Many of them said, in effect, that the books were beneath their dignity. Yet when he asked them what contemporary books they had been reading in the past year, he discovered that many of the books they had been reading in the past year were our selections."[17]

The real objection to the middlebrow was that it threatened a social and intellectual elite that had already lost its financial exclusivity and now saw its educational and cultural distinction slipping away. Reading Keats and Milton, or Joyce and Faulkner, would lose its cachet if the owner of a shoe factory could read them too. (It was bad enough that the factory owner's son might be in the critic's son's class at Yale.) The most vivid expression of this discomfort comes from the fictional Flora Poste, heroine of the 1932 novel *Cold Comfort Farm:* "One of the disadvantages of almost universal education was the fact that all kinds of persons acquired a familiarity with one's favourite writers. It gave one a curious feeling; it was like seeing a drunken stranger wrapped in one's dressing-gown."[18]

The lowbrows, with their "mass culture," were not a threat. It was easy to draw the line between low and high, but the middle blurred seemingly important distinctions. The critics' solution was cultural apartheid with sharp lines drawn between black and white, but no room for the cultural equivalent of South Africa's "coloureds." From England, Virginia Woolf advised lowbrows to resist the siren call of the middle and remain pure; this sounds suspiciously like being told to know one's place. "The true battle," she wrote, "lies not between the highbrows and the lowbrows joined together in blood brotherhood but against the bloodless and pernicious pest who comes between. . . . Highbrows and lowbrows must band together to exterminate a pest which is the bane of all thinking and living." In the United

States, Macdonald was even clearer about the need "to recognize that two cultures have developed in this country and that it is to the national interest to keep them separate. . . . [L]et the masses have their Masscult, let the few who care about good writing, painting, music, architecture, philosophy, etc., have their High Culture, and don't fuzz up the distinction with Midcult." And although his essay is somewhat tongue-in-cheek, Russell Lynes used an image that must have been even more offensive in 1949 than it is today: "The middlebrows are influential today, but neither the highbrows nor the lowbrows like them; and if we ever have intellectual totalitarianism, it may well be the lowbrows and the highbrows who will run things, and the middlebrows who will be exiled in boxcars to a collecting point probably in the vicinity of Independence, Missouri."[19]

Macdonald, writing in 1960, was fighting a losing battle. Most of the institutions of middlebrow culture vanished, others continue to thrive, and some new candidates for the title emerged; but the *idea* of the middlebrow faded away. It became increasingly difficult to distinguish middle from high, and cultural critics and scholars alike lost the compulsion to set themselves apart. The caste of brows simply could not survive another well-educated, intellectually confident generation, one whose members changed class as readily as they changed jobs and clothes. As cultural critic John Frow points out, "whereas once . . . high culture was unequivocally the culture of the ruling class, this hierarchical structure is no longer the organizing principle of the cultural system."[20] In contemporary American society, it is not clear that the "ruling class" participates in high culture except for tax-deductible corporate contributions. At least at the prosperous end of American society, cultural capital and economic capital are increasingly separable; neither is linked invariably to social status; and cultural capital is less easy to pass from one generation to another than the economic variety.

One attack on the notion of brows came from the advent of cultural studies, which transformed the lowbrow into the subject of scholarly investigation. The media annually ridicule sessions of the Modern Language Association about Elvis Presley, Madonna, sitcoms, and other phenomena that are decidedly not highbrow. This blurring of brows may be related to an important fact about the way people choose their entertainment: most people read, listen to music, and watch television and movies that fall into various categories of culture. Psychologist Victor Nell refuted "'the elitist fallacy'—the belief that as sophistication grows, coarser tastes wither away.

. . . On the contrary: though sophisticated readers have the capacity and the desire to enjoy deeply felt and delicately wrought literature, and habitually do so, they continue, on occasion and if their consciences allow them, to delight in the childlike triumphs of His Majesty the Ego." Sociologist Harold Wilensky, in a less tolerant comment, concluded that "there is little doubt from my data as well as others' that educated strata—even products of graduate and professional schools—are becoming full participants in mass culture; they spend a reduced fraction of time in exposure to quality print and film. This trend extends to the professors, writers, artists, scientists—the keepers of high culture themselves."[21] Listeners enjoy Mozart *and* Mariah Carey, television viewers watch PBS *and* Comedy Central, and readers lose themselves in A. S. Byatt *and* Danielle Steel. My own survey of readers of serious nonfiction showed that more than half also read mystery novels, more than a quarter read science fiction or adventure novels, nearly a quarter read humor, a third read self-help books, and a handful read romance novels.[22] Although it might still be possible to categorize books by brow level, it is not possible to categorize readers in that way.

Even within the theoretical framework offered by Macdonald and other critics, the distinctions are hard to maintain. One basis of distinction was that of culture versus commerce. This was never a very good distinction, because no matter how much the creators of highbrow art disdained commercial success, they still depended on commercial institutions to get their work to their select group of consumers. The institutions might operate on a smaller scale, but they were still manufacturing, marketing, and selling books; exhibiting and selling paintings; and charging listeners for musical performances and recordings. By the end of the twentieth century, the distinction had become totally meaningless: "High culture is fully absorbed within commodity production. . . . Works of high culture are now produced in exactly the same serial forms as those of low culture: the paperback book, the record or disk, film, radio, and television. . . . Within the overall cultural market high culture forms a 'niche' market—but this is also true of many, increasingly differentiated, low cultural products."[23] High, low, and middlebrow books—if they can still be so classified—are all published by the same houses, sold in the same bookstores, differentiated perhaps by nuances of cover design and the sources of blurbs, but otherwise indistinguishable until you read them.

Even reading them is less likely to lead to clear distinctions. In fiction, novels that were written and marketed as high culture become bestsellers: Umberto Eco's *The Name of the Rose* and Annie Proulx's *The Shipping News* are two well-known examples. The phenomenon that brought such crossing over into the headlines, though, was Oprah Winfrey's book club, whose selections range widely over brow levels. Attitudes toward the new lack of distinction went public when Winfrey chose Jonathan Franzen's *The Corrections* in 2001 and he became squeamish about having this fact emblazoned on the cover of his book.[24] Dwight Macdonald was whispering in one ear, "Don't abandon your highbrow standing, even if you lose sales" while his publisher whispered in the other, "Take the sticker, the readers, and the money." Nearly everyone—readers, writers, and critics—sided with the publisher, though they had no financial stake in the matter. The comments in the media suggested that setting oneself apart from the mass of readers was at best silly and at worst deeply offensive. What Frow called "the modernist fantasy of self-definition through opposition to a degraded mass culture" has, in his words "become obsolescent, and indeed has been replaced by rather different practices of fusion of or play between high and low genres and traditions."[25] Readers are now confident enough in their tastes and abilities that they are willing to read—and admit to reading—a variety of books, and the fact that someone less educated than they can also enjoy the book does not reduce their own pleasure.

Popularization has helped to break down the distinctions of brow and illustrates some of the reasons the distinction has become obsolete. The books I have been writing about could be classified as highbrow: their content is difficult and serious; they make readers work and think; they provoke discussion of issues, ideas, and values; many of their readers are highly educated and work at intellectually demanding jobs. Nonfiction retains some of the "good-for-you" cachet awarded in the nineteenth century, leading Victor Nell to suggest that reading nonfiction is sometimes a strategy to justify reading for pleasure.[26] At the same time, though, many of these books succeed in an arena far larger than that of the intellectual elite, becoming bestsellers or at least financially successful publishing ventures. They are by any measure commercial products. If we define the highbrow strictly as a writer's original work, they may not qualify, because the academic authors' work *originally* appeared in journals or books written for their peers. In their trade books they repackage their work for a general audience, adding explanations and context, reducing detail, introducing rhetorical tropes, biographical detail, and even humor. And there is always that handful of reviews and the carping in the halls. A reader with a Ph.D. in physics may poke fun at Richard Feynman yet enjoy Stephen Ambrose; a reader whose doctorate is in history may adore Feynman's books but make snide remarks about Ambrose. Clearly, though, if we allow only those with doctorates in the relevant field to define the highbrow, the system has gotten out of hand. It makes more sense to leave these classifications behind and state simply that these are good books that challenge and inform their readers. Popularization does offer social benefits, but people read these books for intellectual challenge, entertainment, and other reasons as well.

Why We Read Popularizations

Few students of adult reading are cynical enough to believe that people buy books just to look smart. Readers of popular science, history, and the like buy and keep these books, read them in public places, and display them in their living rooms, but keeping up appearances does not explain their large sales. This is especially true of paperback sales, which come after a book's fashionable season has ended. If readers of popularizations choose these books for a social reason it is to be able to discuss their reading with others. These books, and their topics, become the subject of conversation in the workplace, at social gatherings, and in book discussion groups held in living rooms and online. Nearly all readers I surveyed reported discussing their nonfiction reading with colleagues, friends, or family members both informally and in organized reading groups. Anyone observing these conversations can easily distinguish them from the superficial exchanges of people who have read only the reviews. These serious readers are looking for people to talk to and argue with, for reading companions who can help them clarify and consolidate what they are learning. That may be why nonfiction is a frequent choice of book groups, which provide both a venue for discussion and the encouragement that busy people may need to read what they want to read but have difficulty finding time for.[27]

Even this variety of sociability is not an adequate explanation for reading. Harry Scherman, one of the founders of the Book-of-the-Month Club, was perfectly willing to exploit any motive for reading, but he was clear on the difference between buying books for status and reading them for personal satisfaction: "It wasn't that they just wanted to keep up with the good books just to be able to talk about them. That is plain nonsense. . . . The subscriber doesn't want to read books in order to be able to talk about them: he wants to read books! To be sure, he becomes aware of this backsliding when he runs up against people who do read books, and that gives him some sense of guilt, but he would have no sense of guilt if he didn't already have a very active curiosity. It is that which makes people buy books."[28]

Most readers are trying to learn something—a new subject, such as fuzzy logic; a subject that had recently aroused their interest, such as an area of the world suddenly in the news; new developments in subjects they know, such as emerging ideas about evolution; or specific information about a subject that they know only generally, such as greater detail about a historical figure or event portrayed on television. At the same time, though, they want to be entertained. They expect good writing: bad writing, variously described by survey respondents as condescending, repetitious, or pompous, is the main reading for rejecting a book or leaving it unfinished.

Readers distinguish very clearly between reading for information—what we do when consulting reference books or other books useful for finding facts—and reading for understanding and knowledge. They view nonfiction reading as active and intellectually demanding, and this is part of its attraction. The rigors of higher education create a need for intellectual stimulation that lasts beyond the four or more years spent at a university. Once out in the "real world," people often find that their time is occupied by jobs and social life, but their minds are less engaged. "A lot of young women feel frustrated that there isn't the intellectual outlet they had in college," a bookseller notes. The publisher of *Hungry Mind Review* sees a deeper source: "Baby boomers are awakening to the total emptiness of their lives, and reading is something they know is important and haven't quite forgotten how to do." "Literature and reading became part of the boomer self-definition."[29] We need not ascribe "total emptiness" to readers' lives, or consult only baby boomers, to understand the appeal of an intellectual challenge. Even the most interesting job leaves large parts of a well-trained mind idle, and no matter how rewarding parents find their young children, few would argue that childrearing is mainly an intellectual exercise. Brains are not muscles, but they demand exercise.

This explanation resolves a puzzle raised by publishers and scholars alike. In discussing the success of Stephen Hawking's books, Dennis Overbye claims that "the question that still haunts publishers, critics and others, incredulous that there could be as big an audience for a serious discussion of the origin of the universe as for the life of a movie star, is why?" Victor Nell was also puzzled by the fact that readers contradicted one of his basic assumptions: "In Western industrialized societies, we would also expect rankings of literary merit or quality to correlate at significant negative values with preference rankings. This prediction arises from our review of the effects of the social value system and especially the Protestant Ethic, leading us to expect that in these societies, literary quality and unpleasantness would often be seen as synonymous." He resolved the contradiction by concluding that "increased literary sophistication, presumably obtained by those with an education in the liberal arts, attenuates the relationship between merit and difficulty."[30] Readers of popularizations, though, see neither puzzle nor contradiction. The difficulty of a book—so long as it is not created artificially or unnecessarily with poorly explained theory, condescending attitudes, or needless jargon—is part of its attraction.

In online reviews, readers' highest praise is reserved for books that make them think. Readers like nonfiction because it is *demanding* and *thought-provoking.* They like books that *explain difficult ideas, introduce new ideas, spark further interest, make them think differently, make them think for themselves,* and *enhance understanding.* Many of their comments emphasize the importance of being asked to think: one book "could keep you thinking for the rest of your life": "you thought you understood something, and then you find yourself following her arguments and realizing that you didn't understand quite as well as you thought you did"; "I frequently stopped reading to think about what I believed"; it "made me reconsider what I know"; "it was a real pleasure to watch my objection to his argument fall apart as I read the rest of the book."[31] One survey respondent noted that she reads nonfiction "to turn over the mental soil in the garden of thoughts."

Reading popularizations also provides a connection to the authors, pleasurable in part because it re-creates the stimulation of being in a college classroom, but without the apprehension of a final exam looming: "Part of the lure of these books is the chance to reclaim one's citizenship in a troubled and baffling cosmos by hearing the word from the horse's mouth, from someone who has touched the cosmic mystery personally. But another part is surely being treated like an adult, of entering a rough-hewn colleagueship by being trusted to put work into deciphering [complex] statements, or to deal with straight talk of the nature of science and the universe."[32] The absence of a final exam is important, as is the assumption that the reader is a responsible adult. Without a final exam, the reader is not obliged to understand everything, and readers are free to pick and choose, to decide how hard they want to work and how thoroughly they want to understand. In reviewing David Berlinski's book about calculus, Richard Bernstein describes a common experience: "You tend to start out fairly well with these explications of cosmic phenomena, grasping the fundamentals of the early chapters. Then, just as you begin to believe that maybe, finally, you will be permitted to enter into the temple of learning, you find yourself in dismal confrontation with your own limitations. Or perhaps, as Mr. Berlinski warns at the beginning, you just didn't sweat enough, pencil and paper in hand, to follow an argument that is not going to be 'Sesame Street.'" One reader of Hawking's *The Universe in a Nutshell* described a related phenomenon: "It all made beautiful sense as I read it, although it tended to vanish like a dream when I put the book down."[33] If one were being tested on the material, this would create anxiety. Without an exam, readers can enjoy the fleeting moment of comprehension and decide whether or not to go back and work hard enough to make it last.

The author's attitude toward readers is crucial in making difficult material pleasurable and worth working for. Some faculty members enjoy emphasizing the enormous gap between their knowledge and that of their students, and college students have little choice but to tolerate this sort of arrogance. Nonfiction readers do have a choice, and they exercise it regularly. The most common readers' complaints are not about difficulty, but about authors who are *arrogant, condescending, patronizing, self-referential, self-congratulatory,* and *pedantic.* Writers are praised for being *balanced, persuasive, witty, elegant, lively, confident,* and *modest.*

Readers are happiest with books that treat them as collaborators in intellectual activity, books that provide insight into the writer's day-to-day work and methodology, that "bring the reader along the thought trail," as one Amazon reviewer wrote. Readers praise these books as *passionate, moving,* and *humane.* The best authors create a sense of wonder and "remind us why this is such an exciting time to be alive." Popularizations involve readers in the life of the mind, and by making demands on readers' intelligence, they ensure that this involvement is neither passive nor entirely vicarious. Even if we cannot be in the rain forest, the laboratory, the archives, the observatory, or the archeological ruins, we can share in the experience of discovery and learning.

AFTERWORD
Popularization and the Future of the Book

The twenty-first century arrived in the middle of the "information age," at a time when many people were convinced that the book was fast becoming a relic of another era. They reasoned that if you want up-to-the-minute news, stock quotations, treatments for a new disease, or directories to anything from arborists to zoos, the Web is better than a bound volume. Others complained that the Web contains too much information and that its reliability is questionable. These complaints, however, can be applied with equal accuracy to books: there is no shortage of unnecessary and inaccurate information in ink on paper. We have seen, though, that there is more to nonfiction than information.

The authors of popularization are sharing *knowledge*, and their readers are seeking *understanding*. These are more complex commodities than information, and they are more difficult to convey and acquire. The books I have been writing about contain a great deal of information, but it has been very carefully selected and organized. Facts and theories are attached to a framework that both organizes them and makes them easier to understand and learn. They are presented with the aid of rhetorical approaches that increase both understanding and enjoyment. The authors are seeking to connect with their readers, to establish a collaboration in which both have to do a fair amount of thinking. Information on the Web is groceries; serious nonfiction is a gourmet meal.

Books will survive side by side with the Web because the format is well suited to the reader's purpose. Books are portable and durable. You can write in them if you like, and you can share them with friends. When your book discussion group meets, each member can bring a copy and you can compare notes, impressions, questions, and criticisms. And although I treasure my dead-tree books, the new generation of electronic books are close enough to be extremely tempting: same content, comes instantly available, permanently archived, no shelf space.

When considering the continuing life of the book, the distinction between fiction and nonfiction becomes less important than it is in other ways. E. L. Doctorow wrote in 1988 that "there is no longer any such thing as fiction or nonfiction; there's only narrative."[1] Certainly there are blends described by the portmanteau words *docudrama* and *faction*. There are, as we have seen, books posing as one that are in fact the other. Just as memoirists sometimes fictionalize, novelists sometimes run afoul of the libel laws when their characters are too easily identified with real people. Whether writing fiction or nonfiction, writers are writing, and they share concerns about style, narrative, and characterization whether their plots and characters are real or wholly invented. Readers, too, may choose either fiction or nonfiction for some purposes—entertainment or pleasure in good writing, for example. Yet I believe the distinction remains valid and important for both authors and readers, despite some overlap.

The world is not becoming any easier to understand—and not only because scholars have broken it down into smaller units and complicated it. The more we learn, the more knowledge there is to transmit. Only at great intervals does a genuine unifying theory come along that makes understanding a field easier; most of the time, advances in knowledge make understanding more difficult for those outside the inner circles of research. That fact alone generates dozens of books a year. As economics and politics become global, and interdependence among the world's peoples increases, more nations and cultures need to be understood. No sooner have you finished the book about Afghanistan than you need to read about Iraq, and North Korea, and Iran, and Sudan, and Georgia. Editors are always scurrying around looking for someone who knows enough to write a book about the latest hotspot. Lyme disease is replaced by West Nile virus or SARS or swine flu, and understanding viruses, vectors, and vaccines becomes more and more complex. "Music appreciation" used to be about Bach, Beethoven, and Brahms, but now it includes popular music, jazz, and newer genres. The visual arts go well beyond Old Masters. The inclusion of popular culture among the areas worthy of study means keeping up with movies, television shows, and comic books—not just literature and theater. Whether we are keeping up or catching up, books remain the most enjoyable and efficient medium.

Novels are here to stay as well. They may take the form of e-books, brought to life by handheld electronic devices that emulate bound volumes, or they may remain in paper and ink. The diversion, absorption, and fascination of fiction are not an artifact of any particular period of human development. Similarly, the need to connect to other people's minds is not completely satisfied by conversation or lectures. Reading nonfiction keeps us in touch with people who know more, think differently, and add to our understanding. The library of the future may be virtual rather than bricks and mortar, and with any luck it will make it easier for readers to find good books. It will also contain fiction and nonfiction, imagination and understanding, escape and commitment.

New digital media are expanding the possibilities of the book by giving nonspecialists access to original sources, scholarly writing, and research methods once available only to those in research universities. If you are interested in classics, you can find all the texts on line, along with translations, glossaries, illustrations, maps, and commentaries. The human genome is mapped on line, with interpretive material and access to the research literature. Multiple copies of William Blake's books can be compared on your computer screen; the images are searchable; and critical work is a mouse click away.[2] Examples abound, and opportunities to engage in independent learning expand daily. The scholars who have created these resources share the motivation of the academic philanthropists who have popularized their fields, and their audience is the same educated public created by the expansion of higher education. Books and the Web are not competitors but partners in the expansion of knowledge and understanding.

NOTES

1. *NON:* THE PREFIX THAT CHANGES WHAT—AND HOW—WE READ

1. Wayne A. Wiegand, *Irrepressible Reformer: A Biography of Melvil Dewey* (Chicago: American Library Association, 1996).

2. Carl Van Doren, *The American Novel* (New York: Macmillan, 1921), 3.

3. Cathy Davidson, "The Life and Times of *Charlotte Temple*," in *Reading in America: Literature and Social History*, ed. Cathy Davidson (Baltimore: Johns Hopkins University Press, 1989), 147–79; Geoffrey Day, *From Fiction to the Novel* (New York: Routledge & Kegan Paul, 1987), 76–110.

4. Steven Starker, *Evil Influences: Crusades Against the Mass Media* (New Brunswick, N.J.: Transaction, 1989), chap. 4. The quotation is from "Moral and Political Tendency of the Modern Novels," *Church of England Quarterly Review* 11 (1842): 287–88, quoted in Kate Flint, *The Woman Reader, 1837–1914* (Oxford: Clarendon Press, 1993), 12. An excellent account of opposition to fiction, the shift in attitudes toward the genre, and the value of novels to their readers is found in chaps. 3 and 4 of Cathy Davidson, *Revolution and the Word: The Rise of the Novel in America* (New York: Oxford University Press, 1986).

5. Hart, *The Popular Book*, 90. On the popularity of the novel in America, and its classifications, see Nina Baym, *Novels, Readers, and Reviewers: Responses to Fiction in Antebellum America* (Ithaca: Cornell University Press, 1984).

6. Dee Garrison, *Apostles of Culture: The Public Librarian and American Society, 1876–1920* (New York: Free Press, 1979), 33–34, 61, 68, 91.

7. Rebecca Goldstein, "Carried from the Couch on the Wings of Enchantment," *New York Times*, December 15, 2002; see also Esther Jane Carrier, *Fiction in Public Libraries, 1876–1900* (New York: Scarecrow Press, 1965).

8. For an interesting analysis of the writing and reading of domestic novels, see Helen Waite Papashvily, *All the Happy Endings: A Study of the Domestic Novel in America, the Women Who Wrote It, the Women Who Read It, in the Nineteenth Century* (New York: Harper, 1956).

9. Edward Wyatt, "Author Is Kicked Out of Oprah Winfrey's Book Club," *New York Times*, January 27, 2006; Motoko Rich, "Gang Memoir, Turning Pages, Is Pure

Fiction," ibid., March 4, 2008; Motoko Rich, "A Family Tree of Literary Fakes," ibid., March 8, 2008; David Mehegan, "Author Admits Making Up Memoir of Surviving Holocaust," *Boston Globe*, February 28, 2008; Motoko Rich and Joseph Berger, "False Memoir of Holocaust Is Canceled," *New York Times*, December 28, 2008.

10. On the colonial period, see David D. Hall, "Readers and Writers in Early New England," in *History of the Book in America*, vol. 1, *The Colonial Book in the Atlantic World* (New York: Cambridge University Press, 2000), 117–51.

11. Paul C. Gutjahr, "No Longer Left Behind: Amazon.com, Reader Response, and the Changing Fortunes of the Christian Novel in America," *Book History* 5 (2002): 209–36.

12. One of the best general histories of American reading remains Hart's *The Popular Book*, and I have used it extensively. For information on bestsellers I have relied on Frank Luther Mott, *Golden Multitudes: The Story of Best Sellers in the United States* (New York: Macmillan, 1947), and Alice Payne Hackett and James Henry Burke, *80 Years of Best Sellers, 1895–1975* (New York: Bowker, 1977). Mott compiled his lists by calculating 1 percent of the U.S. population for the relevant decade and, using data from earlier studies and publishers' records, determining which titles sold at least that many copies. Hackett and Burke compiled their lists from the bestseller lists in the trade magazine *Publishers Weekly*. For more recent periods I have used the *New York Times* bestseller lists. Bestseller data are notoriously inexact (see Laura J. Miller, "The Best-Seller List as Marketing Tool and Historical Fiction," *Book History* 3 [2000]: 286–304), but for the present purposes these are certainly adequate.

13. Davidson, *Revolution and the Word*, 18.

14. For an account of self-help books in the late nineteenth century see Judy Hilkey, *Character Is Capital: Success Manuals and Manhood in Gilded Age America* (Chapel Hill: University of North Carolina Press, 1997).

15. Charles A. Madison, *Book Publishing in America* (New York: McGraw-Hill, 1966), 24.

16. "Reminiscences of Simon Michael Bessie," 1976, Oral History Project of Columbia University, Butler Library, Columbia University, New York, N.Y., pp. 106–8 of microform transcript.

17. Richard Brodhead, *Cultures of Letters: Scenes of Reading and Writing in Nineteenth-Century America* (Chicago: University of Chicago Press, 1993), 22.

18. Davidson, *Revolution and the Word*, 69.

19. On literary journalism, see Chris Anderson, ed., *Literary Nonfiction: Theory, Criticism, Pedagogy* (Carbondale: Southern Illinois University Press, 1989); John C. Hartsock, *A History of American Literary Journalism: The Emergence of a Modern Narrative Form* (Amherst: University of Massachusetts Press, 2000); Norman Sims, ed., *Literary Journalism in the Twentieth Century* (New York: Oxford University Press, 1990); and W. Ross Winterowd, *The Rhetoric of the "Other" Literature* (Carbondale: Southern Illinois University Press, 1990).

20. Roland Barthes, "Écrivains et écrivants," in *Essais critiques* (Paris: Éditions du Seuil, 1964), 147–54.

21. Robert W. Ehrich to Harold Strauss, June 19, 1955, Alfred A. Knopf Collection, box 164, file 10, Harry Ransom Humanities Research Center, University of Texas at Austin.

22. Gould, *Wonderful Life*, 15–16.

23. Strauss to Ehrich, June 22, 1955, Alfred A. Knopf Collection, box 164, file 10.

24. Gail Godwin, "A Novelist Breaches the Border to Nonfiction," *New York Times*, January 15, 2001.

25. Randall H. Waldron, "Rabbit Revised," *American Literature* 56, no. 1 (March 1984): 51–67.

26. Random House Editorial Files, Anne Freedgood, 1961–1984, box 1338, Rare Book and Manuscript Collection, Butler Library, Columbia University, New York, N.Y.

27. Nell, *Lost in a Book*, 2.

28. Sarton is quoted in Beam, *A Great Idea at the Time*, 86.

29. Ibid.

30. Geertz, *Works and Lives*, 4–5.

2. A BRIEF HISTORY OF POPULARIZATION

1. Porter, introduction to *The Popularization of Medicine*, 3.

2. Thomas Wright, *Popular Treatises on Science Written during the Middle Ages in Anglo-Saxon, Anglo-Norman, and English* (London: Historical Society of Science, 1841), vii; Paivi Pahta and Irina Taavitsainen, "Vernacularisation of Scientific and Medical Writing in Its Sociohistorical Context," in their *Medical and Scientific Writing in Late Medieval English* (Cambridge: Cambridge University Press, 2004), 10, 2. See also Wyn Ford, "The Problem of Literacy in Early Modern England," *History* 78, no. 252 (February 1993): 22–37.

3. M. B. Parkes, *Scribes, Scripts and Readers: Studies in the Communication, Presentation and Dissemination of Medieval Texts* (London: Hambledon Press, 1991), 286.

4. Pahta and Taavitsainen, "Vernacularisation," 17.

5. Parkes, *Scribes, Scripts and Readers*, 275–76.

6. Brian Stock, *The Implications of Literacy: Written Language and Models of Interpretation in the Eleventh and Twelfth Centuries* (Princeton: Princeton University Press, 1983), 13–14, 17; James Westfall Thompson, *The Literacy of the Laity in the Middle Ages* (New York: Burt Franklin, 1963), 9.

7. Parkes, *Scribes, Scripts and Readers*, 275.

8. Ibid., 277, 278, 286.

9. Pahta and Taavitsainen, "Vernacularisation," 11, 14.

10. Michael Ullyot, "English *Auctores* and Authorial Readers: Early Modernizations of Chaucer and Lydgate," in *Reading and Literacy in the Middle Ages and Renaissance*, ed. Ian Frederick Moulton, 45–62 (Turnhout, Belg.: Brepols, 2004), 58.

11. Owen Gingerich, *The Book Nobody Read: Chasing the Revolution of Nicolaus Copernicus* (New York: Walker, 2004), 138.

12. David Cressy, *Literacy and the Social Order: Reading and Writing in Tudor and Stuart England* (Cambridge: Cambridge University Press, 1980), 2.

13. Keith Thomas, "The Meaning of Literacy in Early Modern England," in his *The Written Word: Literacy in Transition*, 97–131 (Oxford: Clarendon Press, 1986), 113.

14. Altick, *English Common Reader*, 19–23.

15. W. B. Stephens, "Literacy in England, Scotland, and Wales, 1500–1900," *History of Education Quarterly* 30, no. 4 (Winter 1990): 555; Cressy, *Literacy and the Social Order*, 183.

16. Brown, *Knowledge Is Power*, 48.

17. Victor Bonham Carter, *Authors by Profession*, vol. 1 (London: Society of Authors, 1978), 18–19.

18. Secord, *Victorian Sensation*, 223–24.

19. Yeo, *Encyclopaedic Visions*, 41.

20. Altick, *English Common Reader*, 47.

21. Yeo, *Encyclopaedic Visions*, xii.

22. Ibid., 26, 27.

23. This was the fifteenth edition. The point is noted by Yeo in *Encyclopaedic Visions*, 32.

24. Kenneth E. Carpenter, *The Dissemination of "The Wealth of Nations" in French and in France, 1776–1843* (New York: Bibliographical Society of America, 2002); see also Cheng-chung Lai, ed., *Adam Smith across Nations: Translation and Reception of "The Wealth of Nations"* (New York: Oxford University Press, 2000).

25. Huntington Cairns, "The Popularization of Law: The Requirements of Popularization," *Michigan Law Review* 40, no. 4 (February 1942): 562.

26. Matthew Ramsey, "The Popularization of Medicine in France, 1650–1900," in Porter, *Popularization of Medicine*, 98–99.

27. Norman Gevitz, "'But All Those Authors Are Foreigners': American Literary Nationalism and Domestic Medical Guides," in Porter, *Popularization of Medicine*, 239–41.

28. Woolf, *Reading History*, 7, 107, 317.

29. Altick, *English Common Reader*, 27.

30. Woolf, *Reading History*, 281–93, 274; Altick, *English Common Reader*, 52–53.

31. Altick, *English Common Reader*, 50.

32. Stephens, "Literacy in England," 555; Cressy, *Literacy and the Social Order*, 177.

33. Carl F. Kaestle, "Studying the History of Literacy," in Kaestle et al., *Literacy in the United States*, 25.

34. Altick, *English Common Reader*, 188–204.

35. Ibid., 219–23, 231.

36. Brown, *Knowledge Is Power*, 280.

37. Elizabeth Long, *Book Clubs: Women and the Uses of Reading in Everyday Life*

(Chicago: University of Chicago Press, 2003), 31–58; Elizabeth McHenry, *Forgotten Readers: Recovering the Lost History of African American Literary Societies* (Durham, N.C.: Duke University Press, 2002).

38. Fyfe, *Science and Salvation*, 4, 36.

39. Simon Eliot, "Some Trends in British Book Production, 1800–1919," in *Literature in the Marketplace: Nineteenth-Century British Publishing and Reading Practices*, ed. John O. Jordan and Robert L. Patten, 19–43 (New York: Cambridge University Press, 1995).

40. Altick, *English Common Reader*, 274, 313.

41. Ibid., 194.

42. Fyfe, *Science and Salvation*, 105–6.

43. Jeffrey D. Groves, "The Book Trade Transformed," in *Perspectives in American Book History*, ed. Scott E. Casper, Joanne D. Chaison, and Jeffrey D. Groves (Amherst: University of Massachusetts Press, 2002), 109.

44. William Charvat, *Literary Publishing in America, 1790–1850* (1959; rpr., Amherst: University of Massachusetts Press, 1993), 74–75.

45. Pfitzer, *Popular History and the Literary Marketplace*, 41–43.

46. Casper, *Constructing American Lives*, 5, 238–43.

47. Ronald J. Zboray and Mary Saracino Zboray, *Literary Dollars and Social Sense: A People's History of the Mass Market Book* (New York: Routledge, 2005), xix, xvii–xix.

48. Eugene Exman, *The Brothers Harper* (New York: Harper & Row, 1965); Charles A. Madison, *The Owl Among Colophons: Henry Holt as Publisher and Editor* (New York: Holt, Rinehart & Winston, 1966).

49. Rose, *Intellectual Life*, 20.

50. Both quoted ibid., 130.

51. Secord, *Victorian Sensation*, 336–63, quotes at 341, 346, 351.

52. Charles W. Eliot, quoted in Adam Kirsch, "The 'Five-foot Shelf' Reconsidered," *Harvard Magazine*, November–December 2001, 5–56; quote at 52.

53. Charles W. Eliot, introduction to the Harvard Classics (New York: Collier, 1909), 1.

54. See Beam, *A Great Idea at the Time*, and Rubin, *Middlebrow Culture*.

55. Rubin, *Middlebrow Culture*, 237.

56. Ibid., 263.

3. A HIGHLY EDUCATED PUBLIC

1. The most recent historical study is William J. Reese, *America's Public Schools: From the Common School to "No Child Left Behind"* (Baltimore: Johns Hopkins University Press, 2005). R. Freeman Butts, *Public Education in the United States: From Revolution to Reform* (New York: Holt, Rinehart & Winston, 1978) contains useful bibliographical notes. For an analysis of educational history relating specifically to race, class, and ethnicity, see Ira Katznelson and Margaret Weir, *Schooling for All: Class, Race, and the Decline of the Democratic Ideal* (New York: Basic Books,

1985). On early literacy, see E. Jennifer Monaghan, *Learning to Read and Write in Colonial America* (Amherst: University of Massachusetts Press, 2005); William J. Gilmore-Lehne, *Reading Becomes a Necessity of Life: Material and Cultural Life in Rural New England, 1780–1835* (Knoxville: University of Tennessee Press, 1989); and Kenneth A. Lockridge, *Literacy in Colonial New England: An Enquiry into the Social Context of Literacy in the Early Modern West* (New York: W. W. Norton, 1974). For the late nineteenth and early twentieth centuries, see Kaestle et al., *Literacy in the United States.*

2. George S. Counts, *The Selective Character of American Secondary Education* (Chicago: University of Chicago, 1922; rpr., New York: Arno Press and the *New York Times*, 1969), 3, 135–48; Butts, *Public Education*, chap. 11.

3. Studies that show the relationship between reading and education, performed throughout the twentieth century, include Lester Asheim, "What Do Adults Read," in *Adult Reading: The Fifty-fifth Yearbook of the National Society for the Study of Education* (Chicago: University of Chicago Press, 1956); William S. Gray and Ruth Monroe, *The Reading Interests and Habits of Adults* (New York: Macmillan, 1930); William S. Gray and Bernice Rogers, *Maturity in Reading* (Chicago: University of Chicago Press, 1956); Herbert H. Hyman, Charles R. Wright, and John Shelton Reed, *The Enduring Effects of Education* (Chicago: University of Chicago Press, 1975); Henry C. Link and Harry Arthur Hopf, *People and Books* (New York: Book Industry Committee, Book Manufacturers' Institute, 1945); Larry J. Mikulecky, Nancy Leavitt Shanklin, and David C. Caverly, *Adult Reading Habits, Attitudes, and Motivations: A Cross-Sectional Study* (Bloomington: Indiana University School of Education, 1979); Rhey Boyd Parsons, "A Study of Adult Reading" (master's thesis, University of Chicago, 1923); Amiel T. Sharon, "What Do Adults Read," *Reading Research Quarterly* 9, no. 2 (1973–74): 148–69; and Nicholas Zill and Marianne Winglee, *Who Reads Literature: The Future of the United States as a Nation of Readers* (Washington, D.C.: Seven Locks Press, 1990).

4. James Dickey, interview on *Fresh Air*, NPR, September 30, 1993; John Y. Cole, ed., *Books in Action: The Armed Services Editions* (Washington, D.C.: Library of Congress, 1984), 9–10.

5. Eudora Welty, *One Writer's Beginnings* (New York: Warner, 1984), 5, 9; Jorge Luis Borges, "Libraries, Books and Reading," in *Reading for All* (Newark, Del.: International Reading Association, 1973), 4; Richard Rodriguez, *Hunger of Memory: The Education of Richard Rodriguez: An Autobiography* (New York: Bantam, 1983), 61–62.

6. Hyman, Wright, and Reed, *Enduring Effects*, 85–91; John P. Robinson, "Mass Media Usage by the College Graduate," in *A Degree and What Else: Correlates and Consequences of a College Education*, ed. Stephen B Withey (New York: McGraw-Hill, 1971), 95–109.

7. Robinson, "Mass Media Usage," 95; Leonard Wood, "Demographics of Mass Market Consumers," *Book Research Quarterly* 3, no.1 (Spring 1987): 31–39; response to the author's survey, described in chapter 8, n. 22.

8. Gallup study cited in Leonard A. Wood, "Demographics of Mass Market Consumers," *Book Research Quarterly* 3 (Spring 1987): 35–36; reader quote from the author's survey.

9. Pierre Bourdieu, *Distinction: A Social Critique of the Judgement of Taste*, translated by Richard Nice (London: Routledge & Kegan Paul, 1984), 22–28; Jennifer Moses, "Don't Take Boswell to the Beach," *New York Times*, July 8, 2001.

10. "The Reminiscences of Harry Scherman," interviews conducted by Louis M. Starr, December 1954–November 1955, 117–20, Oral History Collection of Columbia University, Series I, Butler Library, Columbia University, New York, N.Y.

11. Lawrence Lipking, "Competitive Reading," *New Republic*, October 2, 1989, 28–35; Moses, "Don't Take Boswell."

12. Link and Hopf, *People and Books*, 155–56.

13. Peter F. Drucker, "Politics in the West: Totalitarian and Democratic," in *The Democratic Imagination: Dialogues on the Work of Irving Louis Horowitz*, ed. Ray C. Rist (New Brunswick, N.J.: Transaction, 1994), 106. Figures on enrollment vary, depending on whether one uses data from the American Council on Education, the U.S. Office of Education, or the U.S. Census. The numbers in this paragraph are drawn from Joseph Ben-David, *American Higher Education: Directions Old and New* (New York: McGraw-Hill, 1972), 1; Clark Kerr, "Higher Education Cannot Escape History: The 1990s," in *An Agenda for the New Decade*, ed. Larry W. Jones and Franz A. Nowotny (San Francisco: Jossey-Bass, 1990), 6; Alain Touraine, *The Academic System in American Society* (New York: McGraw-Hill, 1974); and the U.S. Census for 2000.

14. Clark Kerr, *The Great Transformation in Higher Education, 1960–1980* (Albany: SUNY Press, 1991), xiii; GAO-03-341, *A Report to the Secretary of Education*, February 2003.

15. Julian B. Roebuck and Komanduri S. Murty, *Historically Black Colleges and Universities: Their Place in American Higher Education* (Westport, Conn.: Praeger, 1993), chap. 2; Kerr, "Higher Education Cannot Escape History," 10; Richard M. Freeland, *Academia's Golden Age: Universities in Massachusetts, 1945–1970* (New York: Oxford University Press, 1992), 88.

16. Kerr, "Higher Education Cannot Escape History," 10.

17. "McGuffey Was Never Like This," *Fortune*, December 1959, 109.

18. Eugene Exman, *The House of Harper: One Hundred and Fifty Years of Publishing* (New York: Harper & Row, 1967), 299–302; Tebbel, *The Great Change*, 167.

19. A. Wayne Anderson, ed., *Wiley: One Hundred and Seventy-five Years of Publishing* (New York: John Wiley, 1982), 151; Donald S. Lamm, "A Brief History of W. W. Norton & Company," manuscript, October 4, 1993, author's possession.

20. *American Library Annual* (New York: Bowker, 1956), 83; *Bowker Annual* 6 (1961): 53; Kenneth C. Davis, *Two-Bit Culture: The Paperbacking of America* (Boston: Houghton Mifflin, 1984), 266.

21. *Bowker Annual* 6 (1961): 55; 8 (1963): 59; 12 (1967): 46.

22. Kerr, *Great Transformation*, xii, xiii.

23. Christopher Jencks and David Riesman, *The Academic Revolution*, 2d ed. (Garden City, N.Y.: Doubleday, 1968), 23.

24. Warren Bryan Martin, "Alternative Approaches to Curricular Coherence," in *In Opposition to the Core Curriculum: Alternative Models for Undergraduate Education*, ed. James W. Hall with Barbara L. Kevles (Westport, Conn.: Greenwood Press, 1982), 47.

25. The literature on "the canon" is voluminous, but the basic texts are Bloom, *Closing of the American Mind*; Lynne V. Cheney, *Humanities in America: A Report to the President, the Congress, and the American People* (Washington, D.C.: National Endowment for the Humanities, 1988); Darryl J. Gless and Barbara Herrnstein Smith, eds., *The Politics of Liberal Education* (Durham, N.C.: Duke University Press, 1992); Hirsch, *Cultural Literacy*; George Levine, ed., *Speaking for the Humanities*, American Council of Learned Societies Occasional Paper no. 7, 1988; and Arthur M. Schlesinger Jr., *The Disuniting of America: Reflections on a Multicultural Society*, 2d ed. (New York: W. W. Norton, 1998).

26. Ben-David, *American Higher Education*, 67.

27. Kerr, *Great Transformation*, 281; Martin, "Alternative Approaches," 47.

28. G. S. Rousseau, "Science Books and Their Readers in the Eighteenth Century," in *Books and Their Readers in Eighteenth-Century England*, ed. Isabel Rivers (New York: St. Martin's, 1982), 208, 210.

4. FROM SNOW TO SOKAL

1. Green, *Science and the Shabby Curate*, 3.

2. Peter Dizikes, "Our Two Cultures," *New York Times Book Review*, March 22, 2009, 23.

3. Snow, *The Two Cultures*, 2, 5, 17.

4. Leavis, *Two Cultures?*, 10, 15, 22, 26–27.

5. Trilling, "Science, Literature and Culture," 463, 468, 469.

6. Leavis, *Two Cultures?*, 29.

7. John R. Thelin, *A History of American Higher Education* (Baltimore: Johns Hopkins University Press, 2004), chap. 6.

8. Rodney W. Nichols, "Federal Science Policy and Universities: Consequences of Success," *Daedalus* 122, no. 4 (Fall 1993): 197–224.

9. Alain Touraine, *The Academic System in American Society* (New York: McGraw-Hill, 1974), 132.

10. Richard Freeland, *Academia's Golden Age: Universities in Massachusetts, 1945–1970* (New York: Oxford University Press, 1992), 9.

11. Robert Nisbet, *The Degradation of the Academic Dogma: The University in America, 1945–1970* (New York: Basic Books, 1971), 72.

12. U.S.. Bureau of the Census, *Statistical Abstract of the United States, 1993*, tables 149, 417, 975.

13. Walter P. Metzger, "The Academic Profession in the United States," in *The Academic Profession: National, Disciplinary, and Institutional Settings*, ed. Burton R. Clark (Berkeley: University of California Press, 1987), 124, 154.

14. For the history of university presses, see Hawes, *To Advance Knowledge*, chaps.1 and 2. The publication figures are drawn from Hawes, 11–12, and derived from *The Association of American University Presses Directory*, 1982 and 1992.

15. Hawes, *To Advance Knowledge*, 12.

16. Cited in Carolyn J. Mooney, "In 2 Years, a Million Refereed Articles, 300,000 Books, Chapters, Monographs," *Chronicle of Higher Education*, May 22, 1991, A17.

17. Jack Meadows, "Too Much of a Good Thing? Quality Versus Quantity," in *The International Serials Industry*, ed. Hazel Woodward and Stella Pilling (Aldershot, Eng.: Gower Publishing, 1993), 25.

18. Mooney, "In 2 Years," A17; *Scholarly Communication: The Report of the National Enquiry* (Baltimore: Johns Hopkins University Press, 1979), 40; Irving Louis Horowitz, *Communicating Ideas: The Politics of Scholarly Publishing*, 2d ed. (New Brunswick, N.J.: Transaction, 1991), 193.

19. Derek J. De Solla Price, *Little Science, Big Science . . . And Beyond* (New York: Columbia University Press, 1986).

20. David P. Hamilton, "Publishing By—and For?—the Numbers," *Science*, December 7, 1990, 1331–32.

21. Freeland, *Academia's Golden Age*, 95.

22. Gerald Graff, *Professing Literature: An Institutional History* (Chicago: University of Chicago Press, 1987), 121.

23. *Scholarly Communication*, 46–47.

24. Stephen E. Atkins, *The Academic Library in the American University* (Chicago: American Library Association, 1991), 127 (table 5.1).

25. Nisbet, *Degradation*, 108–9.

26. Atkins, *Academic Library*, 130 (table 5.3), drawn from Burton R. Clark, *The Academic Life: Small Worlds, Different Worlds* (Princeton: Carnegie Foundation for the Advancement of Teaching, 1987), 77.

27. Freeland, *Academia's Golden Age*, 103.

28. Henry Rosovsky, *The University: An Owner's Manual* (New York: W. W. Norton, 1990), 89.

29. Levy is quoted in Freeland, *Academia's Golden Age*, 107.

30. W. H. Auden, *The Dyer's Hand*, quoted in Green, *Science and the Shabby Curate*, facing p. 1.

31. *Nature* 384 (December 12, 1996): 497; ellipses in original.

32. Quoted in Orlando Patterson, "The Last Sociologist," *New York Times*, May 19, 2002.

33. Ibid.

34. John Higham, *History: Professional Scholarship in America*, rev. ed. (Baltimore: Johns Hopkins University Press, 1989), 68–69.

35. Pfitzer, *Popular History and the Literary Marketplace*, 61–64.

36. Higham, *History*, 78.

37. Bruce Kuklick, *The Rise of American Philosophy: Cambridge, Massachusetts, 1860–1930* (New Haven: Yale University Press, 1977), 571, 572.

38. Jeffrey Henderson, "The Training of Classicists," 91, in *Classics: A Discipline and Profession in Crisis?*, ed. Phyllis Culham and Lowell Edmunds (Lanham, Md.: University Press of America, 1989).

39. Vincent B. Leitch, *American Literary Criticism from the Thirties to the Eighties* (New York: Columbia University Press, 1988), 62.

40. Elizabeth Bruss, *Beautiful Theories: The Spectacle of Discourse in Contemporary Criticism* (Baltimore: Johns Hopkins University Press, 1982), 14.

41. Ibid., 20.

42. Ibid., 4; Frank Lentricchia, *After the New Criticism* (Chicago: University of Chicago Press, 1980), xiii.

43. Harold Perkin, *The Rise of Professional Society: England Since 1880* (New York: Routledge, 1989), 397–98.

44. Sokal, "Transgressing the Boundaries," 217.

45. Sokal, "A Physicist Experiments," 62.

46. "Science Wars and the Need for Respect and Rigour," *Nature* 385 (January 30, 1997): 373.

5. ACADEMIC PHILANTHROPISTS

1. Paulos, *Innumeracy*, 80.

2. Freidson, *Professional Powers*, 15–16.

3. Keay Davidson, *Carl Sagan: A Life* (New York: John Wiley, 1999), 391–92.

4. Ferris, "Risks and Rewards," 264.

5. Quoted in Ian Parker, "Richard Dawkins's Evolution," *New Yorker*, September 9, 1996, 43.

6. Raymond A. Sokolov, "Talk with Stephen Jay Gould," *New York Times Book Review*, November 20, 1977, 50, 52.

7. Thomas Balogh, review of *The Age of Uncertainty*, *Journal of Economic Literature* 15, no. 3 (1977): 932–33.

8. Larissa MacFarquhar, "The Prophet of Decline," *New Yorker*, September 30, 2002, 94.

9. Mizzi van der Pluijm, "Non-fiction and the Netherlands: A Problematic Relationship," *Publishing Research Quarterly* 14, no. 2 (1998): 27.

10. Luey, "Are Fame and Fortune the Kiss of Death?"

11. Quoted in William E. Mitchell, "Communicating Culture: Margaret Mead and the Practice of Popular Anthropology," in MacClancy and McDonaugh, *Popularizing Anthropology*, 123.

12. Robert E. Ricklefs, review of *The Diversity of Life*, *Science* 259, no. 5102 (1993): 1774; Alan B. Spitzer, review of *Citizens*, *Journal of Modern History* 65, no. 1 (1993): 176.

13. Alan Campbell, "Tricky Tropes: Styles of the Popular and the Pompous," in MacClancy and McDonaugh, *Popularizing Anthropology*, 73.

14. Morris Janowitz, *American Journal of Sociology* 80, no. 1 (1974): 235; Keith

Curry Lance, *Social Science Quarterly* 62, no. 2 (1981): 394; Linda Brodkey, *Academic Writing as Social Practice* (Philadelphia: Temple University Press, 1987), 25.

15. Christian de Duve, *Nature* 383 (October 31, 1996): 771–72.

16. Stephen Jay Gould, interview by Michael Krasny, *Mother Jones*, January/February 1997, www.motherjones.com/politics/1997/01/stephen-jay-gould, accessed August 31, 2009.

17. Bibby, *Testimony of the Spade*, vii.

18. Galbraith, *A Life in Our Times*, 535–36.

19. Donald P. Hayes, "The Growing Inaccessibility of Science," *Nature* 356 (April 30, 1992): 739–40.

20. Ibid., 740.

21. Patricia Nelson Limerick, "Dancing with Professors: The Trouble with Academic Prose," *New York Times Book Review*, October 31, 1993, 22–24.

22. Paul Starr, *The Social Transformation of American Medicine* (New York: Basic Books, 1982), 32, 34, 87.

23. Haber, *Quest for Authority*, 15.

24. Hudson, *Jargon of the Professions.*

25. Denis Dutton, "Language Crimes," *Wall Street Journal*, February 5, 1999; also available at www.denisdutton.com/language_crimes.htm.

26. Carol Berkenhotter, Thomas N. Huckin, and John Ackerman, "Social Context and Socially Constructed Texts: The Initiation of a Graduate Student into a Writing Research Community," in *Textual Dynamics of the Professions: Historical and Contemporary Studies of Writing in Professional Communities*, ed. Charles Bazerman and James Paradis (Madison: University of Wisconsin Press, 1991), 210–11.

27. Campbell, "Tricky Tropes," 79.

28. Paul Fussell, *Doing Battle: The Making of a Skeptic* (Boston: Little, Brown, 1996), 252; Gould is quoted in Claudia Dreifus, "Primordial Beasts, Creationists and the Mighty Yankees," *New York Times*, December 21, 1999.

29. Edward O. Wilson, interview by Toby Lester, "All for One for All," *Atlantic Unbound*, March 18, 1998, www.theatlantic.com/unbound/bookauth/ba980318.htm, accessed August 31, 2009; Dreifus, "Primordial Beasts"; Galbraith, *A Life in Our Times*, 335, 312, 320.

30. *Contemporary Authors* telephone interview, September 15, 1987, in Literature Resource Center 3.1, Author Resource Pages, s.v. Robert Jay Lifton.

31. Edward O. Wilson, interview by Amanda Paulson, *Christian Science Monitor*, April 25, 2002.

32. Steven Pinker, interview by Gayle Feldman, *Publishers Weekly*, December 20, 1993, 27.

33. Quoted in Laura Wood, "Targeting the Educated Lay Audience: Publishers' Perceptions and Strategies" (M.A. thesis, New York University, 1994), 52.

34. Edward O. Wilson, interview by Gregory McNamee, www.human-nature.com/interviews/wilson.html, accessed August 31, 2009.

35. Harold Strauss to Ruth Moore, October 7, 1952, Alfred A. Knopf Collection, Harry Ransom Humanities Research Center, University of Texas at Austin, box 135, file 3.

36. Peter Gay, interview by Wendy Smith, *Publishers Weekly*, January 6, 1984, 87; Paul Fussell, interview by Robert Dahlin, *Publishers Weekly*, October 3, 1980, 8; Leonard V. Smith, "Paul Fussell's *The Great War and Modern Memory*: Twenty-Five Years Later," *History and Theory* 40, no. 2 (May 2001): 245; Editorial Files, Jason Epstein, box 1377, Random House Collection, Columbia Rare Books and Manuscripts Collection, Butler Library, Columbia University, New York, N.Y.; Elaine Pagels, interview by Jenny Schuessler, *Publishers Weekly*, July 31, 1995, 59.

37. Matthew Rose, "History Inc.," *Wall Street Journal*, August 20, 2001.

38. Editorial Files, Anne Freedgood, boxes 1338 and 1339, Random House Collection, Columbia.

6. WRITING TO BE READ

1. Levy and Salvadori, *Why Buildings Fall*, 76–79. In this and subsequent chapters, wherever possible, I have included the sources of quotations in the text itself, with parenthetical page numbers. Complete publication information about these books can be found in the bibliography.

2. Ceram, *Gods, Graves, and Scholars*, vi.

3. Harold Strauss, White Sheet, n.d., Alfred A. Knopf Collection, Harry Ransom Humanities Research Center, University of Texas at Austin, box 1422, file 2.

4. Strauss to Ruth Moore, July 5, 1951, and October 7, 1952, Knopf Collection, box 135, file 3.

5. Simon Schama, interview by Missy Daniel, *Publishers Weekly*, May 17, 1991, 47.

6. Strauss to Moore, June 10, 1953, Knopf Collection, box 135, file 4.

7. Strauss to Moore, June 12, 1958, Knopf Collection, box 239, file 5.

8. Barrow, *Pi in the Sky*, 21.

9. For the fate of the narrative tradition in an earlier period, see Pfitzer, *Popular History and the Literary Marketplace*.

10. "David Riesman, Sociologist Whose 'Lonely Crowd' Became a Best Seller, Dies at 92," *New York Times*, May 11, 2002.

11. Riesman file, Ken McCormick Collection of the Records of Doubleday & Company, Library of Congress, box 95, folder 2.

12. For an excellent account of the writing and reception of *Silent Spring*, see Murphy, *What a Book Can Do*.

13. This paragraph summarizes the findings of one of my students, Elizabeth Pulcini, in "A Comparison of Different Writing Styles in Popular Scientific Literature Describing Viral Outbreaks and Theories in Emerging Viruses," a research paper written at Arizona State University in 2002.

14. Geertz, *Works and Lives*, 110–11.

15. Ibid., 58.

16. Ibid., 44–45.

7. FROM AUTHOR TO READER

1. Michael Korda, *Another Life: A Memoir of Other People* (New York: Random House, 1999), 57–58; Emily Loose, quoted in Laura Wood, "Targeting the Educated Lay Audience: Publishers' Perceptions and Strategies" (M.A. thesis, New York University, 1994), 43; Harold Strauss to Ruth Moore, April 25, 1951, Knopf Collection, Harry Ransom Humanities Research Center, University of Texas at Austin, box 135, file 3.

2. On the *New Yorker* in the postwar years, see Mary F. Corey, *The World Through a Monocle: The New Yorker at Midcentury* (Cambridge: Harvard University Press, 1999).

3. Memo, Jason Epstein to Non Fiction Committee, April 3, 1952, Riesman folder, box 95, folder 2, Ken McCormick Collection of the Records of Doubleday & Company, Library of Congress.

4. Cass Canfield, *Up and Down and Around* (New York: Harper's Magazine Press, 1971), 177.

5. Molly Colin, "Witold Rybczynski: A Self-Described Workaholic, He Chose Leisure as His Latest Subject," *Publishers Weekly*, July 25, 1991, 34; Robert Coles, interview by Dulcy Brainard, *Publishers Weekly*, November 16, 1990, 41.

6. Barber quoted in Wood, "Targeting the Educated Lay Audience," 53.

7. Piatigorsky file, Ken McCormick Collection, Library of Congress, box 87, files 3 and 4.

8. Canfield, *Up and Down*, 202–3.

9. Luey, "Leading the Reader Gently."

10. Canfield, *Up and Down*, 183.

11. Ibid., 202.

12. Editorial Files, Jason Epstein, box 1365, Random House Collection, Rare Books and Manuscripts Library, Butler Library, Columbia University.

13. Emily Loose, quoted in Wood, "Targeting the Educated Lay Audience," 43.

14. Thomas Weyr, "John Brockman and the Science of Deal-Making," *Publishers Weekly*, February 7, 1994, 33–35.

15. Adam Yarmolinsky to Ken McCormick, October 1, 1957, box 19, folder 7, Ken McCormick Collection, Library of Congress.

16. Harold Strauss to Ruth Moore, October 7, 1952, box 135, file 3; to Carleton Coon, September 3, 1957, box 204, file 2; to Geoffrey Bibby, June 29, 1962, box 179, file 8; to Carleton Coon, August 19, 1960, box 279, file 2; all in Knopf Collection, Ransom Humanities Research Center.

17. Carleton Coon, *The Story of Man* (New York: Knopf, 1954), xi.

18. Editorial Files, Anne Freedgood, Freedgood to Sagan, May 27, 1980, box 1338, Random House Collection, Columbia University.

19. For an extended scholarly discussion of paratext see Gennette, *Paratexts*; for a more entertaining, but equally scholarly, survey of the subject see Hauptman, *Documentation*.

20. One exception is Nicholson Baker's *The Mezzanine*, which has genuine notes. On notes to fiction, see Hauptman, *Documentation*, 56–70.

21. On a recent trend toward including bibliographies in fiction, see Julia Bosman, "Loved His New Novel, and What a Bibliography," *New York Times*, December 5, 2006.

22. Bruce Catton to Walter I. Bradbury, September 28, 1950, box 16, folder 1, Ken McCormick Collection, Library of Congress.

23. Kevin Jackson, *Invisible Forms: A Guide to Literary Curiosities* (New York: St. Martin's, 1999), 152.

24. Alan D. Watson, review of Oscar Handlin and Lilian Handlin, *Liberty in America*, *Journal of American History*, 74, no. 2 (1987): 494.

25. Anonymous survey respondent; see note 22, chapter 8.

26. Catton to Bradbury, November 5 and 6, 1951, box 16, folder 2, Ken McCormick Collection, Library of Congress.

27. John C. Burnham, review of Gay in *Journal of the Behavioral Sciences* 26, no. 2 (1990): 196; Eric Schatzberg, review of Petroski, in *Technology and Culture* 40, no. 1 (1999): 153.

28. Forum section, *William and Mary Quarterly* 59, 1 (2002): 203–67. The *New York Times* covered the Bellesiles dispute on September 21, 2000, December 8, 2001, and February 9, October 27, and December 14, 2002; see also History News Network (www.hnn.us), January 14, 2003, and archived articles.

29. See Grafton, *The Footnote*, for the history of the use of footnotes in historical scholarship. Both its title (as arranged on the cover) and the text contain footnotes.

30. Elaine Pagels, interview by Jenny Schuessler, *Publishers Weekly*, July 31, 1995, 59.

31. Alfred A. Knopf to Lyman Butterfield, May 24, 1955, box 162, folder 6, Knopf Collection, Ransom Humanities Research Center.

32. Luey, "Leading the Reader Gently"; John Pitts and Emily Loose, quoted in Wood, "Targeting the Educated Lay Audience," 31–32, 41.

33. Hugh Williamson, *Methods of Book Design*, 3d ed. (New Haven: Yale University Press, 1983), 354–55.

34. Kit Allen, quoted in Wood, "Targeting the Educated Lay Audience," 46.

35. Emily Loose, quoted in Wood, "Targeting the Educated Lay Audience," 47.

36. Williamson, *Methods*, 354–55.

37. Doniger used this description in a June 1992 address to the Association of American University Presses. She confirmed the quote and gave permission for its use in an e-mail of December 4, 2002. See also her "The Academic Snob Goes to Market," *Scholarly Publishing* 24, 1 (October 1992): 3–12.

38. Angus Cameron to Fred Rosenau, September 11 and 21, 1961, box 328, file 6, Knopf Collection, Ransom Humanities Research Center.

39. Kit Allen, quoted in Wood, "Targeting the Educated Lay Audience," 46.

40. On bookselling, see Laura J. Miller, *Reluctant Capitalists: Bookselling and the Culture of Consumption* (Chicago: University of Chicago Press, 2007).

8. WHY WE READ

1. Italo Calvino, *If on a Winter's Night a Traveler*, trans. William Weaver (New York: Harcourt Brace, 1981): 49, 149.

2. Nell, *Lost in a Book*, 238–39, 236.

3. See also Wendy Simonds, *Women and Self-Help Culture: Reading Between the Lines* (New Brunswick, N.J.: Rutgers University Press, 1992), 216.

4. Russell Lynes, "Highbrow, Lowbrow, Middlebrow," *Harper's*, February 1949, reprinted as chap. 17 of his *The Tastemakers* (New York: Harper & Bros., 1954), 333.

5. Seneca [the Younger], *De tranquillitate animi*, in *Four Dialogues*, ed. C. D. N. Costa, trans. L. D. Reynolds (Warminster, Eng.: Aris and Phillips, 1994), 77–79; F. Scott Fitzgerald, *The Great Gatsby*, chap. 3.

6. Benton, "Too Many Books," 268–97; Baker, "Books as Furniture," 88.

7. Baker, "Books as Furniture," 89.

8. Simonds, *Women and Self-Help Culture*, 44.

9. Escarpit, *Sociology of Literature*, 16.

10. Rose Cohen, *Out of the Shadow* (New York: George H. Doran Co., 1918), 249, quoted in Lee Soltow and Edward Stevens, *The Rise of Literacy and the Common School in the United States: A Socioeconomic Analysis to 1870* (Chicago: University of Chicago Press, 1981), 36.

11. Both quoted in G. Robert Carlsen and Anna Sherrill, *Voices of Readers: How We Come to Love Books* (Urbana, Ill.: National Council of Teachers of English, 1988), 21.

12. Gerald Howard, "The Cultural Ecology of Book Reviewing," *Media Studies Journal* 6, 3 (Summer 1992): 95; Mark Alan Stamaty, "Boox," *New York Times Book Review*, July 21, 2002, 23; Pierre Bayard, *How to Talk About Books You Haven't Read*, trans. Jeffrey Mehlman (New York: Bloomsbury, 2007). Murphy analyzes the importance of reviews in generating discussion in *What a Book Can Do*.

13. Levine, *Highbrow/Lowbrow*, 206, 227. John Carey, *The Intellectuals and the Masses* (Boston: Faber & Faber, 1992), analyzes the similar British ambivalence toward the newly literate at the turn of the twentieth century.

14. Lynes, "Highbrow, Lowbrow, Middlebrow," 313; Dwight Macdonald, "Masscult and Midcult," part 2, *Partisan Review* (Fall 1960): 593, 609, 592.

15. Rubin gives an excellent account of many of these institutions in *Middlebrow Culture*.

16. Rebecca Goldstein, "Carried from the Couch on the Wings of Enchantment," *New York Times*, December 15, 2002. For another reader's responses to Book-of-the-Month Club selections, as well as an analysis of the club, see Radway, *A Feeling for Books*.

17. Interviews with Warren Lynch conducted by Louis M. Starr, 1954, Book-of-the-Month Club, Series IV, Oral History Collection of Columbia University, Butler Library, Columbia University, New York, N.Y., p. 6 of microform transcript.

18. Stella Gibbons, *Cold Comfort Farm* (1932; New York: Penguin, 1994), 105.

19. Woolf is quoted in Lynes, "Highbrow, Lowbrow, Middlebrow," 320; Macdonald, "Masscult and Midcult," part 2, 628; Lynes, 311.

20. Frow, *Cultural Studies*, 23–24.

21. Nell, *Lost in a Book*, 4; Harold L. Wilensky, "Mass Society and Mass Culture: Interdependence or Independence," *American Sociological Review* 29, 2 (April 1964): 173–97; quote from 190.

22. Luey, "Who Reads Nonfiction?" This article reports on a survey based on 53 questionnaires distributed to readers of serious nonfiction. The article also includes the questionnaire. Throughout this book, quotations from anonymous readers not otherwise attributed are drawn from these questionnaires or from further questionnaires collected after the article was written.

23. Frow, *Cultural Studies*, 23.

24. The brouhaha was covered in the *New York Times* on October 21, 24, and 29, and November 4 and 15, 2001, with an editorial appearing on October 30. Letters to the editor appeared on October 25 and November 2 and 4.

25. Frow, *Cultural Studies*, 25.

26. Nell, *Lost in a Book*, 45.

27. On reading groups, see Elizabeth Long, "The Book as Mass Commodity: The Audience Perspective," *Book Research Quarterly* 3, no.1 (Spring 1987): 9–30; "Textual Interpretation as Collective Action" in *The Ethnography of Reading*, ed. Jonathan Boyarin (Berkeley: University of California Press, 1993), 180–211; and *Book Clubs: Women and the Uses of Reading in Everyday Life* (Chicago: University of Chicago Press, 2003).

28. "The Reminiscences of Harry Scherman," interviews conducted by Louis M. Starr, December 1954–November 1955, Book-of-the-Month Club, Series I, Oral History Collection of Columbia University, Butler Library, Columbia University, New York, N.Y., p. 119 of microform transcript.

29. Bookseller and publisher quoted in Walter Kern, "Rediscovering the Joy of Text," *Time*, April 21, 1997, 104; Carolyn K. Reidy, Simon & Schuster, quoted in Dinitia Smith, "In Book Publishing World, Some Reasons for Optimism," *New York Times*, December 6, 2002.

30. Dennis Overbye, "Cracking the Cosmic Code with a Little Help from Dr. Hawking," *New York Times*, December 11, 2001; Nell, *Lost in a Book*, 140, 164.

31. Reader reviews on Amazon.com for twenty-five of the titles discussed in this book.

32. Overbye, "Cracking the Cosmic Code."

33. Richard Bernstein, "Calculus for the Literacy, if Not for the Numbers," *New York Times*, February 7, 1996; reader quoted in Overbye, "Cracking the Cosmic Code."

AFTERWORD: POPULARIZATION AND THE FUTURE OF THE BOOK

1. *New York Times Book Review*, January 27, 1988.

2. See www.perseus.tufts.edu; www.genome.gov; www.blakearchive.org.

SELECTED BIBLIOGRAPHY

Altick, Richard D. *The English Common Reader: A Social History of the Mass Reading Public, 1800–1900.* 2d ed. Columbus: Ohio State University Press, 1998.

Ambrose, Stephen. *Undaunted Courage: Meriwether Lewis, Thomas Jefferson, and the Opening of the American West.* New York: Simon & Schuster, 1996.

Baker, Nicholson. "Books as Furniture." *New Yorker,* June 12, 1995, 84–92.

Barrow, John D. *The Origin of the Universe.* New York: Basic Books, 1994.

———. *Pi in the Sky.* Oxford: Clarendon, 1992.

Beam, Alex. *A Great Idea at the Time: The Rise, Fall, and Curious Afterlife of the Great Books.* New York: Public Affairs, 2008.

Bell, Daniel. *The Coming of Post-Industrial Society.* New York: Basic Books, 1973.

———. *The End of Ideology.* Glencoe, Ill.: Free Press, 1960.

Bellesiles, Michael. *Arming America: The Origins of a National Gun Culture.* New York: Knopf, 2000.

Bemis, Samuel Flagg. *John Quincy Adams and the Foundations of American Foreign Policy.* New York: Knopf, 1949.

Benton, Megan. "'Too Many Books': Book Ownership and Cultural Identity in the 1920s." *American Quarterly* 49, no. 2 (1997): 268–97.

Berlinski, David. *A Tour of the Calculus.* New York: Pantheon, 1995.

Bibby, Geoffrey. *The Testimony of the Spade.* New York: Knopf, 1956.

Bloom, Allan. *The Closing of the American Mind.* New York: Simon & Schuster, 1987.

Brodie, Fawn. *Thomas Jefferson: An Intimate History.* New York: W. W. Norton, 1974.

Bronowski, Jacob. *The Ascent of Man.* Boston: Little, Brown, 1974.

Brown, Richard D. *Knowledge Is Power: The Diffusion of Information in Early America, 1700–1865.* New York: Oxford University Press, 1989.

Carson, Rachel. *Silent Spring.* Boston: Houghton Mifflin, 1962.

Carter, Stephen. *The Culture of Disbelief: How American Law and Politics Trivialize Religious Devotion.* New York: Basic Books, 1993.

Casper, Scott E. *Constructing American Lives: Biography and Culture in Nineteenth-Century America.* Chapel Hill: University of North Carolina Press, 1999.

Catton, Bruce. *Glory Road*. Garden City, N.Y.: Doubleday, 1952.

———. *Mr. Lincoln's Army*. Garden City, N.Y.: Doubleday, 1962.

Ceram, C. W. [Kurt Marek]. *Gods, Graves, and Scholars*. New York: Knopf, 1951.

Clark, Kenneth. *Civilisation: A Personal View*. New York: Harper & Row, 1969.

Cooke, Alistair. *America*. New York: Knopf, 1973.

Darwin, Charles. *On the Origin of Species*. London: J. Murray, 1859.

———. *The Voyage of the Beagle*. London: Smith, Elder, 1839.

Degler, Carl N. *At Odds*. New York: Oxford University Press, 1980.

de Kruif, Paul. *The Microbe Hunters*. New York: Harcourt, Brace, 1932.

Durant, Will. *The Story of Philosophy*. New York: Simon & Schuster, 1926.

Durant, Will, and Ariel Durant. *The Story of Civilization*. New York: Simon & Schuster, 1935–75.

Escarpit, Robert. *Sociology of Literature*. Translated by Ernest Pick. Painesville, Ohio: Lake Erie College Press, 1965.

Ferris, Timothy. "The Risks and Rewards of Popularizing Science." *Chronicle of Higher Education*, April 4, 1997, 264.

Fortey, Richard. *Trilobite! Eyewitness to Evolution*. New York: Knopf, 2000.

Freidson, Eliot. *Professional Powers: A Study of the Institutionalization of Formal Knowledge*. Chicago: University of Chicago Press, 1986.

Frow, John. *Cultural Studies and Cultural Value*. Oxford: Clarendon Press, 1995.

Fukuyama, Francis. *The End of History and the Last Man*. New York: Free Press, 1992.

Fussell, Paul. *The Great War and Modern Memory*. New York: Oxford University Press, 1975.

Fyfe, Aileen. *Science and Salvation: Evangelical Popular Science Publishing in Victorian Britain*. Chicago: University of Chicago Press, 2004.

Galbraith, John Kenneth. *The Affluent Society*. Boston: Houghton Mifflin, 1958.

———. *The Age of Uncertainty*. Boston: Houghton Mifflin, 1977.

———. *A Life in Our Times: Memoirs*. Boston: Houghton Mifflin, 1981.

———. *The New Industrial State*. Boston: Houghton Mifflin, 1967.

Garrett, Laurie. *Betrayal of Trust: The Collapse of Global Public Health*. New York: Hyperion, 2000.

———. *The Coming Plague: Newly Emerging Diseases in a World Out of Balance*. New York: Farrar, Straus & Giroux, 1994.

Gay, Peter. *The Education of the Senses*. New York: Oxford University Press, 1984.

———. *Freud: A Life for Our Times*. New York: W. W. Norton, 1988.

Geertz, Clifford. *Works and Lives: The Anthropologist as Author*. Stanford: Stanford University Press, 1988.

Gennette, Gérard. *Paratexts: Thresholds of Interpretation*. Translated by Jane E. Lewitt. New York: Cambridge University Press, 1997.

Gordon-Reed, Annette. *The Hemingses of Monticello: An American Family*. New York: W. W. Norton, 2008.

Gould, Stephen Jay. *Full House: The Spread of Excellence from Plato to Darwin*. New York: Harmony, 1996.

————. *The Mismeasure of Man.* New York: W. W. Norton, 1981.

————. *Wonderful Life: The Burgess Shale and the Nature of History.* New York: W. W. Norton, 1989.

Grafton, Anthony. *The Footnote: A Curious History.* Cambridge: Harvard University Press, 1997.

Green, Martin. *Science and the Shabby Curate of Poetry: Essays About the Two Cultures.* New York: W. W. Norton, 1965.

Guillen, Michael. *Bridges to Infinity: The Human Side of Mathematics.* Boston: Houghton Mifflin, 1983.

————. *Five Equations that Changed the World: The Power and Poetry of Mathematics.* New York: Hyperion, 1995.

Haber, Samuel. *The Quest for Authority and Honor in the American Professions, 1750–1900.* Chicago: University of Chicago Press, 1991.

Handlin, Oscar. *The Uprooted: The Epic Story of the Great Migrations That Made the American People.* Boston: Little, Brown, 1951.

Hart, James D. *The Popular Book: A History of America's Literary Taste.* New York: Oxford University Press, 1950.

Hauptman, Robert. *Documentation: A History and Critique of Attribution, Commentary, Glosses, Marginalia, Notes, Bibliographies, Works-Cited Lists, and Citation Indexing and Analysis.* Jefferson, N.C.: McFarland, 2008.

Hawes, Gene R. *To Advance Knowledge: A Handbook on University Press Publishing.* New York: American University Press Services, 1967.

Hawking, Stephen. *A Brief History of Time: From the Big Bang to Black Holes.* New York: Bantam, 1988.

————. *The Universe in a Nutshell.* New York: Bantam, 2001.

Heilbroner, Robert. *The Worldly Philosophers: The Lives, Times, and Ideas of the Great Economic Thinkers.* New York: Simon & Schuster, 1953.

Henig, Robin Marantz. *A Dancing Matrix.* New York: Knopf, 1993.

Herrnstein, Richard J., and Charles Murray. *The Bell Curve: Intelligence and Class Structure in American Life.* New York: Free Press, 1994.

Hirsch, E. D. *Cultural Literacy: What Every American Needs to Know.* Boston: Houghton Mifflin, 1987.

Hudson, Kenneth. *The Jargon of the Professions.* London: Macmillan, 1978.

Kaestle, Carl F., Helen Damon-Moore, Lawrence C. Stedman, Katherine Tinsley, and William Vance Trollinger Jr. *Literacy in the United States: Readers and Reading since 1880.* New Haven: Yale University Press, 1991.

Kennedy, Paul M. *The Rise and Fall of the Great Powers: Economic Change and Military Conflict from 1500–2000.* New York: Random House, 1987.

Lasch, Christopher. *The New Radicalism in America, 1889–1963: The Intellectual as a Social Type.* New York: Knopf, 1965.

Leakey, Richard. *The Origin of Humankind.* New York: Basic Books, 1994.

Leavis, F. R. *Two Cultures? The Significance of C. P. Snow.* With an essay on Sir Charles Snow's Rede Lecture by Michael Yudkin. London: Chatto & Windus, 1962.

Levine, Lawrence W. *Highbrow/Lowbrow: The Emergence of Cultural Hierarchy in America.* Cambridge: Harvard University Press, 1988.

Levy, Matthys, and Mario Salvadori. *Why Buildings Fall Down: How Structures Fail.* New York: W. W. Norton, 1992.

Luey, Beth. "Are Fame and Fortune the Kiss of Death?" *Publishing Research Quarterly* 19, no. 3 (Winter 2007): 36–47.

———. "'Leading the Reader Gently': Popular Science Books in the 1950s." *Book History* 2 (1999): 218–53.

———. "Who Reads Nonfiction?" *Publishing Research Quarterly* 14, no. 1 (Spring 1998): 21–35.

MacClancy, Jeremy, and Chris McDonaugh, eds. *Popularizing Anthropology.* New York: Routledge, 1996.

McCormick, Joseph B., Susan Fisher-Hoch, and Leslie Alan Horwitz. *Level 4: Virus Hunters of the CDC.* Atlanta: Turner, 1996.

McCullough, David. *Mornings on Horseback.* New York: Simon & Schuster, 1981.

Moore, Ruth. *Man, Time, and Fossils.* New York: Knopf, 1953.

Murphy, Priscilla Coit. *What a Book Can Do: The Publication and Reception of "Silent Spring."* Amherst: University of Massachusetts Press, 2004.

Nader, Ralph. *Unsafe at Any Speed: The Designed-In Dangers of the American Automobile.* New York: Grossman, 1965.

Nell, Victor. *Lost in a Book: The Psychology of Reading for Pleasure.* New Haven: Yale University Press, 1988.

Nozick, Robert. *Anarchy, State, and Utopia.* New York: Basic Books, 1974.

Pagels, Elaine. *The Gnostic Gospels.* New York: Random House, 1979.

Paulos, John Allen. *Innumeracy: Mathematical Illiteracy and Its Consequences.* New York: Hill & Wang, 1988.

———. *A Mathematician Reads the Newspaper.* New York: Basic Books, 1995.

———. *Once Upon a Number: The Hidden Mathematical Logic of Stories.* New York: Basic Books, 1998.

Peters, C. J., and Mark Olshaker. *Virus Hunter: Thirty Years of Battling Hot Viruses around the World.* New York: Anchor, 1997.

Petroski, Henry. *Beyond Engineering: Essays and Other Attempts to Figure without Equations.* New York: St. Martin's, 1986.

———. *The Book on the Bookshelf.* New York: Knopf, 1999.

———. *The Pencil: A History of Design and Circumstance.* New York: Knopf, 1990.

Pfitzer, Gregory M. *Popular History and the Literary Marketplace, 1840–1920.* Amherst: University of Massachusetts Press, 2008.

Piatigorsky, Gregor. *Cellist.* Garden City, N.Y.: Doubleday, 1965.

Piel, Gerard. *Science in the Cause of Man.* New York: Knopf, 1961.

Pinker, Steven. *The Language Instinct.* New York: Morrow, 1994.

———. *Words and Rules.* New York: Basic Books, 1999.

Pollan, Michael. *The Botany of Desire: A Plant's-Eye View of the World.* New York: Random House, 2001.

Porter, Roy, ed. *The Popularization of Medicine, 1650–1850*. New York: Routledge, 1992.

Preston, Richard. *The Hot Zone*. New York: Random House, 1994.

Radway, Janice A. *A Feeling for Books: The Book-of-the-Month Club, Literary Taste, and Middle-Class Desire*. Chapel Hill: University of North Carolina Press, 1997.

Rashid, Ahmed. *Taliban: Militant Islam, Oil, and Fundamentalism in Central Asia*. New Haven: Yale University Press, 2000.

Rawls, John. *A Theory of Justice*. Cambridge: Harvard University Press, 1971.

Regis, Ed. *Virus Ground Zero: Stalking the Killer Viruses with the Centers for Disease Control*. New York: Pocket Books, 1996.

Reich, Charles. *The Greening of America: How the Youth Revolution Is Trying to Make America Livable*. New York: Random House, 1970.

Riesman, David. *The Lonely Crowd*. New Haven: Yale University Press, 1961.

Rose, Jonathan. *The Intellectual Life of the British Working Classes*. New Haven: Yale University Press, 2001.

Rubin, Joan Shelley. *The Making of Middlebrow Culture*. Chapel Hill: University of North Carolina Press, 1992.

Ryan, Frank. *Virus X: Tracking the New Killer Plagues*. Boston: Little, Brown, 1997.

Rybczynski, Witold. *Waiting for the Weekend*. New York: Viking, 1991.

Sagan, Carl. *Broca's Brain: Reflections on the Romance of Science*. New York: Random House, 1979.

———. *The Cosmic Connection: An Extraterrestrial Perspective*. Garden City, N.Y.: Doubleday Anchor, 1973.

———. *Cosmos*. New York: Random House, 1980.

———. *Dragons of Eden: Speculations on the Evolution of Human Intelligence*. New York: Random House, 1977.

Schama, Simon. *Citizens: A Chronicle of the French Revolution*. New York: Knopf, 1989.

———. *Dead Certainties (Unwarranted Speculations)*. New York: Knopf, 1991.

Secord, James A. *Victorian Sensation: The Extraordinary Publication, Reception, and Secret Authorship of "Vestiges of the Natural History of Creation."* Chicago: University of Chicago Press, 2000.

Shumway, David R. *Creating American Civilization: A Genealogy of American Liberature as an Academic Discipline*. Minneapolis: University of Minnesota Press, 1994.

Skinner, B. F. *Walden Two*. New York: Macmillan, 1948.

Snow, C. P. *The Two Cultures: And a Second Look*. Cambridge: Cambridge University Press, 1964.

Sobel, Dava. *Longitude: The True Story of a Lone Genius Who Solved the Greatest Scientific Problem of His Time*. New York: Walker, 1995.

Sokal, Alan D. "A Physicist Experiments with Cultural Studies." *Lingua Franca*, May/June 1996, 62.

———. "Transgressing the Boundaries: Towards a Transformative Hermeneutics of Quantum Gravity." *Social Text* 46/47 (Spring/Summer 1996): 217–52.

Spence, Jonathan. *The Death of Woman Wang*. New York: Viking, 1978.

———. *The Memory Palace of Matteo Ricci.* New York: Viking, 1984.

———. *The Question of Hu.* New York: Knopf, 1988.

Strouse, Jean. *Alice James: A Biography.* Boston: Houghton Mifflin, 1980.

Tannen, Deborah. *Gender and Discourse.* New York: Oxford University Press, 1994.

———. *You Just Don't Understand.* New York: Morrow, 1990.

Tebbel, John R. *The Great Change, 1940–1980.* Vol. 4 of *A History of Book Publishing in the United States.* New York: Bowker, 1981.

Thurow, Lester. *The Zero-Sum Society: Distribution and the Possibilities for Economic Change.* New York: Basic Books, 1980.

Trilling, Lionel. "Science, Literature, and Culture: A Comment on the Leavis-Snow Controversy." *Commentary,* June 1962, 461–77.

Ulrich, Laurel Thatcher. *A Midwife's Tale: The Life of Martha Ballard, Based on Her Diary, 1785–1812.* New York: Knopf, 1990.

Watson, James D. *The Double Helix: A Personal Account of the Discovery of the Structure of DNA.* New York: Atheneum, 1968.

Weiner, Jonathan. *The Beak of the Finch: A Story of Evolution in Our Time.* New York: Knopf, 1994.

Whyte, William. *The Organization Man.* New York: Simon & Schuster, 1956.

Wilson, Edward O. *Consilience: The Unity of Knowledge.* New York: Knopf, 1998.

———. *The Diversity of Life.* Cambridge: Belknap Press of Harvard University Press, 1992.

Woolf, Daniel R. *Reading History in Early Modern England.* Cambridge: Cambridge University Press, 2000.

Yeo, Richard. *Encyclopaedic Visions: Scientific Dictionaries and Enlightenment Culture.* Cambridge: Cambridge University Press, 2001.

INDEX

218   INDEX